LIPA IN PICTURES

THE FIRST TEN YEARS

LIPA IN PICTURES
THE FIRST TEN YEARS

THE LIVERPOOL INSTITUTE FOR PERFORMING ARTS

British Library Cataloguing in Publication Data.
A catalogue record for this book is available
from the British Library.

ISBN 0-9539423-2-5

Photographs and illustrations:
Jon Barraclough, Chris Brown, Paul Carey,
Raymond Farley, Mark Featherstone-Witty,
Joel Fildes, Roger Huggett, Robin Maryon,
Roger Morris, Stephen Morris, Brian Slater,
Ian Southerin, Tim Spilman, John Spinks,
Liz White, *Private Eye*, *Marie Claire*, *The Stage*,
The Sunday Times, *The Daily Post*, Liverpool,
The Daily Telegraph, *The Liverpool Echo*,
The Independent.

Every effort has been made to contact the
holders of copyright material, but if any have
been inadvertently overlooked, the publisher will
be pleased to make the necessary arrangements
at the first opportunity.

Designed and typeset by
Roger Huggett / Sinc Design Consultants.
Printed and bound in the United Kingdom by
The Lavenham Press.

Above: The unrenovated Institute appears just above the tree line, lit by the afternoon sun.

WHILE WRITING this celebratory book, I was struck by the incidence of luck and underplay of the effort — the enduring effort. For, as we often say to our students: "Hard work makes luck possible".

Aside from Paul McCartney, who gave me a second chance to live my dream, particular thanks for the creation of LIPA go to the people either listed in the text or in Section 8. They have also been acknowledged, with still others, in my earlier book *Optimistic, Even Then*.

For the creation of this book, I gratefully acknowledge Mitzi Bales, who edited the words, Jane Tatam, who managed the production process and Christine Webster for helping the process here at LIPA. The look of the book was Roger Huggett's contribution and, as the apearance of a picture book defines its quality, his achievement speaks for itself.

The material for the book gathered itself over the years; photographs taken, newspaper articles collected and mementoes kept. All were thrown into cupboards since they weren't immediately necessary to achieve the many pressing tasks. In choosing the material for the book, the moment of reckoning came. This meant sorting and selecting material from those cupboards.

It also became clear that even the best material cannot convey the moment when learning happens – the reason why teachers teach and students learn.

Our journey can never be over. For, as Winston Churchill once said, "It's the end of the beginning".

MARK FEATHERSTONE-WITTY
FOUNDING PRINCIPAL / CEO

Jesse reaches for the stars IN CALIFORNIA

California based LIPA graduate Jesse Harlin is working with the stars... *Star Wars* that is.

He is a composer with LucasArts, the company headed by famous director and movie-maker George Lucas.
Jesse, an American, who graduated in Music in 1999, said: "Mostly, I write for videogames. Currently, I'm composing a largely original soundtrack for *Star Wars: Republic Commando*, our new first person shooter."
He is also editing music, including the original John Williams' *Star Wars* scores, for use in new games at LucasArts.
Said Jesse of his time at LIPA: "It was fantastic. LIPA was everything I had been looking for in a college." Later adding: "It was the attention to the business of being a professional musician that made LIPA really special."

● *See page 14 for the Big Q&A interview with Jesse.*

ABOUT THE BOOK SPONSORS

YAMAHA

Yamaha has supported the LIPA dream from early concept stage through to what it is today - one of the world's most vibrant artistic hubs for emerging talent. We regularly collaborate on a range of schemes including masterclasses, summer schools and are proud to be a founding partner of the acclaimed MIBI (Make It, Break It) Awards for Young Songwriters www.makeitbreakit.org

LIVERPOOL 08

It's thanks to our cultural institutions like LIPA that Liverpool was chosen as the European Capital of Culture for 2008. Congratulations on making LIPA one of the most successful performing arts schools in the world in 10 short years.

EMI

Congratulations to LIPA on a resounding first ten years. We are proud to offer our continued support and look forward to the next ten.

THE BPI/BRIT TRUST

Congratulations LIPA on reaching your 10th anniversary. The BPI/BRIT Trust is proud to be associated with the Liverpool Institute for Performing Arts and supports its commitment to the training of talented and motivated individuals.

GREENBERG GLASS

Greenberg Glass is proud to have been associated with LIPA over the past decade. We wish Mark and his team continued success with this exciting venture. Well done!

HIGH END SYSTEMS

Never underestimate the power of lighting design. We're proud to enable students to express and learn the art of color, texture, motion and dimension in light by providing them with the newest technology. Along with the art, LIPA is teaching the business side of entertainment – a skill that's often overlooked but much needed to be successfully creative in the real world.

BROCK CARMICHAEL

Specialists in historic building conservation and the imaginative regeneration of old buildings, Brock Carmichael Architects are proud to have been associated with LIPA from inception to the present day.

WALFORDS

It seems like only yesterday that we began our association with LIPA. Through all the good and hard times, Walfords have been proud to provide professional services, and we wish LIPA every success in the future.

LIPA IN PICTURES

1 THE DREAM

Paul McCartney — *Let It Be Liverpool* — 1990

Band on the dock ... Paul, Linda and fellow musicians in high spirits before the concert

Famous future for old school

THE
LIVERPOOL INSTITUTE
FOUNDED 1825
HIGH SCHOOL
FOR BOYS

THE road to fame is a step nearer for Merseyside youngsters, pledged Paul McCartney last night.

His former school, the Liverpool Institute, is set to emerge as the focus for artistic excellence, he told an international Press conference last night.

Future

And it is all thanks to the Echo.

Paul said: "I was sad to see my old school in such a state recently and I wrote to the people of Liverpool last year through the Echo to see what they thought of launching it towards a new future.

□ *THE Liverpool Institute's most famous former pupil raises the curtain on his old school's new role as a centre for performing arts. NEIL HODGSON reports*

"As the paper said a few days later, Echo readers have given a big thumbs up," said Macca last night.

And last night Paul set the Liverpool Institute for Performing Arts up and running with a star-studded fanfare.

Former Beatles producer George Martin gave the scheme his full support, saying: "Liverpool is a wonderful city which is better than it's ever been — you can really sock it to them around the world.

"I remember when the Beatles knocked the world sideways with their talent.

"Liverpool did that — congratulations Liverpool ... do it again."

And Mark Featherstone-Witty, co-driving force behind the centre with Paul, said: "I don't know of any leading artist who has gone back to his home town to give local people a greater chance than he had.

"What we are launching this evening is an institution which will

put not just Liverpool, but this country at the forefront of music and performing arts education — it might sound grand, but this is the scale of our dreams."

The final word belonged to the man of the night.

"Liverpool people have always had a lot of talent, I can't write a note of music, I just write down what sounds good.

"So, hopefully this school will tap that talent, rather than the academic thing."

He added: "When I was talking to the Liverpool band the Christians about setting this up they asked me what I was going to teach at the school.

"I said I might call in with my guitar and sit around with the kids and if I'm there I can point them in the right direction.

Hope

"It won't necessarily be teaching, but it will be some kind of assistance."

And Paul said: "I don't want to be a Paul Getty character and come here throwing money about.

"But I just want to give hope to some of the kids who haven't got the avenues, which was what it was like for me."

George Martin ... the Beatles' producer

George Martin: 'The Beatles knocked the world sideways ... do it again, Liverpool'

The Institute ... schoolhouse rock

Macca: 'I want to give hope to the kids without avenues ... like it was for me'

1 THE DREAM

WHILE MANY people made important contributions to the creation of the Liverpool Institute for Performing Arts, it can be said that two people figured most prominently in its founding: Paul McCartney and Mark Featherstone-Witty. Both had had different life journeys when they met. But they were united by their optimism in aiming to create a new higher education institution for both aspiring performers and those who made performance possible.

Mark had first written to Paul in 1983 about his hopes of establishing a performing arts school in London. Unbeknownst to him, Paul had paid a sentimental visit around his dilapidated old school in Liverpool in the mid 1980s. Without any particular plan in mind, Paul hoped that somehow the building could be restored. Shortly after this, George Martin, the Beatles producer who was working with Mark to establish the London school, brought about a meeting between Paul and Mark.

By the time the two met in May 1989, each had been motivated differently to put dedication and energy behind the possibility of turning a dilapidated nineteenth-century building into a new kind of performing arts institute.

Above: Paul McCartney and Mark Featherstone-Witty seal the partnership to establish LIPA. It seems that they were fated to meet when they did.

Right: The crucial second letter to Paul from Mark that gained Paul's favourable response to the idea of transforming his old school into a new school for performing arts. Its timing was fortunate in that Paul had just taken his sentimental journey through the building and was looking for a way to preserve it.

Mark had been an actor and director as well as an educator in his life, and, without exactly realising it, he had long been wondering how education and training could provide for a sustained career in the performing arts – often the shakiest career choice. Part of the answer seemed to come to him watching the Hollywood film *Fame*. One of the teenagers auditioning for a place at the New York High School for Performing Arts mentioned to other hopefuls that they had to be able to sing and dance as well as act to gain admission – what Americans call "the triple threat" and what the British think of as versatility.

It struck him forcefully that a versatile performer had to be more employable than a single-skill performer. This make him think further that a school where students could gain proficiency in all the skills that made a production work might have a route to a positive alternative in the entertainment world, if their dream job didn't materialise. His own dream, then, was a school where one body of students, interacting together, delivered every needed skill for a successful production. This dream galvanised him into a 16-year campaign to establish such a school just in the United Kingdom.

Mark spent four years from 1980 to 1984 exploring his ideas with some 120 practitioners, asking each: "From where you are now, what

Above left: George Martin in the studio named after him at LIPA. Because he had been the most helpful patron during the critical early phase of the work, Mark calls him the godfather of LIPA.

Top and below right: The cover and an inside page of the brochure about the charity that had been created to promote a performing arts school in London and elsewhere, if possible.

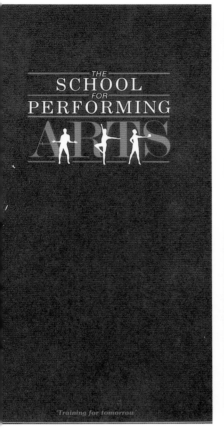

Above: George and Mark in conversation at the launch of the BRIT School in London, which preceded their joint involvement in LIPA. Tim Rice is in the foreground.

Left: Sir Alan Parker being interviewed at LIPA.

Melvyn Bragg

'The School for Performing Arts is a first rate idea and has long been necessary. Without The School and as a parent, one has had to consider the best available and this is often overseas. We need a school like this here'.

Richard Branson

'At the moment, there is no training ground for the music entertainment industry. Additionally, there is no provision for youngsters to come to grips with the technical innovations which have and will continue to revolutionize the industry. We need The School for Performing Arts to train youngsters to keep the music world vibrant and alive'.

Judi Dench

'The School for Performing Arts is not more of the same. New, original, novel — whatever the word, The School for Performing Arts is not only building upon the best existing practices, but also pioneering. I hope people reading our Appeal Document will immediately appreciate this'.

Jonathan Miller

'Although the theatrical and music industries need young people with a fluency in vocational skills, they also need entrants with a first class general education. This means not only the usual school subjects, but the skills needed to manage a commercial life. I am delighted The School for Performing Arts aims to provide just this'.

Victoria Wood

'So many potential young performers do not know what performing art to pursue, particularly now when versatility is so often demanded and can mean survival. My training consisted of a university drama course, which probably suited me better than a conventional drama school, but certainly was not ideal. I wish The School for Performing Arts had been around then'.

would you like to have known then?" Pete Townshend, for one, told him: "My abiding metaphor for the rock industry is people rushing forward to throw themselves onto a bonfire" – an observation that encouraged Mark to feel he was heading down the right track.

One of the first influential people he met was Alan Parker, the director of *Fame*, who advised him to visit schools in the US as they existed in a culture unembarrassed about calling entertainment an economic activity. By diligence and good fortune, Mark met Anthony Field. Apart from working at the Arts Council for 25 years as its finance director, Tony was fired up by all aspects of the theatre. For example, he had assisted embryonic producers Cameron Mackintosh and Thelma Holt, among

others, and initiated the first university course for arts administration in the UK. They focussed on London as the venue for the school.

In 1985 the Schools for Performing Arts (SPA) Trust was created with Tony as Chair. During the following years of modest fundraising, the City Technology College Trust was approached. At first unresponsive, the Trust later supported the idea of a specialist school for performance technology with some courses for aspiring performers as well. George Martin, then the Appeals Chairperson of the SPA, introduced the idea to the British Phonographic Industry (BPI), the trade association of British record companies, which also became interested. The catalysts were Richard Branson and George himself, who had already spoken with Paul McCartney

Above: Recreating the Beatles' famous shot during the launch of the BRIT School in London. Kenneth Baker, then Secretary of State for Education leads supporters Richard Branson, Virgin Group Chairperson; David Puttnam, then a film producer; Matt Goss of the boy band Bros; George Martin, record producer and Mark.

Left: Newspaper coverage of the BRIT School launch.

A shot from Paul's home movie of him walking around his old school as he reminisced about his school days. This was released as a DVD with the recording of his Liverpool Oratorio.

about supporting the London school.

Just at that time, Paul was considering something else. As he explained: "Late one night I made a sentimental visit to my old school, the Liverpool Institute. I found the place in a dilapidated state but was still intrigued by being in a place where so many of my early years had been spent. I took a film cameraman around and reminisced about the teachers, the pupils (one of them George Harrison) and some of the events that took place in this once lovely building. Making this film inspired me to start talking to people about ideas to save the building."

Paul discovered that the building was governed by a charitable trust, managed by Liverpool City Council. The Council had a number of impressive unoccupied buildings without an obvious use. Even if the site were sold, the money would have to be applied to meet the objectives of the existing trust. So, although the building was decaying and unused, it was impossible to consider renovation or restoration without an identified and sustainable use. It also happened during this period that a resident in Liverpool's postal code 8 – the scene of the 1980s' riot and a district close to the school – mentioned to him that Liverpool needed a performing arts school.

DO YOU WANT FAME?

...asks Paul McCartney in an open letter to Liverpool

Magic of city's famous Institute

I have never written a letter to the Liverpool Echo before, but it seems to me the best way to reach the people of the city.

I recently revisited my old school, the Liverpool Institute, which, as most people will know, was closed down a few years ago. It was sad for me to see the old place in such a state of disintegration but despite this it still seemed to me to be a very fine old building.

My visit there reminded me of something that a Liverpool friend from Upper Parliament Street had said to me right after the Toxteth riots.

He suggested that it would be a great idea for Liverpool to have a School for the Performing Arts — in other words a "Fame" school, the idea being that local working-class youngsters would have an opportunity to pursue a career in the performing arts without having to pay the huge fees normally associated with such institutions.

At the time I was so impressed with the idea that I mentioned it to another friend, ex-Beatles producer George Martin, who also felt it had great potential. George, not having the same Liverpool connections, has since been involved in setting up a similar school down south which appears to be going well.

My visit to the Institute made me think that the old building (built in 1825) might be a perfect location for a school.

With this in mind I made one or two inquiries and it now seems to be a good moment to throw the question open to the people of Liverpool.

If the interest in such an idea is low then of course there is no point in carrying on. If on the other hand, people were interested in something that would give ordinary kids such a great opportunity, then I would be more than happy to give my support to a campaign to establish a "Fame" type school in Liverpool.

I got a great start in life courtesy of the Liverpool Institute and would love to see other local people being given the same chance. I hope very much that the

Liverpool Institute ... could it become a city "Fame" school?

Paul McCartney ... support

Liverpool Echo and its readers feel this is something worth pursuing and I am sure that if the answer is a positive one we will be able to attract interest from many other sources.

WHAT is the magic of Liverpool Institute?
News of secret talks to turn it into a Fame Academy came as no surprise to hundreds of old boys.

For the glorious building has already brought out the drama and artistic talent of dozens of ex-pupils.

They include comedian Arthur Askey, broadcaster Peter Sissons and ex-Coronation Street star and theatre impresario Bill Kenwright as well as Paul McCartney.

The prestige of Liverpool's Institute was summed up by its last headmaster and former pupil Jack Sweeney just before its doors shut in 1985.

"The Institute encouraged us all to be individuals. It gave us an atmosphere in which we could all develop."

WHAT DO YOU THINK?

What do YOU think readers?

Should a Fame school be set up in Liverpool Institute? Should it be supported by Paul McCartney? Now you can have your say.

Write in with your comments to Paul McCartney, Liverpool Echo, PO Box 48, Old Hall Street, Liverpool L69 3EB.

We have also set up a special 'phone vote system.

If you think Paul should support a Fame school call 0077 554422.

If you think he should not call 0077 554433.

Lines will stay open until midnight on Sunday and calls will cost just 5p.

RING-A-DING VOTE BACKS PAUL'S BID FOR FAME!

DO YOU WANT FAME? ...asks Paul McCartney in an open letter to Liverpool

Echo letter ... how Paul launched his campaign

Readers say yes to school of performing arts on Merseyside

Paul McCartney ... wins backing

By Paul Byrne

ECHO readers have given a big thumbs-up to Paul McCartney's idea for a "Fame" school in Liverpool.

In an open letter to the paper Paul asked the readers if they would support a school for the performing arts being set up in the city.

Former Beatle Paul believes his old school, the Liverpool Institute, would be the perfect home for the venture.

Through the Echo he asked the people of

Yoko Ono, have indicated they would support a campaign to set up the school.

And the man behind the new School for Performing Arts in London, Mark Featherstone-Witty, is being invited up to Liverpool later this week by the city council.

Mr Featherstone-Witty is understood to have already spoken to Paul McCartney

McCartney and any other performers, classical and pop musicians, comedians or actors who wish to be involved in a centre for performing arts in the city.

"I'm delighted so many people telephoned the Echo poll, including myself.

"Councillors and officers have been working to establish such a centre for 12 months now. We have already successfully set up part of the project based in the

Paul's open letter to Merseysiders through *The Liverpool Echo* and the follow-up article about the public's supportive response.

The cover of the Liverpool Council's Music City Report. This report was instrumental in winning official backing for LIPA.

The timing of incidents: a miracle?

Not long after this chance meeting, another fortuitous incident occurred. Some Liverpool City Councillors were considering how music could play a part in regenerating the city. Keith Hackett, then chairperson of finance, had an intense belief in the capacity of the arts to rejuvenate inner cities. Pete Fulwell, then managing The Christians, was commissioned to write a report proposing how, who and which kind of music elements could sustain popular music in the city.

A chain of contacts ensued: Pete contacted the MD of The Christians' record label who suggested he contact George Martin who suggested he contact Mark. Suddenly, the city and Paul were asking Mark the same question: "What would a new school for performing arts be like and how would it fit in with the city's current providers of learning?"

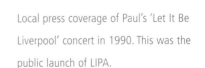

The first time the public heard about the possibility of the Liverpool Institute for Performing Arts (LIPA) was in *The Liverpool Echo* on 24 February 1989.

Before he became too involved, Paul wanted to find out what the people of Liverpool felt about a Fame-type school in their city. People were invited to have their say by ringing a dedicated phone number. Four days later, the result was announced: overwhelming enthusiasm.

This was happening at almost the exact moment that the BRIT School was launched, it being the result of the original SPA campaign to establish a school for performing arts in London.

Local press coverage of Paul's 'Let It Be Liverpool' concert in 1990. This was the public launch of LIPA.

The launch. Meeting Paul at the reception (middle right) are Jack Sweeny (left), one of Paul's former teachers in his days at the Liverpool Institute for Boys, and Roger Morris (right), another former student who became a loyal trustee of LIPA.

Mark Featherstone-Witty,
the Administrative Director of
The Liverpool Institute for Performing Arts,
invites

to a Reception backstage before
Paul McCartney's 'Let It Be Liverpool' Concert
on Thursday, 28th June, 1990 at 6.30 p.m.

Directions are overleaf

There can be no admission without this invitation

R.S.V.P. immediately
The Liverpool Institute for Performing Arts
c/o 47 Red Lion Street
LONDON WC1R 4PF

2 RAISING THE MONEY

LIVERPOOL INSTITUTE
AND SCHOOL OF ART . 1825

THE
LIVERPOOL
INSTITUTE
FOR
PERFORMING
ARTS

"I and others want to be involved in a place where we can pass on the skills and experience that have contributed to our success"

Paul McCartney

2 RAISING THE MONEY

Above: Bergen Peck and Mark at work in LIPA's first office. It was converted from a couple of old storerooms and quickly overflowed (right).

THE NEWS was out, but there was a financial mountain to climb. Although Paul was willing to support a small team, plus casuals and volunteers, he did not intend to be the main financial backer. Mark became painfully aware that the UK public sector, both local and national, would not assume this role either. Somehow big sums had to be raised with this in mind.

Mark and Bergen Peck, his friend and an enthusiast, began to work around the corner from Paul's old school in a building that had been Britain's first homeopathic hospital and then Liverpool Polytechnic, soon to become Liverpool John Moores University. Their priority was to produce a fundraising brochure.

The difficulty in this endeavour was discovering the true cost of restoration and renovation. This was complicated by two major factors: first, it was hard to survey the existing old school accurately, particularly when it was not under the LIPA project's ownership; second, the curriculum had yet to be formulated and so had to be expressed in broad outline until staff could be appointed to work out the details. The budget, too, could only be projected in broad terms.

There were other problems in the climb up the mountain. How to create a document that was attractive and exuded confidence without

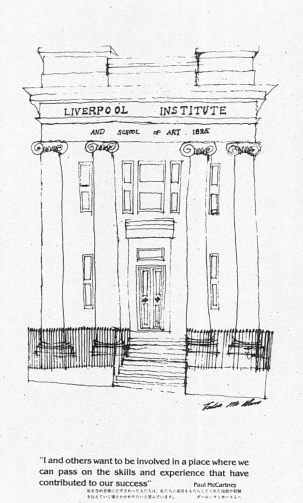

LIVERPOOL INSTITUTE
AND SCHOOL of ART 1825

THE
LIVERPOOL
INSTITUTE
FOR
PERFORMING
ARTS

"I and others want to be involved in a place where we can pass on the skills and experience that have contributed to our success" Paul McCartney
私を含む音楽にたずさわった人たちは、私たちに成功をもたらしてくれた技能や経験を伝えていく場とかかわりたいと望んでいます。 ポール・マッカートニー

comment by George Martin

ジョージ・マーティン
写真：ジョン・スチュアート・ファリア

ジョージ・マーティンのコメント

音楽は、私たちの豊かな生活を支える未来型生活産業のなかで、ますますその中心的な役割をはたしていくものと思われます。たとえば、音楽は、広告やマーケティングの強力な戦力として、私たちが購入する商品、衣服、さらには食べ物にいたるまで、私たちの生活全般にわたって大きな影響を与えているのです。

音楽を中心とするパフォーミング・アートが経済に与える影響は、外貨の獲得や新しいタイプの雇用の創造などにおいて多大な貢献が認められます。「1988 - 1989年度の芸術による国外収益報告」によれば、芸術による外貨収益は60億ポンドにおよび、石油産業と並ぶ業績をあげています。

では、音楽やパフォーミング・アートの業界の発展のためのキー・ポイントは何なのでしょうか。業界を担っていく人材の教育や訓練によって、この業界はどのように変化していくのか。私には非常に興味深いところです。私が特に気にしているのは、他の業界と違ってこの業界には将来を担っていく人材を養成するための教育機関が未だに存在していないことです。数年前、私はこの種の教育機関の設立をめざしているパフォーミング・アート・スクール設立準備機構の後援者となりました。私たちは、その最初の学校として、クロイドンにブリティッシュ・レコード・インダストリー・トラスト・スクールを設立しました。

giving potential supporters the idea that the project would spend rashly? How to give a glimpse of the future when the building hadn't been obtained or designed? In addition, Paul was wary about being too much the centre of attention.

One answer was to show care by printing the document on recycled paper. Another was to produce an accompanying video with endorsements from famous Liverpool performers. Such a video was produced creatively and cost effectively by a gifted amateur. On it were Holly Johnson (Frankie Goes to Hollywood) and Keith Mullin (The Farm), among others.

Fundraising was exhilarating, if a slog. While Bergen initially concentrated on the building and training side, Mark threw himself wholeheartedly into the total project. By nature optimistic, he took on much of the sheer grunt work such as investigating and applying for grants, contacting individuals known to have expendable funds and organising fundraising events. Among the latter were four lunches.

Paul was willing to attend the fundraising lunches, which took intensive planning and organising. The first was held in London at the Performing Right Society (PRS), which collects the revenues attached to a music creator's copyright. The lunch was a fund raising success, with all

Above: LIPA's Appeal document in its Japanese translation by Tetsuo Hamada, Paul's envoy in Japan and a loyal LIPA collaborator.

Right: The group photograph that ended the PRS lunch, a practice adopted for every fund raising lunch thereafter. Back row: Pete Waterman, Jonathan Simon, Michael Freeguard, Robert Abrahams, Mark, Steve Lindsay, Jon Crawley, Charles Armitage, Peter Cox, Richard Ogden. Middle row standing: Ken Berry, John Eastman, Paul Curran, Peter Dadswell, Stewart Slater, Stephen Howard, Steve Lewis, Stuart Hornall, Donald Mitchell, Andrew Potter, Robin Godfrey-Cass, Lucien Grainge, Joanne Cohen. Middle row seated: Bob Wise, Vivian Ellis, Linda, Paul, Wayne Bickerton, Chris Wright, Jim Fifield. Front row: John Axon, David Hockman, Humphrey Walwyn, Tony Silov, Tony Field, Nigel Elderton, John Billingham, Peter Reichardt, Marshall Lees. (Also attended) James Little, Steven Norris MP, Adam White.

Below: Feeling buoyant before the PRS lunch are Steve Lewis, Mark, Linda McCartney, David Hockman, Peter Waterman and Paul.

Right: Paul, Michael Portillo (then Minister of State with special responsibility for Merseyside) and Mark in the school woodwork room which was falling apart bit by bit.

Below: The Liverpool City Challenge prospectus for developing Liverpool City East. This affected LIPA as it covered the area where the old Institute for Boys was located.

reaching new heights

LIVERPOOL CITY CENTRE EAST

DEVELOPMENT PLAN

LIVERPOOL CITY CHALLENGE

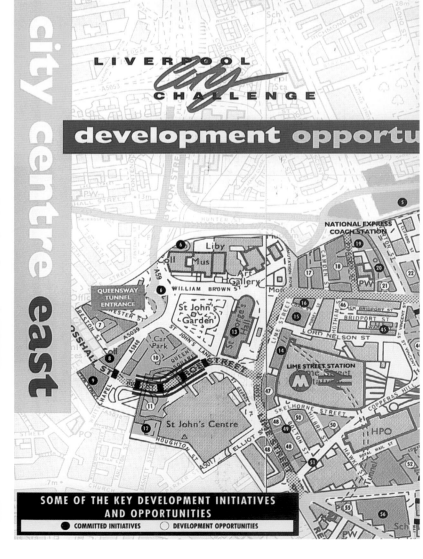

city centre east

LIVERPOOL City CHALLENGE

development opportu

NATIONAL EXPRESS COACH STATION

SOME OF THE KEY DEVELOPMENT INITIATIVES AND OPPORTUNITIES

● COMMITTED INITIATIVES   ○ DEVELOPMENT OPPORTUNITIES

DEPARTMENT OF THE ENVIRONMENT
2 MARSHAM STREET LONDON SW1P 3EB
071-276 3000

My ref   SQ/PSO/25767/92
Your ref

4 DEC 1992

Dear Mr Featherstone-Witty

Your letter of 17 November was most helpful in bringing me up to date on the various significant fund raising achievements to date and the proposals for next year, particularly revolving around Paul McCartney's World Tour.

You will by now be aware that I recently gave approval to the funding of works on the roof and high-level masonry at Liverpool Institute through Liverpool City Challenge, and it is pleasing to see progress on all fronts towards the realisation of the LIPA project.

I certainly hope that an opportunity will arise next year for me to meet you and see for myself the Institute buildings.

Yours sincerely

ROBIN SQUIRE

Mark Featherstone-Witty Esq

Above: The restoration of the roof starts with funding by the Department of the Environment.

POST CARD

Dear Mark
Give received the feasability study now and hope to chat soon. Things going well for us in Japan. Rock and roll is alive and well in Tokyo! Regards. Paul + Linda

MARK FEATHERSTONE WITY
C/o SPA
47 RED LION ST.
LONDON WC1R 4PF
ENGLAND.

Above : Paul and Mark keep in touch continuously.

but two participants making a contribution. The most generous came from EMI, the Beatles' label.

Meanwhile, another miracle was materialising. Michael Heseltine, then Secretary of State for the Environment, decided to allocate a small percentage of urban grants throughout the country to galvanise local authorities to come up with imaginative regeneration schemes. The 'small percentage' created a pot of £350m for 10 winners, each being allotted £35m. Liverpool asked Paul to sign its bid document to make an impact.

While bids from across the nation were being considered by bureaucrats, Michael Portillo, then MP and a minister with responsibility for Liverpool, visited the proposed LIPA site. This was prompted by the fact that the Merseyside Task Force, a body reporting to him, had agreed to help fund LIPA's business plan. It appeared that those in government perceived LIPA as a good thing. Since his visit was on the day of the Liverpool premier of Paul's *Liverpool Oratorio*, Paul joined him on the tour of his old school.

The group photograph from the European Union launch. Back row: David Walker, Steffen Smidt, Ros Reuter, Etienne Reuter, Richard Ogden, Begona Rodriguez, Peter Coldrick, John Morley, Robert Davies, Geoffrey Brown. Middle row: Steve Bagnell, Jeremy Harrison, Petrus Cornelissen, Mme. Lutti, Patricia Rawlings, Sir Jack Stewart-Clark, Ken Stewart, Christine Morley, Jean Flamson, Enrico Boarretto, Keith Hackett. Front row: Dame Jocelyn Barrow, Hywel Ceri Jones, Humphrey Walwyn, Mark, Linda, Paul, Vasso Papandreou, John Flamson, Graham Meadows, Will Haire, Mary Banotti. (Not pictured is Colette Flesch, who attended the launch but had to leave early.)

In due course, Liverpool was one of the winning cities for regeneration funds, earmarked for Liverpool City East. This is where the proposed LIPA site lay, so LIPA was to be a flagship project.

While the LIPA team met with various Liverpool bureaucrats, it emerged that they wanted to prevent further decay by repairing the roof of the school, without compromising any final decision about LIPA. This proved positive for publicity purposes as the building was already being restored, though it also presented financial difficulties because the final use for the building could lead to alterations and additional cost.

While creating the business plan, the project team had a new thought: as the EU had created a special fund for the Parthenon in Athens, recognising it as the birthplace of European civilisation, could not Liverpool represent the birthplace of European popular culture? Could the EU be persuaded to help fund LIPA in the same way? This optimistic and fanciful idea opened the mental door to European structural funds – and so to the second fundraising lunch in Brussels. It took three months to pull the event together.

The Brussels lunch in the end proved to be the most strategically and

financially significant of all four lunches, partly because EU structural funds were granted as a result and met roughly one third of the capital cost, and partly because it brought on board Grundig, the well-known German electronics company, as the largest corporate sponsor. There were five speakers: Sir Jack Stewart-Clark for the European Parliament; John Flamson for the Liverpool City Challenge initiative, Commissioner Vasso Papandreou for the EU, Mark and Paul for LIPA. The Commissioner ended her gentle, informal speech saying: "This is a worthwhile project; we wish you all the best and we shall do the most we can do".

All the while, donations were coming in, some in five figures, some small – even from schoolchildren. A Star Trek donation also arrived. So it was time for a supporters' newsletter. Eventually, five newsletters were issued.

★ ★ ★
★ LIVERPOOL INSTITUTE PERFORMING ★
★ ARTS ★
★ ★ ★

PAUL McCARTNEY

INVITES

....

FOR LUNCH AT 12.45 P.M.

ON THURSDAY 2nd JULY 1992

AT CONCERT NOBLE

RUE D'ARLON 82

1040 BRUSSELS

RSVP THE DEVELOPMENT OFFICE, LIPA
THE HAHNEMANN BUILDING, 42 HOPE STREET, LIVERPOOL L1 9HW UK
TELEPHONE/FAX: 44 51 707 0002
(THIS LUNCH IS SPONSORED BY VOLKSWAGEN)

Top left: Paul and Vasso Papandreou, a key European Commissioner whose support for LIPA was important and enthusiastic.

Above and top right: The invitation and menu to the European Union launch held in Brussels.

Right: Seeking to raise match funding is turned into a challenge by Geoff Baker, then Paul's publicist.

Menu

Bavarois de légumes de saison
en chemise d'épinards
et son coulis de tomates

* * *

Raviolis de Saffran
garniture d'asperges du pays
et sauce à la creme légères

* * *

Le bavarois aux fraises

This luncheon is sponsored by
VOLKSWAGEN

The success of the Brussels lunch was not repeated in London or Japan, the third and fourth of such planned fundraisers.

Since Paul was touring most of the 1990s, he decided to try to raise money on tour by offering a 'LIPA Ticket' at a special price. Initially this was pitched at the corporate market, but insufficient time for responses affected take-up. It was Paul's fans who responded with enthusiasm.

Lorne Michaels, the US film and television producer, had answered Paul's request for support by donating the takings of the premieres of *Wayne's World 2*. The first was held in the Empire cinema, Leicester Square, London – the very same cinema where Mark had first seen *Fame*. After the London premier, the Hard Rock Café hosted a reception at their Hyde Park venue and donated £25,000.

Living their lives publicly in the years of slog was a shock to the LIPA project team. Every media pundit was eager to offer his or her opinion. It seemed that no one could mention performing arts or performing arts training

A little help from my friend

Paul McCartney

THE Prime Minister has made a £4 million wager with Paul McCartney — pledging the money for his Fame-style school if he can raise the same himself.

The ex-Beatle wants the money to convert his old school into the Liverpool Institute for the Performing Arts, a college for would-be pop stars and managers.

MAJOR IN £4M GAMBLE TO BACK McCARTNEY'S SCHOOL OF FAME

Mr Major's pound-for-pound gamble with McCartney guarantees him £4 million of Government money, provided he can raise the same amount in donations by the end of this year.

It leaves McCartney just six months to reach his target.

But the pledge is certain to boost his international drive to raise £13 million by 1995.

McCartney said yesterday:

"Things are going well, there's still a long way to go but I'm convinced we'll make it."

The Queen has already given the scheme her personal endorsement by unexpectedly sending McCartney a cheque for the school.

Mr Major sent McCartney a message of support and official Government backing on his first day in charge of the EC presidency.

McCartney will relay the message to top-level EC politicians when he flies to Brussels today to seek their support.

Already £1.5 million has been raised for the project following large donations from the singer and The Music Publishers' Association.

When LIPA opens on the site of McCartney's disused old school, the Liverpool Institute, it will provide courses for 2,500 students. The former Beatle may even teach some courses.

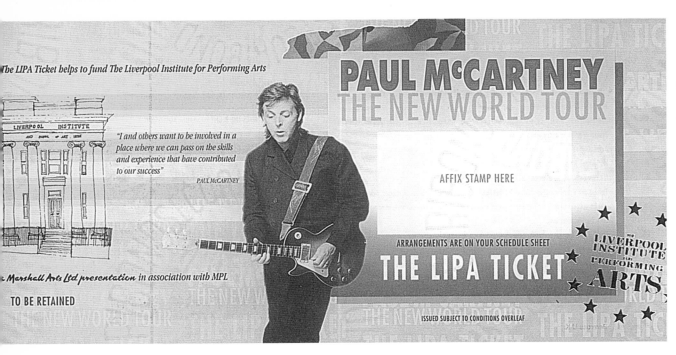

The LIPA Ticket helps to fund The Liverpool Institute for Performing Arts

PAUL McCARTNEY
THE NEW WORLD TOUR

"I and others want to be involved in a place where we can pass on the skills and experience that have contributed to our success"
PAUL McCARTNEY

AFFIX STAMP HERE

ARRANGEMENTS ARE ON YOUR SCHEDULE SHEET
THE LIPA TICKET

THE LIVERPOOL INSTITUTE FOR PERFORMING ARTS

A Marshall Arts Ltd presentation in association with MPL

TO BE RETAINED

ISSUED SUBJECT TO CONDITIONS OVERLEAF

Right: The guests at the *Wayne's World 2* benefit for LIPA in London included (left to right) Jerry Hall, Jools Holland, Paul, Peter Sissons (a schoolboy contemporary of Paul's), Chrissie Hynde, Twiggy, Linda McCartney, Naomi Campbell and Mike Myers.

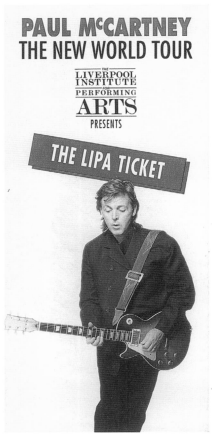

PAUL McCARTNEY
THE NEW WORLD TOUR

THE LIVERPOOL INSTITUTE FOR PERFORMING ARTS
PRESENTS

THE LIPA TICKET

Above and right: The LIPA Ticket on Paul's world tour to raise funds. On some occasions, it gave fans the unique experience of meeting Paul after the sound check, as pictured in Australia.

EUROPEAN CHARITY PREMIERE

IN AID OF

THE LIVERPOOL INSTITUTE FOR PERFORMING ARTS
SUPPORTED BY GRUNDIG

WAYNE'S WORLD 2

OFFICIAL RADIO STATION · Virgin radio 1215 AM · WAYNE'S WORLD 2

Hard Rock CAFE

PAY **THE LIVERPOOL INSTITUTE FOR PERFORMING ARTS**

DATE JAN 28 1994

TWENTY FIVE THOUSAND POUNDS

IN RECOGNITION OF THE SALE OF LINDA McCARTNEY'S VEGGIE BURGERS

£ 25,000.00

FOR AND ON BEHALF OF THE HARD ROCK INTERNATIONAL FOUNDATION

Right: Some of the guests at the *Wayne's World 2* benefit in Liverpool included Adrian Henri, Russell Christian, Mike Myers, Janice Long, Ian McCulloch and Mick Hucknall.

Below: Newspapers across the world ran articles about the creation of LIPA.

Right: Two major fund raising initiatives announced at the same time: EU support and Grundig's title sponsorship.

Something to celebrate: Paul and Linda McCartney arriving in London yesterday to break the good news about LIPA.

EC backs McCartney 'Fame' school

POP STAR Paul McCartney's plans to open a "Fame" school in Liverpool was given a £6m boost yesterday.

The EC's European Regional Development Fund has given it a £4m grant and electronic giant Grundig is making a donation estimated at £2m.

Grundig yesterday committed itself to "a long-term investment over four years", providing 50 per cent of the required private sector funding and putting the school on course to open in September 1995.

The ex-Beatle has already don-ated £1m of his own money to turn his old school into a college for aspiring musicians and rock executives, as far afield as the £12m target has been raised for The Liverpool Institute for Performing Arts, where the McCartney, 50, hopes to teach classes.

He said yesterday: "Obviously I'm delighted at the news. It's great to have the backing of so many people from so many different walks of life — from kids who sent us their pocket money through the EC.

A private donation from the Queen was made last June and the Prime Minister pledged the Government would give £4m if the singer/songwriter matched it through fundraising.

Former Beatles Ringo Starr and George Harrison have made hefty personal donations, as have many other pop stars.

LIPA chief executive Mark Featherstone-Witty said: "LIPA is now truly up and running. Paul McCartney's dream was that Liverpool will one day boast the finest school of its type in the world. Industry is sharing Paul's vision and the dream of LIPA is becoming a firm reality."

Mr McCartney has agreed for the first time to allow one of his songs to be used in commercials. C'mon People, from his current album Off The Ground, will feature in a series of radio and TV ads to promote LIPA.

■ Linda McCartney was also celebrating yesterday — she has sold her 50 millionth vegetarian meal and was presented with a special "Golden Dish" award by frozen food company Ross to mark the occasion.

- Beatle dons doublet and hose for fame school TV debut -

PAUL HAM-LETS IT UP IN SCREEN AD

● Head-liner ... Beatle Paul dons his disguise

By Jayne Atherton

PAUL McCartney has made his first TV and cinema commercial — to promote his Liverpool Fame School.

Ex-Beatle Paul swopped his rock and roll stage gear for Elizabethan costume, mortar board and paint-brush for the commercial which will be flashed across the world.

Variety

His fans will see him as a paint-splattered artist, Shakespearian actor and a headmaster to show the variety of courses at the new Liverpool Institute of Performing Arts.

MTV and Eurosport channels will carry the ad in the UK, while Viva will also broadcast it across Europe. It will also be seen in German cinemas.

LIPA, housed in the old Liverpool Institute building — Paul's former school — has already received 1,500 applications from would-be students who want to attend its first classes in September 1995.

The school will have unrivalled facilities in Britain including a 500-seat auditorim, four recording studios and video and radio suites.

Paul told the ECHO today: "I want this to be the best school of its kind in the world. I and others in the industry want to be able to pass on skills and experiences that have contributed to our success.

"It's great to see the day dawning when my old school will have students back in its corridors and that Liverpool will be the world's target for tomorrow's talent."

April 8, 1993

Letter launches star's scheme

By Alex Hunt

FOUR years ago, Paul McCartney wrote to the Echo asking Merseysiders whether they wanted a Fame school.

A telephone poll brought the res-ounding answer — YES!

Since then, the region has been joined by the Queen and a whole host of celebrities in backing the venture.

They include Eddie Murphy, Mark Knopfler, Paul Simon, Dudley Moore, Alan Parker and Andre Previn as well as George Harrison, Ringo Starr and Yoko Ono through Apple.

The target for the fund-raising has been £12m to get LIPA up and running, plus a further £3m endowment fund for students who cannot get grants.

McCartney has given £1m, Grundig £2m, and a further £1m has come from the public and showbiz circles.

EC funding announced today pushes up the total by £4m with the govern-ment having pledged £4m of City Chal-lenge money to match the privately raised money.

The school will cater for students 18-years-old upwards. With 2,300 part-time places, there will be plenty of opportun-ities for going back to school.

Processing admissions for courses will start next year.

Subjects covered will range from per-forming of music to marketing, music industry management to photography.

PAUL'S DREAM IS TO BE FULFILLED

Up to £12m pledged to help Fame school

PAUL McCartney today announced that his dream to build a Fame school in Liverpool had become a reality — thanks to a £6m boost in funds.

The former Beatle revealed that £4m has been given by the EC and £2m from a sponsorship deal with German electronics company Grundig.

The government has pledged to match money raised pound for pound.

Today Paul looked ahead to taking his first class at the Liverpool Institute for Performing Arts in 1995.

Informal

He said: "The first thing I say when I go into class has got to be: 'OK kids, I don't know how to do this, so let's try and work out a way.'

"I'll show them how I started, some chords and then: 'Right, go away and write a song.'

"It will be informal, anything I teach, because I'm not a great academic."

The long-term Grundig deal includes using McCartney's music in adverts for the first time.

Estimates for the value of the Grundig adverts for LIPA over the next few years range up to £8m.

LIPA chief executive Mark Featherstone-Witty said today: "This is truly excellent news. "LIPA is now two-thirds of the way towards its 1995 target of raising £12m.

"Paul McCartney's dream was that Liverpool will one day boast the finest school of its type in the world and that dream is now reality."

Since McCartney first sought backing for a Fame school in the Echo four years ago, he has attracted the backing of the Queen, John Major and a host of showbiz friends.

Grundig spokesman Jochan Van Splunter said: "Now industry too can hold this dream and together we can all work to let a new opportunity begin for the young people."

Builders have already moved into the LIPA building in Hope Street, where 550 full-time and 2,300 part-time students are expected to be registered for its first term in autumn 1995.

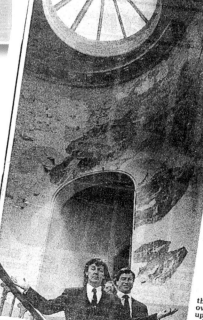

Flashback ... Paul McCartney with minister Michael Portillo at the Liverpool Institute

---

£2M BOOST FOR FAME SCHOOL

McCartney's dream comes a step nearer to reality

PAUL McCartney's Merseyside Fame School is to get a £2m boost from German electronics company Grundig.

By Alex Hunt

Details of the deal for the Liverpool Institute for Performing Arts are expected to be announced tomorrow.

The donation ends a long struggle to find a major private sector sponsor for the project to breathe new life into McCartney's old school, the Liverpool Institute.

receive its first students at the con-verted school building in September 1995, with the number of full-timers building up to 550 within three years.

Grundig is also expec-ted to announce a major sponsorship of

The Grundig sponsorship is launched with a press conference in London.

Far Right: Paul in the Grundig TV commercial that visually captured LIPA's multi-skilling philosophy.

Sponsorship deal nets £1 million for 'Fame' school

Advance – Grundig director Johan van Splunter (left) with LIPA patron Paul McCartney and director Mark Featherstone-Witty

BY TARA CONLAN

Liverpool Institute of Performing Arts has signed a sponsorship deal with electrical manufacturer Grundig worth more than £1 million.

The so-called 'Fame' school, whose chief patron is Paul McCartney, will use the money over the next four years to help out with the day to day running costs of the company. It will also be channelled into attracting students to LIPA from all over Europe. Grundig has already set up information centres across the continent and LIPA workshops have been organised.

This is the second sponsorship from Grundig. The first was in 1993 when the school was founded. The new four year contract will run into the next millennium.

Grundig director Johan van Splunter commented: "We hope that our continued support will contribute to the advancement and education of young people not only from the UK, but across Europe as well."

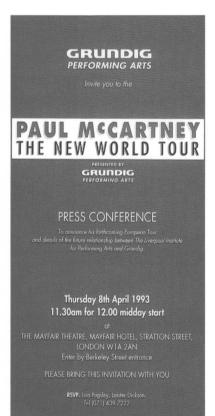

GRUNDIG
PERFORMING ARTS

Invite you to the

PAUL McCARTNEY
THE NEW WORLD TOUR

PRESENTED BY
GRUNDIG
PERFORMING ARTS

PRESS CONFERENCE

To announce his forthcoming European Tour
and details of the future relationship between The Liverpool Institute
for Performing Arts and Grundig.

Thursday 8th April 1993
11.30am for 12.00 midday start
at
THE MAYFAIR THEATRE, MAYFAIR HOTEL, STRATTON STREET,
LONDON W1A 2AN
Enter by Berkeley Street entrance

PLEASE BRING THIS INVITATION WITH YOU

RSVP. Lisa Pugsley, Laister Dickson.
Tel (071) 439 7222

without some reference to LIPA. Many times the criticisms were unfounded and the comments hurtful. It took a hardening of the skin to maintain optimism and equilibrium.

Aiming to revitalise their brand for a younger market, Grundig felt that it needed to engage with youth through sport and the performing arts. Of the two, their engagement with the performing arts was non-existent. LIPA provided the engagement. The link between LIPA, Paul and Grundig called for negotiations that proved complicated and protracted, if congenial and constructive. One very tricky negotiation involved a TV advert in which Grundig wanted Paul to appear, but which Paul resisted on his principle of not endorsing products. The problem was resolved by creating the advert in two parts: one with Paul about LIPA and one solely about Grunding products.

The London launch of the link between Grundig and LIPA was the chance to mention, slightly early, the EU commitment of £4m to fund the project.

The money to launch LIPA had been raised. So far so good. The project was actively moving towards putting the money to work. This meant different mountains to climb; some, however, turned out to be remarkably familiar.

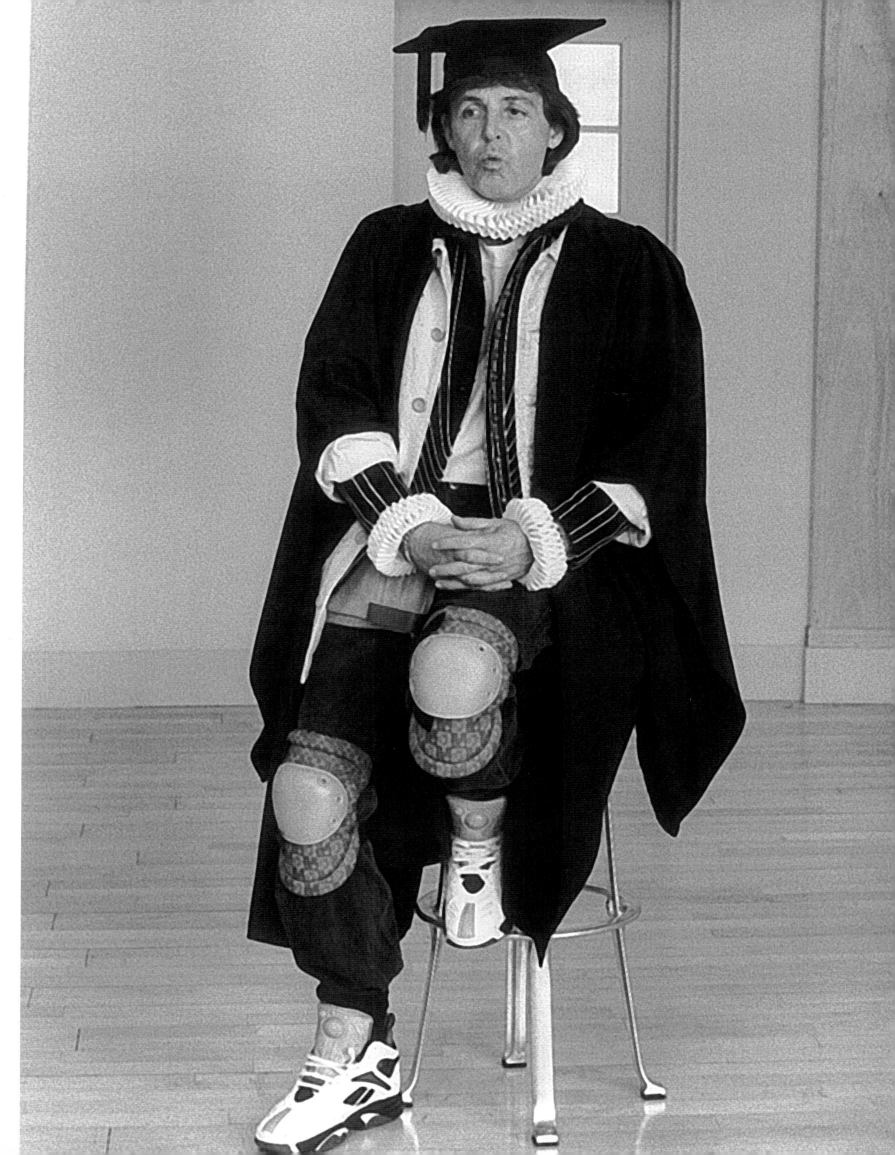

LIPA IN PICTURES

3 PUTTING THE MONEY TO WORK

3 PUTTING THE MONEY TO WORK

One of the scary moments in the renovation of the old school: the need to support the walls after the removal of three floors in the front of the building.

THE FIRST demand for a huge input of money was restoration and renovation. The existing three floors on the front of the old school were shaky, decayed and unable to take the weight of even normal student activity. They had to be removed and a new edifice built within the walls of the old one. The catalogue of things needing to be done included mechanical ventilation, fire detection, lighting protection, security, voice evacuation, data, telephones, computers, audio visual cabling, theatre lighting and sound systems. The aim was to route these services undetected throughout the building – taking 36 miles of cabling.

46

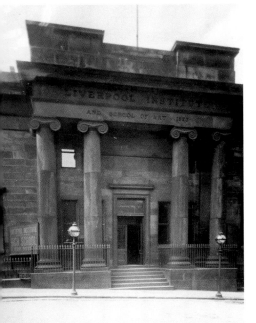

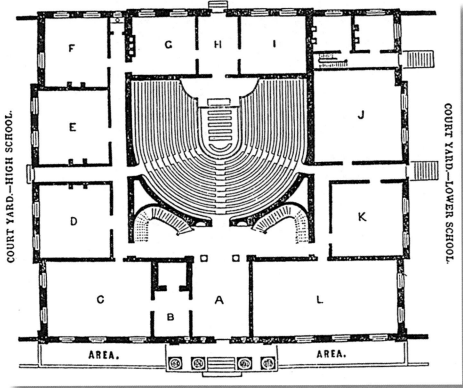

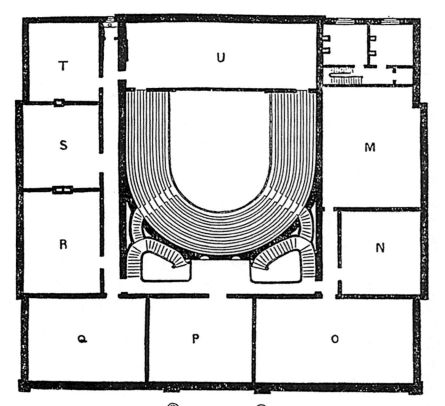

REFERENCE TO PLAN.

A. Vestibule.	H. Back Vestibule.
B. Secretary's Office.	I. Chemical Department in High
C. Library.	and Lower Schools.
D. Board Room.	Lecture Room.
G. Laboratory.	U. Museum.

HIGH SCHOOL.

E. Mathematical Department.	O. English Department.
F. Philosophical Department of High and	P. Writing Department.
Lower Schools.	Q. Classical Department.
M. Writing Department of Preparatory	R. French Department, No. 1.
School.	S. French Department, No. 2.
N. Mathematical Department, No. 2.	

LOWER SCHOOL.

L. English Department.	K. Mathematical and Philosophical De-
J. Writing and Drawing Department.	partment.

EVENING SCHOOL.

L. Mathematical Department.	N. Mechanical Drawing and Naval Archi-
P. Writing Department.	tecture Department.
J. Landscape, Drawing, and Perspective	T. Figure Drawing, Ornamental Painting,
Department.	Modelling, and Ornamental Drawing
M. Architectural Drawing Department.	Department.

The original building was square, as seen in the plans.

Paul's old school had an interesting history. It started as the Mechanics' School of Arts, opening in 1837 to offer education through lectures. By the time the original school moved into the current Mount Street building, the range and popularity of the lectures had greatly increased, as did the scope and cost. Great names of visiting lecturers included the American author and philosopher Ralph Waldo Emerson, the Irish dramatist James Sheridan Knowles, and the English author and sometimes performer Charles Dickens. In 1847–8 the 82 lectures included 33 on literary topics, 25 on science, 8 on music and 4 each on history and oratory.

The date on the front pillars of LIPA is in fact the date when the idea of a Mechanics' Institute was presented to various local master craftsmen. It was the dream of Thomas Traill, vice president of the Liverpool Royal Institution, who developed the idea from another Scot, John Anderson. This idea was to afford 'the mechanic the means of acquiring some knowledge on which the operation of his art was founded'. So art was linked with knowledge for workers and, by extension, the general public.

Like many public buildings of the time, the old school reflected the confidence of a thriving city based on wealth and was subject to being adapted as new ideas emerged. In 1840 the school had been transferred to the Liverpool City Council and became the Liverpool Institute for Boys. In turn, the Liverpool Institute became Liverpool's pre-eminent classical grammar school, then a comprehensive before closing in 1985. Years of marginal upkeep and two years of vandalism reduced the building to a handsome, rotting shell in a setting to rival continental European cities.

Charles Dickens was one of the famous lecturers at the Liverpool Institute for Boys during its life in the 19th century.

SOIREE AT THE LIVERPOOL MECHANICS' INSTITUTION, ON MONDAY LAST.—MR. DICKENS'S ADDRESS.

48

Brock Carmichael (Liverpool) won the national competition to find an architect. David Watkins led the design team. The model first presented had to be adapted when it was discovered that the floors supported the bulging walls in the old gym to the right of the main building.

By the time actual restoration began, costs had escalated with a continuous need for money. Luckily, the National Lottery had just started up and grants from that organisation were substantial enough to keep things going.

By this time, LIPA's Council (its Board of Governors) had been chosen. These were the people to whom Mark reported. There was also a small team of employees that he managed.

Old photos of the former Institute including schoolboys at their studies. It was an outstanding grammar school. By 1917, a Nobel Prize winner was among its eminent old boys.

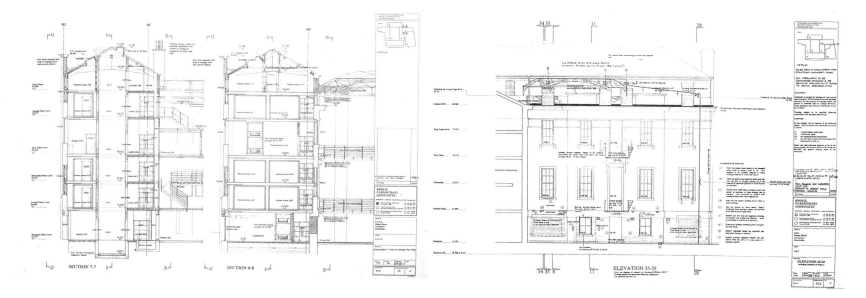

SECTION 7-7   SECTION 8-8   ELEVATION 35-35

The Design Team gather in front of the model. Back row: Bergen Peck, Peter Carmichael (Brock Carmichael Associates); Roy Billington (Roy Billington Associates), structural engineers; Richard Spencer (Walfords) quantity surveyors; Mark. Front row: Geoffrey Manning (C E Griffiths & Son) mechanical engineers; David Watkins (Brock Carmichael Associates), architect; Paul Cleworth (E C Harris Project Management), project manager; Brian Edmondson (Roy Billington Associates) and Peter Thomas (Walfords). Not pictured is Collin Thompson (Walfords).

Top and right: Renovation, reconstruction plans, model and personnel Gantt chart.

LIVERPOOL INSTITUTE FOR PERFORMING ARTS.
PROPOSED PROGRAMME: PERSONNEL

Left: Before and after pictures of the auditorium (top), the back of the building (middle) and one of the main staircases (bottom).

Right: Work on the front interior.

Left: The colours for the interior walls were derived from a painting by André Derain (shown).

Right: Before, during and after pictures of the front dance studio (top), a main staircase (second row), a lower passageway (third row) and the main hall (bottom).

Overleaf: The building changes.

NON NOBIS SOLUM SED TOTI MUNDO NATI

THE PAUL McCARTNEY AUDITORIUM

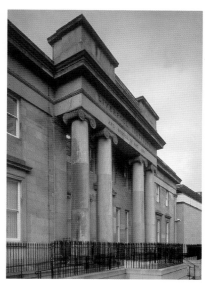

The old school gym (top). It was removed to house 21st-century facilities of five recording studios a lecture theatre/second auditorium and other rooms and spaces, which was a design challenge (middle and bottom).

The renovation of the building (right). The design challenge was to erect a new structure (below) in a historic street and as part of a Grade II listed building without resorting to pastiche.

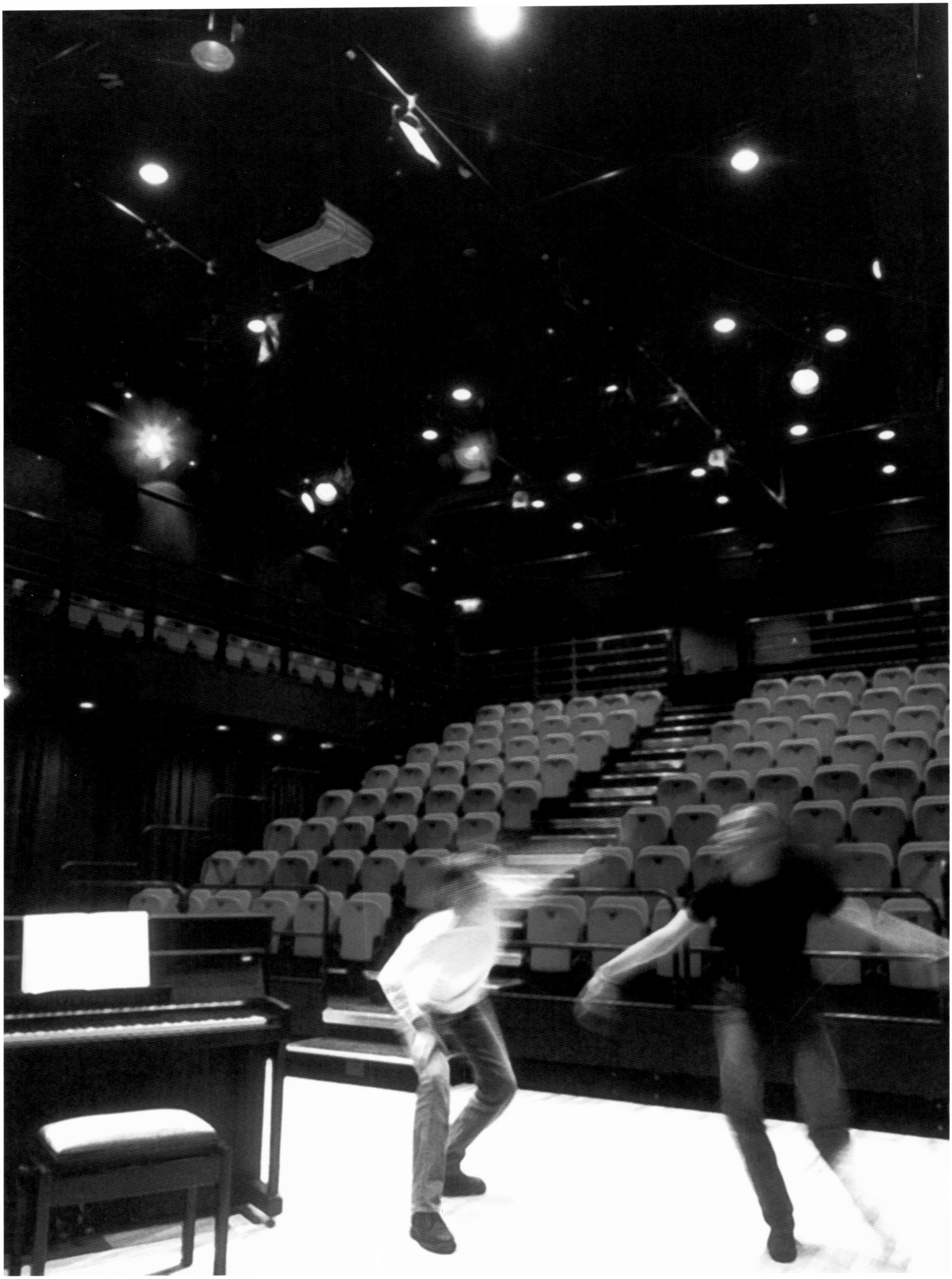

Left: The new studio/dance/lecture theatre.

Right: The largest recording studio in the school. It was named The George Martin Studio to honour his contribution.

Below: The atrium that joins the old building with the new.

LIPA IN PICTURES

4 TESTING THE PHILOSOPHY

4 TESTING THE PHILOSOPHY

The pilot courses get started.
This one is Image and Style.

A S WORK began on the building, the LIPA project team launched a series of four free pilot courses for 10 local bands, soloists and a theatre group to test both the content and delivery of its programme. Apart from business and marketing, the courses covered areas that active performers simply didn't or couldn't spend time thinking about. One course, for example, was called Image and Style. In it, the invited

THE LIVERPOOL INSTITUTE FOR PERFORMING ARTS PROSPECTUS 1995

CONTENTS. THE LIPA PROSPECTUS, 1995 ENTRY Application Form. Audio-tape.
SIDE A: Introducing LIPA Presented by Peter Sissons. Interviews with Joan Armatrading, Cameron Mackintosh, Paul McCartney, George Martin and David Puttnam.
SIDE B: THE LIPA PROSPECTUS on Tape. Read by Peter Sissons.
ACKNOWLEDGEMENTS We want to thank the following people and organisations who have helped us to produce our first prospectus by providing goods and services at no or minimal cost: Nick Angell for providing his studio, Angell Sound EMI for supplying and copying the tapes, Steve Kelly for mixing Side A, Liam O'Donoghue for conceiving Side A, Billy Mawhinney for conceiving the design and artwork, J & C Moores for their contribution to printing costs, Radio City, Liverpool for mixing facilities, Peter Sissons and featured Patrons.

RUNNING TIME 3 YEARS APPROX
18 Suitable only for persons of 18 years and over
Not to be supplied to any person below that age

051 70   70003

The copyright of all the prospectus material is held by The Liverpool Institute for Performing Arts, Mount Street, Liverpool L1 9HF

Right: A jokey video cover, itself a piece of industry hardware, for the first prospectus: spot the bar code in the shape of LIPA's front pillars and the running time of approximatly three years. The designer was Billy Mawhinney.

Below: The prospectus rolls off the press.

Left: A glimpse at various pilot courses. The LIPA philosophy underpinning these is that, whatever their specific ambition, students must acquire diverse skills, for example, in directing, lighting, costume design and business planning.

participants were asked to develop a coherent strategy as to how to present themselves to the public, either as a group or soloist, and to get across the concept behind their music and performance. Practising graphic and fashion designers, as well as photographers, were drafted in to help them achieve a strategy.

In addition to appointing staff, the LIPA team needed to issue the first prospectus, which had the formidable task of selling an institution that didn't yet exist. No pictures. No students. No curriculum. No achieving alumni. This dilemma was solved by producing the prospectus in a form common to media industries: a video along with the more usual printed version.

Then, too, there were formal standards of higher education to meet and the curriculum to create before the first auditions could be held. These

Music is one of the UK's three top earners of foreign income. In this respect it out performs steel, oil refining and pharmaceuticals. On one level, LIPA exists to support this industry and to ensure that music and other arts continue to retain their hold on the world stage.

However, this is one aspect only of LIPA's mission for although money and commerce may be important, they are not everything.

music

Pages from the second prospectus.

"ANY TRAINING IN ART
IS
AT LEAST

A PARTIAL TRAINING IN
ANARCHY"
JOHN CAGE

'To do is to be' Plato

'To be is to do' Socrates

'do be do be do' Frank Sinatra

(graffiti - anon)

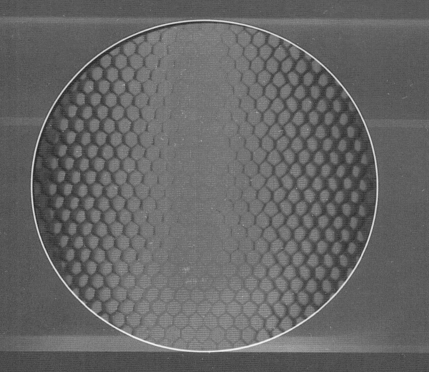

entry96/97

Cover of the second prospectus. Producing
this was a formidable challenge since it
had to be issued before the first teaching
year was underway. No students and no
activities to photograph. The solution was
to present the LIPA concept and sprinkle
the text with quotes and anecdotes. One is
attributed to Ira Gershwin. When asked:
"Which comes first, the words or the
music?" His response was: "The contract".

THE LIVERPOOL INSTITUTE FOR PERFORMING ARTS

Ex-Beatle gründet Pop-Uni —
so und ähnlich lauteten die
hlagzeilen, als bekannt wurde.
ß Rockstar Paul McCartney in
iner Heimatstadt Liverpool eine
ochschule für Unterhaltungs-
nst zu gründen gedenke. Mittler-
eile hat sich die Sache soweit
onkretisiert, daß die ersten 180

Paul McCartney als Lehrmeister für Showbiz-Experten

Augustin beginnt demnächst e
ool Institute for Performing Ar

Student steers for the stars

TALENTED singer and drama student Samira Rankin (left), looks all set to reach for the stars after gaining a coveted place at a North West academy for performing arts.

Samira, 19, of Whittingham Lane, Broughton, Preston, had to undergo a full day audition, competing against hundreds of hopefuls — some of them from abroad — for a place at the Liverpool International Institute of Performing Arts.

Former Beatles star Paul McCartney, was heavily involved in setting up the centre which throws open its doors for the first time in September to the select students.

Samira, an ex-pupil at Broughton High School, is currently spending five weeks' holiday at her aunt's home in Canada. Her excited mum, Elaine, phoned her with the good news that she had got a place and they both cried with joy.

Mother-of-five Mrs Rankin said: "She has really worked hard for this and it is something she really wants to do with her life."

ach "Performing Design" (Au-
ihrungsgestaltung). „Eine einma-
ge Chance", freut sich der
4jäh
ur R

Da
ls M
lte L
isse
erhi
Ex-Beatle in den Sparstrumpf und
tartete eine Kampagne zur Umge-
taltung der Schule in Europas
erste E
gelang
ung, da
Unterha
und vie
der Sho
begeiste
das Lip
ät ange
EU und
behörd
schulin
konnte
Ged
ger für

FAME OF SCHOOL GOES WORLD-WIDE

Darf bei
McCartn
die Lehre
Gerd Wil
aus Sank
stin hat a
von nur z
Deutsche
der weltw
gehrten S
plätze an
verpool I
for Perfo

Julie's set for the big time!

SINGER songwriter Julie Thompson from Sprowston has got a ticket to ride.

by ABIGAIL SALTMARSH

She's on her way to Merseyside to study at the Liverpool Institute of Performing Arts, whose famous patron is former Beatle Paul McCartney.

Julie, who has just finished her A-levels, has already been approached about record deals — but originally set them aside until after her exams.

And now she has decided she will put them off again because she wants to study further before aiming for the big time.

"It is tempting when they offer you lots of money and say 'come and record with us'," said Julie, 18. "But if you look at the small print they end up getting it back from you 10 times over."

Julie hopes doing a three-year music degree will give her the experience she needs

"It is just that it will give me more skills and I will not be at their mercy," she explained.

Among Julie's lecturers will be McCartney himself and Elvis Costello. The students are encouraged to go gigging with big groups to gain experience.

Julie launched her musical career when she was just 10, singing cover versions in local pubs.

She won a songwriting contest at the British Song Writing Fair at 11 and has already played solo in venues such as the Astoria and the Rock Garden in London.

"When I was nine I left Brownies and did not want to go on to Guides but my Dad said I had to take up something else," Julie said.

"He suggested the keyboard and in the end I agreed and I

jene, die bei Roch
iz- und Theaterau
icals oder Revuer
ter den Kulissen
le Bedingungen
m solchen Showb
öchte Gerd Willss
ol heranreifen.
t und Kreativitä
nte Energieele
s mit: Nachden

Dancer Leanne Frear is jumping for joy after beating thousands of hopefuls to grab one of the first 200 places at the new Liverpool Institute for the Performing Arts. For Leanne, who lives with her parents, Carole and Bill Frear, at Barton Turns, the offer is her best birthday present ever. She starts the three-year BA Honours degree course in the performing arts at the Paul McCartney-backed school on Monday — two days after her 20th birthday.
● Full story — P.9.
● Picture: Neil Barker

Left: The search for students. Search teams initially went across Europe and Scandinavia, starting in Norway.

Right: Auditions.

Below: A LIPA representative answers questions from a prospective student.

Lou Reed (right) headlined the New York launch at Paul's invitation. For wider publicity, the imminent release of Paul's latest album, *Free as a Bird*, was announced at the same time.

DAILY POST. 16/3/95.

Fame school wins applause from Big Apple

By Chris Parker
Daily Post Staff

PAUL McCartney's fame school dream became the toast of Manhattan as rock stars sang its praises yesterday.

Lou Reed, Bruce Springsteen's drummer Max Weinberg and Led Zeppelin producer Eddie Kramér were the focus of dozens of radio and television stations as they introduced America to the Liverpool Institute for Performing Arts.

A corporate sponsor made the surprise announcement that it is to sponsor an American student's three-year study at LIPA.

New York's Planet Hollywood restaurant played host to the stars, who were joined by LIPA chief executive Mark Featherstone-Witty.

Lou Reed described LIPA as offering a unique service by teaching young artists about the machinations of the entertainment industry.

He said: "My experience with management has been a little disappointing. I had to fight for 12 years to get payment for Walk on the Wild Side.

"I wish a course like this had been available to me when I was starting out."

Reed read out a faxed message from the college's main patron, Paul McCartney.

The former Beatle took the opportunity to announce that a number of new songs by the three surviving band members would be released at the end of the year.

His message read: "I'm sorry I can't be with you, but I've got the best possible excuse.

"I'm working in the studio on a couple of tracks from a '60s beat groups you may have heard of — called the Beatles."

He added: "I want to give something back to my old home town of Liverpool."

Alison Holbourn, director of communications at LIPA, said: "Everyone in New York loves the idea of coming to Liverpool.

LIPA is considering further campaigns in California and Japan after its success in Norway.

LIPA managers revealed they will spend the next four days at Manhattan's La Guardia School for Performing Arts, the institution which inspired the television series Fame, to tell young hopefuls how they can apply for a LIPA place.

started in January 1995. Since multiskilling was a key part of the LIPA approach, each hopeful had to undertake a variety of tests. The worlds of words, lobbying, committees and general tasking vanished into the reality of people who might become students. Soon afterwards, audition teams were travelling the world. By the time the selection was made, there were students from 11 countries. The second prospectus was produced a year later, still as a concept.

Paul asked Lou Reed, the US singer and songwriter, to headline the

Above: Press coverage followed the cost overruns and the building delays.

New York launch in March 1995. Lou immediately understood the focus on business skills when he said: "My experience with managers has been a textbook study of what not to do. Although I had a university degree, once my friends and I were in rock, we just wanted to make a record. No one paid attention past that. It took me 12 years to regain the rights to *Walk on the Wild Side*."

Another appeal was launched, this time for equipment. Although the original costings had covered equipment, the escalating costs of everything soon outran the available funds. In fact, time and cost overruns delayed the start of the teaching year. Staff members were itching to teach and students anxious to learn. Finally, students visited Liverpool for the first time in November 1995 for an induction programme.

The cost overruns meant that the governing body was meeting more regularly than planned. As a body of volunteers, their loyalty to the project was tested hard. To LIPA's good fortune, no one failed the test.

Right top: High End Systems donates their latest model lighting table. The presentaton was made by the CEO, Lowell Fowler (far right) with David Catterall, the UK executive of the company, in attendance.

Right bottom: Grundig board member, Johan van Splunter, in front of the Internet cafe donated by his company, the major commercial sponsor of LIPA.

Far right: The cover of the second appeal. It was directed towards acquiring equipment.

Fame school faces the final curtai

McCartney: cash crisis

THE Liverpool Institute for Performing Arts (Lipa) — better known as Paul McCartney's Fame school — is teetering on the edge of insolvency, its principal has admitted. It is seeking to avoid closure by imposing a £500 emergency "facility fee" on its students. Mark Featherstone-Witty, the principal, last week predicted further storms ahead for the college, *write John Harlow and Cherry Norton*.

Since Lipa was opened by the Queen last summer it has failed to attract enough high-paying foreign students to pay its way. It is also battling with builders who claim they are owed £3m for converting McCartney's former grammar school into a rock college.

Lipa is running on a shoe-string, admits Featherstone-Witty. "The £45,000 we shall raise from the new charges, which are access fees for musical instruments and other facilities, makes all the difference between success and insolvency," he said.

Donors who originally contributed to the school have made it clear they will not bail it out now. These include McCartney, the former Beatle who gave more than £1m; Elvis Costello, the rock musician; Wayne Sleep, the dancer; David Hockney, the painter; and American film stars Eddie Murphy and Jane Fonda.

Although McCartney has shunned the business side of Lipa, he has committed himself to lecturing at the college at least once a year. Other patrons who are also expected to visit include Sir Cameron Mackintosh, the theatrical im-

On the way out? Emergency fees may be imposed

presario; Melvyn Bragg, the broadcaster; Dame Judi Dench, the actress; and actors Dudley Moore and Derek Jacobi.

For the first time Featherstone-Witty, a former actor, has admitted that he made mistakes while establishing Lipa. In retrospect, he said, he should have employed extra staff to recruit more foreigners, who were expected to make up a quarter of the 200 students but, in fact, number just a handful. "We shall make up for this next year," he said.

Featherstone-Witty, 40, ran into similar problems in the early 1980s when, as co-founder and managing director of Fleury Education, he was running a group of private colleges dedicated to publishing and insurance. He complained later in a written summary of his achievements that he had to struggle to reach financial targets because of an unexpected shortage of foreign students. This he blamed on laws restricting the number of such visitors to Britain.

He has since dissolved Fleury Education, as well as the Anglo-American Performing Arts Club, which he set up to bring American audiences to

see British musicals. [...] many ideas, it is remembering all of said last week.

He also underes running costs of ar In 1989, with th Alan Parker who inal Fame film, J the writer, and the Beatles' helped establi school in Croy teaches mus addition to r subjects.

Almost a the Croyd financial proble ton, a spokesma "The industrial invest £1m more inally expected learn to worl budgets."

Featherstone Brit without p the similarities pool institute. love lost betwee It all went rather time George N troduced me to ney, who said tribute to anothe but this time it Liverpool."

Mark Featherstone-Witty Liverpool Institute for Performing Arts

A REPORT on the Liverpool Institute for Performing Arts (November 10) stated that the Institute was "teetering on the edge of insolvency", and referred to financial problems faced by other organisations with which Mark Featherstone-Witty, LIPA's founder and chief executive, had been involved, inferring that Mr Featherstone-Witty was responsible for these problems.

In fact, Fleury Education was financially successful and was sold to an American company, and Mr Featherstone-Witty was not involved in the management of the Brit School. The Anglo-American Performing Arts Club never traded. We ac-

cept that the inference was unjustified and apologise for any distress caused.

It is true that the cost of refurbishing the building occupied by LIPA is causing a financial headache for LIPA's subsidiary (which is responsible for the refurbishment) and active steps are being taken to raise further capital funds.

However, the Institute itself is in sound financial health. LIPA is not in deficit and is on course to remain in the black for the foreseeable future.

There is no danger of it closing down and students are currently being recruited for the next academic year.

It took some years after the opening to erase the overruns, but all the partners achieved this through contributions.

Cost overruns were avidly seized upon as big news by the press, often with adverse comment. The press also harped on planning problems. This didn't help fundraising efforts and depressed those trying to make LIPA a success.

Despite these setbacks, the building was ready for occupation by December 1995. LIPA had a home.

News coverage of LIPA's opening. The first students arrive and Gerry Marsden, of Gerry and the Pacemakers, takes a group across the Mersey on the famous ferry.

Opposite: Hooray! We did it.

PHILIP KEY'S Arts diary

CH — Daily Post, Saturday, November 18, 1995

Students ride ferry to fame

By Mark Thomas

The first students at Paul McCartney's "Fame" school were given a traditional welcome to Liverpool today – by catching a ferry across the Mersey.

The 195 full-time students were arriving in the city for a week's introductory study programme before beginning their three-year courses at the Liverpool Institute for Performing Arts in January.

Former Beatle McCartney announced plans to convert his closed-down old school, the Liverpool Institute for Boys, into a "fame" school at a concert he staged in the city in 1990.

It was due to open in September, but delays in renovation work led to a postponement until the New Year.

The students, mostly from the UK, but including a number from Europe, Japan, the USA, Croatia and Korea, will learn to develop their dramatic and musical skills, but also about the business side of show business.

LIPA Chief Executive Mark Featherstone-Witty believes the Institute's programme is unique in the way in which it will teach students the realities of the arts and entertainments industry.

"Performers are a minority in the field," he said. "Far more people are involved in helping the performers reach their potential."

He pointed out that on McCartney's last, relatively small-scale world tour there was a six-piece band but about 120 people behind the scenes.

Typical is Martyn Collins, 34, from Swansea, a singer who has come to LIPA to learn enterprise management.

"I'm very excited about it," he said. I spent a long time working in the music industry on the performance side but haven't been able to marry the two sides properly until now."

Kelly O'Leary, 19, of Kingsclere, near Basingstoke, Hampshire, a singer and cellist embarking on a music course, said: "It was the only place for me to go to. If I hadn't got in I would have tried again next year."

On the ferry students met each other and some of their tutors for the first time. They also had a chance to meet Gerry Marsden, the sixties rock star whose song Ferry Across the Mersey made the river's ferries world famous.

IT'S FAME AT LAST!

Dreams come true as students begin the long and winding road to success—

'There are a lot of talented people here'

By Julie Galaxby

You'll get by with a little help from friends

College for young showbiz hopefuls opens in Paul McCartney's old school

by Catherine Milner
Arts Correspondent

FORGET twanging on a guitar in your bedroom. If you want to be a rock 'n' roll star all you need is £7,000 and three years at the new Liverpool Institute for Performing Arts.

The first students arrived this week at Britain's only government-funded "Fame" institute, situated in Paul McCartney's old school in Toxteth. Strutting around in platform boots and cowboy hats, some of them already looked like roadies for Bon Jovi.

They have come from all over the world. Atsushi, 22, a guitarist from Tokyo, said: "Before I came here, all I knew about Liverpool was that it had a football team, riots and Paul McCartney, but by the time I leave it will be a place buzzing with clubs, recording companies and new bands. And I will have made friends and business contacts useful for me wherever I travel in the world."

Liam Niederst, 25, a singer/songwriter from Nebraska, takes a more intellectual approach. "The cool thing about the institute is that you have all these extreme kinds of people from all these different countries all broadening their minds in an area which they are all crazy about."

Seven hundred students — the majority of whom will be on Government grants — will attend the school, which will be able to award degrees. Aspiring performers will be taught how to write songs

Ripped off: McCartney

and how to sell them; how to dance like John Travolta or act like Kim Basinger. And how to spot unscrupulous agents and film and recording companies.

Special classes will explain how to avoid the infamous rock 'n' roll rows that have broken up many famous bands. There will even be classes in how to cope with fame.

"It's a fantasy to think that people who are successful don't dwell on wealth," said Mark Featherstone-Witty, an entrepreneur who set up the institute in collaboration with McCartney, who last week was made of a Fellow of the Royal College of Music. "The trouble with many young bands is that they get all this money on one hit and then blow it all on some holiday in the Seychelles. We want to try to explain that they'd do better to invest their money so that they can

erous of a long list of illustrious institute benefactors having given £1 million towards the £12 million cost of refurbishing the school with five dance studios, five recording studios and a new theatre.

Other glitterati involved in the project include Joan Armatrading, Eddie Murphy, Carly Simon, David Hockney, Dudley Moore, Wayne Sleep, and Jane Fonda, although the bulk of the money has come from local authorities, the EC and Grundig, the German electronics company which is the main sponsor.

Established pop stars will instruct their fledgling followers in how to make a hit. "But we're not talking about students sitting twanging their guitars in unison," said Mr Featherstone-Witty. "It will be more a question of 'have you thought of doing it this way?' We won't be creating a LIPA style."

Most of the courses appear to have more to do with psychology than showbiz. "Transactional Analysis Classes" will instruct students into the wiles of getting on with people.

And in an increasingly media-influenced world, students will learn how to project a suitably cool image. "If you are a pop musician you are selling yourself as much as your work. Your hairstyle, clothes, logo and how you market yourself all matter enormously. You also need to learn how to handle interviews properly."

All this might sound ludicrous to anybody who ever thought of great rock stars as scruffy, anarchic rabble rousers rather than a set of clones poring over spreadsheet

First stage: Takaya Tsukura and Liam Niederst hope the college will launch them on a successful career   *Photograph: John Robertson*

LIPA IN PICTURES

5 THE FIRST YEAR

5 THE FIRST YEAR

O N 8 JANUARY 1996 the first group of students gathered for the first whole student body meeting of LIPA. Twenty-two days later, they found themselves on risers on the stage of the newly named Paul McCartney Auditorium. In darkness behind the curtain, they awaited the start of the Inauguration.

This was the moment when the people who helped create LIPA and the people for whom LIPA was created sat in the same room. After the curtain rose, both groups gazed at each other. As so often happens, the initial response was profound silence. Although there was music and a light show, hearts were stilled.

Mark began compèring the show by reading a notice he had seen in a bureaucrat's office, entitled The Six Stages of a Project. The stages were: enthusiasm, disillusionment, panic, search for the guilty parties,

The Inauguration ceremony in The Paul McCartney Auditorium. Students perform for an audience of supporters, administrative and teaching staffs and invited guests.

participants. He thanked everyone for not making that scenario come true at LIPA.

The event started by a recount of the story so far, so it was natural that the first speaker was George Martin, followed by Tony Field. Then came Peter Bounds (for Liverpool City Council), John Flamson (for Liverpool City Challenge), Peter Reichardt (for EMI Music Publishing), Padraig Flynn (for the European Commission), Hans Bartel (for Grundig), Brigitta Unger-Soylka (for the German state of Baden-Wurrtemberg), Sir Paul Beresford (for the Department of the Environment) and Peter Toyne (for Liverpool John Moores University).

Mark introduced Paul by welcoming him to his new old school. After acknowledging that the moment was all too much for him, Paul went on to describe the hope the old school had given him as a lad from Speke and how it was possible to succeed "given enough love, passion and [being] prepared to put in enough hard work". He went on, "Obviously one of my feelings now is how proud my mum and dad would have been..." He stopped, thumped the lectern and said: "But I won't go into that because I'll start crying".

Above: Some of the inaugural speakers (clockwise from top left). These included George Martin, Mark, Paul, John Flamson (CEO of Liverpool City Challenge) and Hans Bartel (promotions director of Grundig).

Right: One of the first students meets
the Lead Patron.

Below left: Paul and Mark in a moment
of quiet reflection at the inauguration.

Below right: The celebration cake is cut.

Mark, also struggling to maintain composure, turned his back on the audience to address the first student body directly: "My only hope is that you, at some point in your career, experience the fulfilment I am experiencing now. After all this time, now that LIPA is finally here, now that you are LIPA, my dearest wish is that you will achieve your dreams or a reality you enjoy as much. We'll do our best to help you on your way."

Despite, or maybe because of, the intense emotions, the first student body and the staff buckled down to an accelerated programme. The other reason for the intensity was that the late start meant the first term had to

IO DOWNING STREET
LONDON SW1A 2AA

THE PRIME MINISTER

I have been following the progress of the Institute with great interest. It is a project which has captured the imagination of both local and central Government and the support of the European Community as well as private and individual sponsors and, above all, the people of Liverpool and far beyond.

For many of us Liverpool and the performing arts go hand-in-hand and LIPA is a fitting expression of that relationship. That music making and performance should become an element in the city's regeneration is - to me - entirely appropriate.

I congratulate the Institute's founders for their vision, and all those who have worked to make this vision the reality it is today. I am delighted that the Institute is now open and I wish it - and everyone associated with it - every success.

December 1995

HOUSE OF COMMONS
LONDON SW1A 0AA

The Office of the
Leader of The Opposition

Britain is justifiably proud of her performing arts and no city has done more to discover and nurture this talent than the city of Liverpool. It is therefore a great pleasure to be sending a message of support to the Liverpool Institute for Performing Arts. LIPA is committed to offering its students a first class education for a career in an industry that provides a wide range of job opportunities.

The arts are important to individuals, to communities and to our economy; they give pleasure to millions; they release the talent of countless others; and they deserve our support at local and national level. Arts entertain and educate, bringing people together for enjoyment and learning. LIPA will make a great contribution to this by developing its Community Arts programme. As a result, people who would otherwise have no contact with the arts will get the opportunity to experience all that they offer.

I wish you a very successful launch and look forward to great achievements in the future.

Tony Blair

Rt Hon Tony Blair MP

EVITA

ALAN PARKER

I'm sorry I cannot be with you today for the launch of LIPA, but unfortunately I am in Argentina filming 'EVITA'.

It's thirteen years since Mark Featherstone-Witty first talked to me about the possibility of a school for performing arts in Britain and I'm glad that my film 'FAME' in some small way inspired the notion.

The long, gargantuan, mostly up-hill struggle now has come to fruition, largely due to Mark's extraordinary passion, persistence and courage in never giving up on that dream. I take my hat off to him and send my very best wishes for the future to everyone involved.

I cross my fingers for you all.

Alan Parker

ALAN PARKER

The Rt Hon Paddy Ashdown MP

HOUSE OF COMMONS
LONDON SW1A 0AA

Message of Support

I am delighted to lend my support to the launch of The Liverpool Institute for Performing Arts. Not only will LIPA provide a platform for the talent and enthusiasm of young artists, it will ensure they have access to the back-up and resources they need to succeed. In addition, technical and business training will provide the entertainment industry with the skilled professionals it requires. The Institute is set to continue Liverpool's proud tradition as a centre of excellence in the performing arts - a tradition which has contributed in no small part to our country's dominant position in the global entertainment and leisure industries. I wish LIPA every success for the future, and look forward to seeing its students excel in all areas of the performing arts.

Paddy Ashdown

Paddy Ashdown MP

Letters from the leaders of the three main political parties and from film director Sir Alan Parker.

Right: A singing class in the early days.

reason for the intensity was that the late start meant the first term had to be shoehorned into just seven months. At the end of this period and after a month's break, everyone returned for the second year, along with an intake of new students.

To underscore the collaborative nature of the institute learning processes, a student/staff choir was formed during the first year. It was organised and led by Nick Phillips, a talented staff member. One of the pieces the choir worked on was his own composition called *The Red Ribbon*

Top: The first year gets underway with an in-school performance of Into the Woods by Stephen Sondheim (left) and musical entertainment in Liverpool's main shopping centre (right).

Above and right: Lighting designers, dancers and singers start their first year studies.

reportage des monats

TICKET ZUM RUHM

Helen aus Manchester beim Theater-Workshop (rechts), daneben Schulgründer Paul McCartney. Unten: Tanz-lehrer Stephen Fant (vorn) ge-hörte zur Truppe von Martha Graham und Alvin Ailey.

In Liverpool gibt es die erste Show-busineß-Uni der Welt. Die Idee hatte Paul McCartney, die Lehrer heißen Lou Reed oder Joan Armatrading. Wer da kein Star wird, ist selbst schuld

Left: The multi-culturalism of music.

Top right: Former student Ramesh Meyyappan, from Singapore, is now touring with his own show in England, Switzerland, Austria, Poland and Italy.

Right: LIPA students featured in *Marie Claire*. The popular fashion magazine ran an article on LIPA in the issue of January 1997.

Top left: Part of the audience at the first LIPA concert in a Liverpool park. It was well supported by fellow students.

Middle left: Students help to raise funds, collecting donations in the main shopping square.

Bottom left: A design student at work on a poster for a LIPA event.

Top right: The first group of students to graduate, on stage before the ceremony.

Below right: The first Hallowe'en in the LIPA bar. It was so successful that it has become an annual event.

Above: A rehearsal for a community show. Community Arts is an essential part of the curriculum.

Left: A designer works on an entry in a 'wacky races' event.

Right: Students at work.

Requiem.

A series of 'Conversations With' and Master Classes also began. Mark Knopfler and Ben Elton were among the first leading entertainment figures to participate.

Before the first teaching year ended, the Queen officially opened the building on 7 June 1996. The visit was timed to the minute and yet

94

round the building, there were small groups of people representing various contributions to the project (like the building team, the funders and the governing body). Her Majesty also watched students working. This element ended with a medley show in the main auditorium, after which the Queen met students and received an impromptu three cheers.

It took some time to achieve LIPA's hope for a mix of goals. A performing arts institute was a major part. Taking a role in the future of the city and the region was another. Yet another was to provide performing arts learning via the internet.

During the early years, LIPA bid for a variety of local and regional projects funded by the European Social Fund, usually to assist those who were in serious need of financial support. Over time, the institute participated or led some 20 initiatives.

The hectic first teaching year ended with The Royal Opening as the Queen greets and meets the LIPA people.

Below right: Enthusiastic to the end, students peek out of the window to watch the Queen depart.

6 UP AND RUNNING

6 UP AND RUNNING

As the Institute got into its stride, the social programmes continued to evolve. The embracing title of Flexible Learning and Enterprise Support (FLES) was used.

One foundation programme was the Music Industry and Media Innovation Centre (MIMIC). This was a research and support facility for music entrepreneurs. It included the course called Get Serious, designed to help local musicians become more aware of some of the skills and issues that could enhance careers in the music industry. This programme interacted with some 37 bands. In 1999, one of the participating bands was named by *The New Music Express* as one of the country's best unsigned bands of the year. This led to a research project to assess the use of the internet to provide music initiatives at a variety of local sites.

Right: The poster promoting the Get Serious programme for musicians (detail).

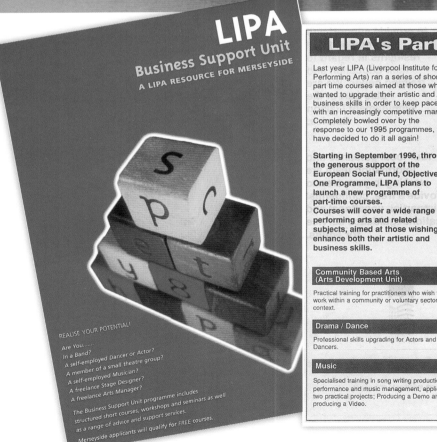

LIPA
Business Support Unit
A LIPA RESOURCE FOR MERSEYSIDE

REALISE YOUR POTENTIAL!

Are You......
In a Band?
A self-employed Dancer or Actor?
A member of a small theatre group?
A self-employed Musician?
A freelance Stage Designer?
A freelance Arts Manager?

The Business Support Unit programme includes structured short courses, workshops and seminars as well as a range of advice and support services.

Merseyside applicants will qualify for FREE courses.

LIPA's Part-Time Courses

Last year LIPA (Liverpool Institute for Performing Arts) ran a series of short part time courses aimed at those who wanted to upgrade their artistic and business skills in order to keep pace with an increasingly competitive market. Completely bowled over by the response to our 1995 programmes, we have decided to do it all again!

Starting in September 1996, through the generous support of the European Social Fund, Objective One Programme, LIPA plans to launch a new programme of part-time courses.
Courses will cover a wide range of performing arts and related subjects, aimed at those wishing to enhance both their artistic and business skills.

Community Based Arts
(Arts Development Unit)

Practical training for practitioners who wish to work within a community or voluntary sector context.

Drama / Dance

Professional skills upgrading for Actors and Dancers.

Music

Specialised training in song writing production performance and music management, applied to two practical projects; Producing a Demo and producing a Video.

Business Support
(Business Support Unit)

A range of flexible training programmes, distance learning and advice which aim to meet the needs of performing arts practitioners seeking to develop viable businesses and careers.

Glass Ceiling Programme
(Business Support Unit)

Training aimed at women on Merseyside and offers opportunities to women who wish to develop skills such as interpersonal skills, information technology, business planning for the cultural sector.

Sound Recording and Production Techniques

A range of practical programmes, coupled with a solid theoretical framework in sound engineering and production techniques.

* Places for the above part time courses are FREE to Merseyside applicants.

* Applicants must be aged 16 years and over.

* Child care facilities are available for the Glass Ceiling Programme.

For further details contact:

Sue Murphy or Michelle Ross
(LIPA Outreach Co-Ordinators)
The Liverpool Institute for Performing Arts
Mount Street, Liverpool L1 9HF

Tel: 0151 330 3240 / Fax: 0151 330 3131

THE
LIVERPOOL INSTITUTE
PERFORMING ARTS
Supported by GRUNDIG

EUROPEAN
SOCIAL FUND

Above: More promotion for the Get Serious course.

Far left: The Business Support Unit brochure.

Left: Advertising the part-time courses.

By 1999, LIPA gained its first contract to organise the Music Open and Distance Learning programme. This led to The Open Learning programme in 2002, a Modern Apprenticeship Programme and further programmes rooted in the city and the region.

→ THE CAMEO PROJECT

CAMEO

_EQUALITY, OPPORTUNITY, SUCCESS
Trailblazing entrepreneurial apprenticeship scheme
_EMPOWERING ENTREPRENEURS
From unemployed to a company director at 22
_WITHOUT BOUNDARIES
Effective partnership working, regionally,
nationally, and transnationally

LIPA
THE LIVERPOOL INSTITUTE FOR PERFORMING ARTS
Lead Patron
Sir Paul McCartney

**New Deal for Musicians
with the Liverpool Institute
for Performing Arts**

Open learning programme –
lasting up to six months
**for unemployed
musicians and DJs,
aged 18 to 24**

**New Deal
Your gig
for life**

The New Deal for Musicians open learning
programme offers you:

■ Mentoring from music industry experts
■ Practical work packs designed by music
  industry movers and shakers
■ Chance to attend masterclasses and
  workshops
■ Networking opportunities
■ Performance slots at showcase gigs
■ Access to state-of-the-art music and learning
  resources

new deal✱   LIPA
THE LIVERPOOL INSTITUTE FOR PERFORMING ARTS

Above: The widely disseminated CAMEO report, the flyer for The New Deal for Musicians programme and FLES participants.

Most recently LIPA ran The New Deal for Musicians programme for the North West Coastal district from Cumbria to South Cheshire, as well as the new transnational programme EQUAL and a three-year project, again for music entrepreneurs, called Coaching and Mentoring for Empowerment and Opportunity (CAMEO).

Under FLES, the institute began a Saturday part-time performing arts academy for 4 to 19 year-olds (LIPA 4:19). Currently, some 400 children and youngsters attend acting, dancing and singing classes, with special classes during the week for students who need more advanced training.

LIPA 4:19

The part-time performing arts academy caters for ages 4 to 19, as the title states.

Born To Perform

Tuesday 5th July and Wednesday 6th July 2005

Friday 8th July and Saturday 9th July 2005

Sunday 10th July 2005

LIPA
4:19

live it

LIPA
4:19

The world-famous Liverpool Institute for Performing Arts is launching a new part-time performing arts school for 4 to 19 year olds this September.

Classes are split in to four age groups - 4 to 6 year olds, 7 to 10 year olds, 11 to 13 year olds and 14 year plus.

Our unique classes for both 4 to 6 and 7 to 10 year olds will stretch imaginations, build self-confidence and bring all the magic of performing arts activities to life.

Classes run on Saturdays over 12 week terms starting September 2003. LIPA offers fantastic facilities and a safe and encouraging learning environment.

Find out more tel: 0151 330 3009
email: 419enquiries@lipa.ac.uk

LIPA
The Liverpool Institute for Performing Arts
Mount Street
Liverpool
L1 9HH

MIMIC magazine – June 1999

MIMIC IS PART FUNDED THROUGH THE ESF ADAPT INITIATIVE

MIMIC WEB SITE http://www.lipa.ac.uk/mimic

MIMIC - MUSIC INDUSTRY AND MULTI MEDIA INNOVATION CENTRE

The Liverpool Institute for Performing Arts (LIPA) began operating in 1995. LIPA is a fantastic centre which is at the leading edge for new technology in the performing arts. The MIMIC centre was formed to be a research and support facility for music enterprises as they grappled with the notion of new and advancing multimedia applications. This covered a range of aspects from new recording techniques, through to developing the use of the WEB to market products and services.

The project began as an in depth research into the effect of new technology on the music industry through an audit of Merseyside based music enterprises. This was headed up by Pete Fulwell who had developed a great interest in this area of research a number of years prior to the project. (See Back Page)

MIMIC began its life as an ADAPT project in 1997. ADAPT is an initiative of the European Social Fund to assist areas which have suffered from large scale redundancies as the result of industrial decline. The ADAPT initiative is designed to help us to do something about it, through the use of new technology.

The audit function was to gain valuable information on the current level of IT activity within local music enterprises. From this information we were able to ascertain what level of support would be needed to enable these enterprises to ADAPT to the changes.

A number of exciting events have emerged since we began the project.

For further details of what we have done and what we will be doing, look us up on our WEB page. The project will undoubtedly change almost constantly. We will change with it but the underlying theme will remain new ways of working for our local music enterprises and hopefully ways of creating wealth for the area which produces the talent.

INTRODUCTION BY GED MCKENNA

GIG FOR KOSOVO

See inside for details!

GRUNDIG
made for you

LIPA

THE LIVERPOOL INSTITUTE FOR PERFORMING ARTS

LIPA
THE LIVERPOOL INSTITUTE FOR PERFORMING ARTS

acting *dance* *song*

Postgraduate Diploma in Acting

A journey to make you weep, laugh, sing, dance, **succeed.**

LIPA
THE LIVERPOOL INSTITUTE FOR PERFORMING ARTS

Three new DIPLOMAS IN PERFORMING ARTS
popular Diploma in Popular Music and Sound Technology

Above: Publicity for LIPA's integrated diplomas and the Postgraduate Diploma in Acting.

Left: The cover of the Music Industry and Media Innovation Centre (MIMIC) prospectus.

Higher education, too, continued to evolve.

From the start, LIPA ran a one year diploma in Popular Music and Sound Technology, partly for musicians who just wanted a year to upgrade their knowledge and partly as a foundation for direct entry to music programmes elsewhere. Eight years later, this diploma was joined by three integrated diplomas in acting, dance and song. A postgraduate diploma in acting was also added.

With these developments, sufficient performance space became an issue, so the hope is to build another facility on site to house six new dance and rehearsal spaces, as well as a dedicated building for embryonic arts and entertainment businesses.

With LIPA well underway, two issues remained that were both critical and energy draining. The first was solving the cost overrun. The original anticipated cost of renovating and equipping the building, together with development costs to opening, was £12.2m. In reality, it was £20.5m. Paul

'CONVERSATIONS WITH' AND MASTER CLASSES

About 80 established professional have shared their experiences with, and tested the skills of, those aiming to enter the same professions.

Clockwise from top right: Ken Campbell, writer and all-round entertainer; Andy McLuskey, record producer and singer-songwriter; The Bangles, singer-songwriter; Willy Russell and Tim Firth, playwrights and performers; Corin Redgrave, actor; Amy Winehouse, singer-songwriter; Nickolas Grace, actor.

Clockwise from top left:
Thelma Holt, theatre producer;
Dawn French, comedian;
Richard Wilson, actor-director;
Paul McCartney;
Tim Wheeler, singer-songwriter;
Joan Armatrading, singer-songwriter;
Ed Bicknell, manager Dire Straits,

led the effort to meet the overrun by tripling his original £1m donation on condition that the public funders had to develop a workable funding plan. This was eventually achieved with collaboration from Balfour Beatty, LIPA's builders.

The second was achieving ongoing government funding for each student that was comparable to other specialist performing arts institutions. This, too, was achieved.

Writing this story nearly 10 years after LIPA opened its doors to the first student body, trying to remember when one year started and another year ended and when precisely events took place, is both hard and not how memory works. The experience of living with the lives that LIPA has touched is a continuous present. Particularly when students return to share their career experiences, it's difficult to recall when and if they actually left.

Right: Going to the top to achieve appropriate per student funding. It took a personal approach from Paul to Prime Minister Blair.

LIPA hopes to secure future

BY DIANE MASSEY

Hopes are being fixed on public sector help to secure a firm future for the Liverpool Institute of Performing Arts.

Chief executive Mark Featherstone-Witty said this week that funds to help Britain's newest stage training ground could be secured by the end of the year.

Some 400 full-time students have now enrolled at the college, based in the building which housed patron Paul McCartney's old school and a further 200 are expected next year.

"We are expecting that some money will be forthcoming from public sector sources, including the EU," said Featherstone-Witty. "Our main problem has been that capital expenditure on converting the building has been much higher than anyone foresaw."

LIPA has undertaken a feasibility study on suing the design partnership which oversaw the its building conversion. "We have not yet made a decision on whether to act," said Featherstone-Witty.

The college is spending some running resources on attracting students from overseas.

One project in co-operation with a Japanese technical college will give Japanese LIPA students a 12 month grounding in language and other skills. Fifteen Japanese students are currently enrolled.

Labour to review Fame School funding

PAUL OFFERED LIPA LIFELINE

By Andrew Campbell

EDUCATION Secretary David Blunkett has promised a review of funding for Liverpool's Fame School.

The move follows a campaign, led by Sir Paul McCartney and the Liverpool Institute of Performing Arts, for equal funding for classical and popular music colleges.

In a letter to Sir Paul, the Sheffield MP says: "I do appreciate the anomoly.

"Clearly, with the Popular Music Centre in Sheffield, we are keen to ensure, as you are, that there is parity of esteem and parity of treatment."

He added: "I would be very happy to take a look at this and ensure that, in the changes which will follow the Dearing Committee report into Higher Education, we take the opportunity or ironing out such anomalies.

Quality

"Clearly, the issue of the academic weight verification of qual courses concerned. resumption about lar nature of the art But he warns: "It ne to resolve."

ir Paul also recie dges from former r John Major, sho General Election PA receives less amount per st ical institutions overnment's H Funding Coun Fame School d last year l £2,605 a year red to £6,54 Academy of M

● Give us money . . . that's what the LIPA students need, says

Sir Paul strikes a chord with Blair

SIR Paul McCartney has been invited to Downing Street for the first time - for a high level discussion about his Fame school.

Guitar-playing Prime Minister Tony Blair wants to talk to the former Beatle about the Liverpool Institute for the Performing Arts which could be in line for extra cash.

A friend of Sir Paul said: "This is not a social occasion. It is going to be a serious business meeting.

"Mr Blair is interested in the Institute and wants to know more about it and the work everyone does there."

The college, Sir Paul's idea, was opened in Liverpool last year amid a blaze of publicity and with the ambition of churning out the drama, music and fashion stars of tomorrow.

Funding

It is housed in the old Liverpool Institute High School building in Mount Street, the former school of both Sir Paul and George Harrison, which closed in 1985.

LIPA receives its funding in equal parts from the Liverpool City Challenge Scheme, the European Regional Development Fund and from private backers, including Sir Paul.

But Mr Blair is believed to be considering giving it additional funding, possibly as part of the Government's specialist schools scheme which gives extra cash to colleges with expert tuition in chosen subjects.

"That is a possibility, although the Prime Minister might also want to see what lessons can be learned from

□ FAME: A concert on stage at the Liverpool Institute for the Performing Arts and below, Prime Minister Blair and Sir Paul McCartney

the Institute for the rest of the education system," the friend of Sir Paul explained.

Mark Featherstone-Witty, chief executive of LIPA will also be at the meeting.

He said: "Students who study classical arts get about two thirds more public funding than our students.

"We see that as unfair."

The meeting, scheduled for next Friday, will be the first time Mr Blair has met Sir Paul. But the two are expected to hit it off.

The friend added: "Mr Blair owns and plays a Fender Stratocaster electric guitar so at least they will be barking up the same tree."

By Simeon Tegel
Daily Post Correspondent

Fame school is in line for extra cash

ONCE MORE IN THE PRESS

NOOKS and CORNERS

NEWS from Liverpool, which hopes to be chosen by the Arts Council as "City of Architecture and Design" in 1999.

Perhaps in some ways it deserves to be: after plumbing the depths in the days of Derek Hatton, Liverpool can now point to such things as the conversion of the Albert Dock and the incipient restoration of St George's Hall with justifiable pride.

So it is sad to record that the bad old days of the Shankland-Cox plan, which proposed making central Liverpool a motorway intersection, are not yet over, and the city council is now hoping to drive a new road through the city centre.

One of the pleasant things about Liverpool is how few cars there are: it is like being behind the iron curtain in the good old days. So the good councillors want to drag the city kicking and screaming into the 1960s and solve a non-existent traffic problem by smashing a new road from Leece Street to London Road through the run-down but redeemable urban area between the Metropolitan Cathedral and Lime Street station.

This will involve the demolition of the Pleasant Street School, part of which dates from 1808, as well as a decent row of 18th century buildings on the corner of Renshaw Street and Leece Street, and one listed building: no. 62 Mount Pleasant. Another listed building, no. 64 Mount Pleasant — will be cut in half.

Curiously, the highways and transport department of Liverpool city council claims that the new road "will safeguard listed buildings". It will also ... that is, ... ought to ...

This ... fantasy ... second ... the Cus... "to ... Presuma... then city ... magnifi...

would also have relieved unemployment. Fortunately, even the road-building fanatics of the department of the environment are unimpressed by such nonsense and have called this ridiculous road scheme in.

ANOTHER reason given for this gratuitous new road is that "it will impress tourists and investors". Really? The listed building which is to be mutilated is already much photographed as it is hallowed as the site of the marriage of John Lennon to poor Cynthia. "Culture" in Liverpool, of course, means those four

Four is at long last giving a little cash to his native city.

Paul McCartney — one of the wealthiest men in Britain — offered money to found a Liverpool Institute of Performing Arts: provided, that is, the taxpayer came up with considerably more. This he did thanks to a vapid classless gesture by John Major. Now, with European money promised as well, work is under way to create LIPA in the derelict Liverpool Institution High School for Boys, a handsome neo-Classical building of 1835-37 in Mount Street, which ...

Then the long-suffering residents were obliged to ... as contractors acting for ... council first erected a ten... roof over the building and ... took it down again, leaving ... original roof without slate ... contractors acting for LIP... continued this cavalier destruction and reduced the ... institution to a windowless ... gutted shell. And this was a ... building.

There is worse. Despite opposition from residents and ... amenity societies, listed build... consent was granted for the demolition of the institution's single-storey gymnasium block. This is to be replaced by a five-storey "dance studio", designed by Messrs Brock Carmichael, which will rise higher than the original building and deprive Mount Street of sunlight and views of the Welsh hills. Yet all the required additional accommodation could have been built at the unprepossessing rear of the institution or placed in other disused buildings. The contrast with the treatment of the nearby Liverpool Institution High School for Girls, which is being carefully restored as a centre for women's education without provoking discontent, is marked.

What, indeed, is the point of listing historic buildings if they can still be gratuitously gutted and mutilated? But what are laws and heritage to Liverpool council if it can attach the money-spinning cachet of the name of a posturing ex-Beatle to a development? Were the distant days of Deggsy so very different?

'Piloti'

Watch out she's HOT

FLAME-HAIRED BIANCA KINANE is aiming to be the British Mariah Carey - and steal everyone's hearts in the songbird stakes.

She's already had plenty of practice, of course. She made the final of TV's Stars In Their Eyes as Mariah Carey a year ago.

"I don't regret doing the show at all," she said at the Alex. "It was great fun and it got me a lot of exposure nationwide.

"I did the show because at the time it was the ONLY television series offering opportunities for new singers.

"I may have appeared as Mariah, who I admire very much, but people got the chance to see and hear the way I can sing."

Bianca also appeared recently on

Jonathon Ross' Big Big Talent Show. Although she didn't win, she attracted a lot of fan mail.

"I was given the big build-up by my mum," she said. "That wasn't embarrassing because she's always been very supportive of me.

"Mum used to be a country singer and she was delighted when I started out on a singing career - but she was never pushy.

"She's letting me make my own mind up - and my own mistakes!"

Bianca, of course, is one of the graduates of Paul McCartney's 'Fame' School for the Performing Arts in Liverpool, where she met Jamiroquai.

Listen out for Bianca's new sin-gle The Woman video which w same Spanish Madonna recent And just watch eyes!

BURST INTO FAME: Bianca Kinan, above, and left, as Mariah Carey in

MUSIC PENNED PAUL, GEMMA ...

Concern over Lords ruling on VAT claims

BUSINESSES issuing shares on the open market could find themselves unexpectedly hit by a recent VAT ruling.

The House of Lords' decision in the case of Liverpool Institute of Performing Arts affects the amount of VAT that companies can claim back on purchases or expenses.

It centres on companies which are making VAT-exempt and non-UK supplies.

Businesses making supplies outside the UK will usually recognise the VAT pitfalls involved but if they are also partly exempt, they may fall foul of the new ruling.

And there is also a greater concern is that the Lords' decision could catch out any business engaged in the issue of shares which may be bought by overseas buyers.

Ernst & Young's South coast VAT spokesman Peter Hewitt said: "This latest ruling has obvious implications for any business making exempt and non-UK supplies, but also for those who may inadvertently find themselves in that category through the issue of shares.

IMPLICATIONS: Peter Hewitt of Ernst & Young

"Affected businesses failing to comply with the latest ruling could find themselves paying a 15 per cent misdeclaration penalty as well as repaying any VAT overclaimed."

Businesses should carefully review their potential VAT liability following the House of Lords ruling.

"Making checks is preferable to running unnecessary risks, in an atmosphere where pleading ignorance is no defence," added Mr Hewitt.

Ombudsman to probe fears over Fame school

By Louise Elliott
Daily Post Staff

THE Ombudsman has been called in to investigate allegations that planning committee members acted incorrectly in granting permission for the construction of Paul McCartney's "Fame school."

The inquiry was initiated by a group of residents who are opposed to the way the school has been taking shape in the old Liverpool Institute High School.

They claim the whole atmosphere of the old school, a Grade II listed building, is being completely changed.

And Paul McCartney has been so concerned over the objections of householders in Mount Street, Liverpool, that he has telephoned them personally to apologise for the upset caused.

The Liverpool Institute of Performing Arts was granted planning approval by the city council, despite objections from English Heritage.

But members of the Mount Street Residents' Association last night said they are not happy with the way many members' original concerns seemed to have been "bulldozed" and the plans were granted approval despite various objections.

They are also angry because they do not feel they have been properly consulted on all the plans.

Mike Keating, a member of the residents' association, said last night: "We wrote to the Ombudsman and asked him to get involved in looking into our complaints because we are seriously concerned about the Institute.

"We are worried that plans are not being kept to and we want this investigated. The building is so important to this area we do not want it ruined.

"Because of all the money involved in the scheme, I feel the Ombudsman will take at least a year to investigate and by that time the school will be nearing completion.

"Then it will be too late to do anything about it."

A spokesman for Liverpool ...

Ombudsman to investigate if they have a complaint.

Mr Keating added: "We have no problem at all with Paul McCartney or the scheme which he wants ...

Mark Featherstone-Witty, chief executive of LIPA, said: "All the work which is being carried out is, of course, necessary for the proper development of the ...

□ The Institute, soon to be Paul McCartney's Fame school.

Residents fight for building

Top left: The Private Eye article. It linked LIPA's building programme with Liverpool's bid to be The City of Architecture and Design in 1999.

Above: The impossible story. The claim was not justified because LIPA was not yet in existence.

Top right: LIPA making an unexpected appearance in the House of Lords. This sorted out a VAT problem.

Right: The Ombudsman idea as reported in the The Liverpool Daily Post.

Theatre

Testing time

Technology displaced the classics at this year's Sunday Times National Student Drama Festival, but everyone was eager to experiment, says ROBERT HEWISON

It has been a good festival for Jamie Lloyd, a 20-year-old second-year student at the Liverpool Institute for Performing Arts. Not only did he win the RSC's Buzz Goodbody Award for the best student director, but his production, a crisp and quirky revival of the William Finn/James Lapine musical **Falsettoland**, won the Cameron Mackintosh Award for an outstanding musical contribution. The Bush Theatre, in London, was so impressed that it has offered Lloyd the first of its new bursaries to work on a professional production as assistant director.

Such a deluge of prizes is unusual at the National Student Drama Festival, but Lloyd's talent is not. Since The Sunday Times first helped to launch this celebration in 1956, generations of young people from universities, colleges, schools and youth groups have come together once a year for an intense week of performances, workshops and debates, and have had their lives changed in the process. The future of British theatre starts here.

To this year's festival, held once again at its regular home, Scarborough, have come theatre celebrities such as the directors Michael Attenborough, of the RSC, and John Caird, of the National Theatre, Alan Ayckbourn (whose Scarborough theatre, the Stephen Joseph, housed several productions), Mike Bradwell, of the Bush Theatre, Jatinder Verma, of Tara Arts, the director Clare Venables and the writer Mark Ravenhill, all giving masterclasses in aspects of their craft. Thanks to the Mackintosh Foundation, which has joined The Sunday Times in supporting the festival, the writing and composing team of Alain Boublil and Claude-Michel Schoenberg appeared, disclosing the secrets of their hits, which include Les Misérables and Miss Saigon. The Stephen Joseph Theatre has created a training post for a technician, and the National Theatre a residency for a future producer. More than one show is already lined up for the Edinburgh Festival Fringe.

Lloyd's production of Falsettoland showed just how professional students at the Liverpool Institute for Performing Arts are learning to be, but the most refreshing aspect of this year's festival was the eagerness for experiment. Fully a third of the 15 productions that had been invited to Scarborough from an entry of 115 were collectively devised pieces that explored aspects of new technology or performance art. **Witness Me**, from Warwick University, won an award for physical theatre for its wordless yet emotionally charged exposition of the effects of physical trauma on a quartet of performers who bravely exposed their bodies to a punishing sequence of actions and interactions, set in an environment that was part operating theatre, part morgue. A second piece from Warwick, **dystopia**, had the most ravishing opening moments of the festival, but proved less successful in its use of masks to explore ideas of loneliness and false identity. Helena Sands, who appeared in both pieces, won an individual award for the physical energy of her performances.

Today's students evidently take life seriously, but even when demonstrating the way that modern technology and the media can alienate us from our true feelings, as in Hull University, Scarborough Campus's **... a few more lessons in love ...**, they can still have fun. Another group, also from the Scarborough Campus of Hull University, which supplies much of the volunteer backup for the festival, were commended for **Door 32**, a stylish, well-choreographed piece that took a hotel corridor as a metaphor for existence. Today's students also take life responsibly: we were presented with a performance piece on breast cancer, **Why Wait Till You're Fifty?**, from Brooksby Melton College, and Edinburgh University's revival of an adaptation of the Melvin Burgess novel **Junk** left us in no doubts about the damaging effects of drugs.

'Such was the interest in the use of recorded sound, lighting effects, slide projections and video that my fellow judge complained of 'techno-swamp''

Such was the interest in the use of recorded sound, lighting effects, slide projections and video that Mike Shepherd, the director of Cornwall's Knee High Theatre and — along with the actress Susannah Doyle — my fellow judge, complained of "techno-swamp". Cinematic conventions and B-movie clichés sank Cambridge University's seaborne whale-watchers in **Atlantica**, but you can't have experiment without the risk of failure, and this is one of the few festivals where people are ready and willing to learn from their mistakes.

Experiment and the desire to share creative responsibility do, however, divert ambitions away from tackling classic texts. The oldest play in the festival was by a living writer, Howard Barker. **Judith, a parting from the body** is a brief and bloody encounter between the Old Testament heroine and her victim, Holofernes — in Barker's hands, a characteristic debate about the partnership of desire and death. Sarah Punshon and her trio of Cambridge actors should be congratulated for maintaining a link with the theatre's collective memory, even though their play reached back only as far as 1990.

Devised work and adaptations also left little room for new writing. There was a slight, absurdist piece, Tom Morton-Smith's **Black Boxes and Amber Rooms**, from the University of East Anglia's Minotaur Company, who coupled it with Ashif Verjee's monologue for a cinema-goer, **Rhian and Ripley**. Neither offered competition to last year's winner of The Sunday Times Playwriting Award, Oxford's Peter Morris, who took the prize this year for **A&R**, a reworking of the Faust legend in terms of the American record industry. Black as sin, and lit by cruel shafts of sardonic humour, Morris's three-hander shows the way an "artists and repertoire" executive seduces a would-be recording artist for whom he has as little respect as the audience he exploits.

Though drawing on historical catastrophe and family bitterness, Jennifer Lindsay's **The Grandmother Project** was driven by an American optimism that these things can be worked through. Lindsay portrayed the struggles of her Polish grandmother in post-revolutionary Russia, and the generational battles of her heirs over her memory. Having brought her production all the way from Stanford University, California, Lindsay won a commendation for her creative endeavour, while Emily Dykes, an American student at the Liverpool Institute, who also appeared in Falsettoland, was commended for her supporting roles.

Two productions, above all, can give us hope for the future of the theatre: one through its professionalism, the other through its eccentricity. Liz White's one-woman show, **The Woman Who Walked Into Doors**, demonstrates that Liverpool does not just produce singers and dancers. Created with her directors, Leanne Best and Brian Parsons, who won a commendation for their collaboration, this adaptation of the Roddy Doyle novel took us into the heart of a working-class Dublin woman, who told the story of the triumph of getting a husband, and the disaster of the brutal consequences. As an Irish Shirley Valentine, comic and tragic by turns, White won an award for the best individual performance.

Pull My Strings, from York University, is the sort of gem this festival exists to discover. Whimsical, poignant, but rooted in the pain of losing a parent, it tells the story of a young puppet-maker who has retreated into a private world following the suicide of his father. At night, figures of his own creation play theatre games of psychodrama to persuade him to break out of the barn where he and his puppets hide. As the puppeteer, Samuel Booth used a hypnotic stillness to draw us into a world that out-Pirandellos Pirandello. He, his co-writer and co-director, Anna Sliman, and his company won an award for craft and imagination.

Craft and imagination are what the NSDF celebrates, and it takes craft and imagination to manage the diverse interests of the more than 700 people who made this the best-attended festival yet. This year there has been a new artistic director, Nick Stimson. For him, too, it has been a good festival.

The National Student Drama Festival is sponsored by The Sunday Times, with financial support from the Mackintosh Foundation, the Arts Council of England, Scarborough Borough Council, BBC Talent, the Calouste Gulbenkian Foundation, and the HSBC Disability Access grant. The festival is presented in association with the University of Hull Scarborough Campus, Yorkshire Coast College, Scarborough College, the Ste[...]hen Joseph Theatre an[...] The next [...]ugh from

And the winners were...

Sunday Times Playwriting Award: Peter Morris (Oxford) for A&R
Royal Shakespeare Company Buzz Goodbody Student Director Award: Jamie Lloyd (Liverpool Institute for Performing Arts — LIPA) for Falsettoland
Cameron Mackintosh Award for Outstanding Contribution to Musical Theatre: Falsettoland company (LIPA)
Sunday Times Harold Hobson Student Drama Critic Award: Dan Bye (Leeds)

JUDGES' AWARDS
- **for physical theatre:** the company of Witness Me (Warwick)
- **for craft and imagination:** the company of Pull My Strings (York)
- **for best individual performance:** Liz White, in The Woman Who Walked Into Doors (LIPA)
- **for physical performance:** Helena Sands, in Witness Me and dystopia (Warwick)

JUDGES' COMMENDATIONS
- **for stage adaptation:** the company of The Woman Who Walked Into Doors (LIPA)
- **for style and impact:** the company of Door 32 (Hull University, Scarborough Campus)
- **for creative endeavour:** Jennifer Lindsay of The Grandmother Project (Stanford, California)
- **for performance:** Emily Dykes, in Falsettoland and The Grandmother Project (LIPA)
- **for lighting:** Chris Luffingham, in Witness Me (Warwick)

BURSARIES AND RESIDENCIES
Personal Managers Association writing award: Christopher Dunkley (Exeter University)
Stephen Joseph Theatre technical residency: Neil Hobbes (Edinburgh University)
Royal National Theatre trainee producer: Tracey McGarrigan (Hull, Scarborough Campus)
Bush Theatre directing bursary: Jamie Lloyd (LIPA)

Telling tales: right, Warwick University's Witness Me; above right, Liz White in The Woman Who Walked Into Doors; far right, Falsettoland. Photographs by Allan Titmuss

10 RK

11

Double take at design exhibition

● Designs on city . . . Alke Groppel-Wegener and Nora Krug with their work. *Picture: A*[...]

By Paul Unger

STUDENTS at the Liverpool Institute for Performing Arts are seeing double this week.

A dozen second year students have recreated parts of the city's famous Hope Street as a lesson in set design.

The "Fragments of L1" exhibition includes realistic life-sized models of sections of a garage, a corner of a cathedral, a squat and a pub.

Paul Kleiman, Head of Design at the Institute, said: "There is a whole set of techniques they have lea[...] scenery [...] of polyst[...]

"It's all [...] not be a [...] made un[...]

LIPA transformed by students

The Liverpool Institute of Performing Arts (LIPA) building in Mount Street, Liverpool was recently transformed into a colourful spectacle by two final year students Paul Nulty and Nick Handford.

The *LIPA Lighting Project* took place nightly for a week and was designed by Paul, a final year BA Performance Design student, who wanted to explore the aesthetics of architectural lighting and how equipment can best be utilised, with lighting that emphasised the [...]

technical support and training. With UK distributor Lightfactor Sales, High End supplied additional fixtures for the event.

A total of 16 EC1s, ten Studio Colors and six Cyberlights illuminated the building, while High End also produced high-resolution customised LithoPatterns featuring logos of LIPA and other benefactors.

The fixtures were controlled via LIPA's own Status Cue desk. Programming proved a challenging task as several cues ran simultaneously and the scheme also ran automatically without a 'live' console operator. It was done in several overnight sessions during the previous week by a collection of LIPA students. This democratic process offered everyone a chance to use and understand the equipment.

With the complete gamut of meteorological phenomena occurring during the week, 'LIPAdomes' - a variation on the Ecodome - had to be used to protect the fixtures from the elements.

For Paul, the most galvanising aspect of the project was trying to create depth and texture on what are essential three flat building facades without it looking like a rock 'n' roll show. On a technical and creative level, the project allowed the pair to gain a huge amount of knowledge, hands-on experience and enhanced [...]

Top: Recognition for LIPA actors at *The Sunday Times* National Student Drama Festival.

Above left and right: Recognition for LIPA student designers.

This sensation of a continuous present is reinforced by the age range of students. Since LIPA started, roughly 3,200 people, as young as four and as old as the early 40s, have experienced what the institute offers in its constantly improved, revised and expanded curriculum.

An important aspect of LIPA is its attraction for aspiring performers from all over the world. The latest statistics show that, of all UK higher education institutions, LIPA has the fourth highest intake of international students as a percentage of its undergraduate student body. Currently there are 35 nationalities represented.

Finally, the continuous present is felt through the number and range

The Mail

ON SUNDAY

APRIL 5, 1998

85p

THE COMPLETE SUNDAY PAPER

DYSLEXIA

Could this amazing British breakthrough help your child?

Full story: Pages 8, 9

Two FREE packets of seeds for every reader – See Page 61

In a snapshot ... the new Royal image at the Palace

THE QUEEN OF COOL—OFFICIAL

By Daniel Foggo and Sarah Oliver

THIS is the moment the Queen showed a new face to the nation.

In a break with tradition and Royal protocol, she publicly embraced, for the first time, the generation that will decide the future of the House of Windsor — and won it over.

The picture, which captures an easy rapport between two women who many would have thought had little in common, is the result of a concerted Palace effort to break

LEADER COMMENT:
Page 34

down the barriers between the Monarch and her subjects.

The strategy became apparent on Friday at Buckingham Palace when the Queen hosted the first rock concert to be held at her London residence. It followed an official dinner for visiting heads of state in London for the Asia-Europe Summit.

Afterwards, she met 21-year-old singer Julie Thompson, a performing arts student from Liverpool, who faced her as a symbol of the ordinary people who may have questioned the role of the Monarchy since the death of Diana. The 50-year age gap and the huge cultural divide between them disappeared as they each roared with laughter.

The meeting had an impact on the young Liverpudlian who told The Mail on Sunday:

Continued on Page 3

RELAXED: The Queen shares a joke with Julie Thompson, who described her as 'an amazing woman'

Picture: ADAM BUTLER

Rocker in the pink

Queen's seal of approval boosts punk singer's career

BY BOB McGOWAN AND TOM RAWSTORNE

IT was the night that changed her life . . . when pop unknown Julie Thompson got her first big break thanks to the Queen.

Never in her wildest dreams did the pink-haired punk see herself having a joke with the Queen at Buckingham Palace.

But after "hitting it off" with Her Majesty and receiving the Royal seal of approval, outrageous Julie may now be destined for the top of the charts.

In keeping with the wind of change blowing through the Palace, the Queen had agreed to Julie's band, Camp Houston, playing at Buck House's first rock concert.

Afterwards the Queen, in a relaxed mood, joked about 21-year-old Julie's startling look. The singer, embarrassed about her nose ring, camouflage trousers and gaudy locks, said of her hair: "It's not natural."

The Queen, in green dress and diamonds, quipped that she was glad to hear it — then both dissolved into laughter.

The event was held after a dinner for heads of state attending the Asia-Europe Summit in London.

Julie said: "The Queen really mingled. Maybe she was relaxed because, well, it's her home."

Julie's dad Peter said at his Norwich semi yesterday: "This is a great boost for Julie's career."

Band member Pal Bratelund, 24, said: "This is what we needed to get us on Top of The Pops."

The song they performed, Damon, refers to sex — but the "simulated orgasm" in the number was discreetly missing for the royal performance.

TOP OF THE MOPS: F
new-found fame after s

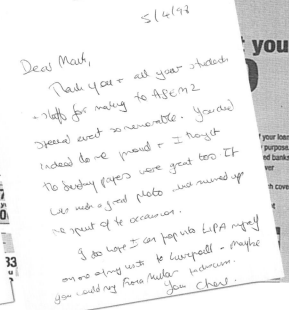

Philip 16 dead

Left and above: A story that appeared across the world, originating in *The Mail on Sunday*.

Inset: Thank you notes from the Blairs. It touched all of us at LIPA.

of events that constantly take place, both inside the institute and across the city.

Early on, there was a request from Cherie Booth Blair, whose family came from Liverpool, for students to perform at Buckingham Palace after a dinner in April 1998 during an Asia-Europe Summit. It seemed a classic example of how a small news item could be blown up to make a splash simply because an exuberant student had dyed hair!

LIPA SHOWS

Over the years, there have been performances of all kinds – some winning local awards and some gaining national praise at the Edinburgh Festival. Since the Institute is 'for performers and those who make performance possible', every show is a collaboration in which students show their skills in performing, sound, lighting, design, front of house and publicity.

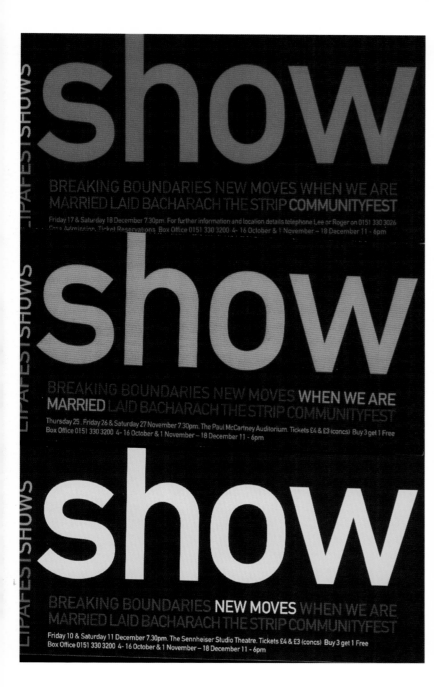

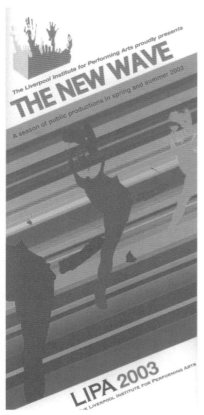

Of the many activities generated by LIPA itself, one example worth noting was Make It, Break It, a national competition run in partnership with Yamaha. Now three years old, this was an annual songwriting and enterprise awards scheme aimed at uncovering and encouraging new talent from young artists and entrepreneurs. The judging panel includes Coldplay's Chris Martin, the promoter Harvey Goldsmith and the producer, Steve Levine.

Right: The Make It, Break It poster. This national competition is in its third year.

Left: Make It, Break It performers trying for the Yamaha prizes.

world of hospitals with a part in BBC
TV's *Casualty*, her first television role.

7 LIFE AFTER LIPA

Bec Phillips calls herself

Queen of Blaggers

Ian Reynolds tried to get a word in

LL she sent was a head-shot. A girl: flame red hair obscuring one eye, red velvet lips curled in 'in your face' defiance. On the phone she asked: 'how will I know you?' I told her 'don't worry, I'll find you.' So it's a good job that the Fab Bar on Portland Street wasn't crammed to capacity or I'd never have heard the barman say 'Hi Bec' as she walked in. Who says the camera never lies?

'I'm like a chameleon', said the tall brunette, happily.

No kidding.

Bec Peters, 25 (though you'd never guess), is a singer, a model; co-owner of a record label, a band manager; a student at Lippa (The Paul McCartney School of Performing Arts) a script writer, a dancer, a DJ, a... You get the picture? She knows what she wants out of life and she pursues her dreams with the dogged determination of an SAS colonel planning a deadly mission. She's not messing about. Bec wants to be famous - and rich, naturally.

Showbiz mum and dad pulling the strings? 'I always knew what I wanted to do but I was no child prodigy. Mum, (Joan), was the first woman to qualify as a football referee, and dad, (Ronnie), was a professional footballer with Burnley'. Of all the kids who dream of playing football, how many make it? And what kind of woman could break down the walls of a male bastion like football? Chez Phillips, there was no such word as 'impossible'

7 LIFE AFTER LIPA

THERE HAVE been eight graduations since the founding of LIPA. Every time, it is difficult to realise that familiar faces will not be seen on a daily basis. But it is comforting that they will fold into the ever-growing, continuous present.

Now comes the inevitable question: How is LIPA doing? For an institute that was created to increase the number of people gainfully employed in the performing arts, the evidence lies partly in show programmes, partly in newspaper coverage and partly in e-mails. But these are not comprehensive. The solid evidence lies in *See Me Now*, a newsletter that comes out annually at graduation. In the centre are profiles of all the graduates of the previous three years who can be located. Roughly 80 per cent are found. Of these, roughly 75 per cent are still working in their chosen field. This seems to be a robust result.

And so, on to the next 10 years . . .

Right: Liam Lynch's album cover. The songs were intelligent parodies of which *The United States of Whatever* became a hit single. It is the shortest hit single ever, lasting 90 seconds.

METROLIFE

DANCE

Richard Alston is thinking big for his company's visit to The Lowry

Trilogy: The Richard Alston Dance Company, with Amanda Weaver and Andrew Obaka (above) will perform at The Lowry

Dancing with the grown-ups

He has been called the father of contemporary dance, but Richard Alston isn't comfortable with that title and, by the tone of his voice, he's more than slightly amused by it: 'I don't feel like a father, in fact I don't think I've ever grown up. I'm more the rebellious prodigal son.'

He firmly assigns that parental responsibility to Robert Cohan, founding artistic director of London Contemporary Dance Theatre, and philanthropist Robin Howard whose humanitarian vision of an institution where dance would develop to benefit society was realised with the opening of The Place in 1969. Indeed, Alston was one of their very first students. Today The Place boasts Alston as artistic director, his career having neatly come full circle. It is also home to Alston's own company. 'In fact,' says Alston, 'I'm just one of The Place's oldest surviving relics!'

Over 30 years experience as choreographer, teacher and from 1986 to 1992, artistic director of Rambert Dance Company, certainly equipped Alston

> If we don't get the level of response, I'll change things around

with all the necessary skills to launch his own successful company in 1994, and no doubt helped earn him his CBE in the 2001 New Year Honours List. Yet Alston retains his youthful energy and enthusiasm, evident in his self-effacing charm and a repertoire of successful works.

He believes that, 'To be a good choreographer you need passion. A burning need to say something about dance, everything else comes from that. Dance is so straightforward, physical, and direct and dancers either work like Trojans or don't make it. An amazing energy comes from them, which stimulates me constantly. It keeps me young.'

More young talent is evident in the first piece of his programme being performed at The Lowry. Strange Company features virtuoso pianist Jason Ridgway playing Schumann's Davidsbundlertanze. 'It's a very romantic piece,' Alston enthuses, 'turbulent, yes, because Schumann was quite a troubled man, but it is extraordinarily attractive, especially when played by Jason.'

When Schumann first published this music, he credited two imaginary characters, Florestan and Eusebius, with its composition. These characters, representing his inner turmoil, and Schumann's wife Clara dominate the dance. They are joined by the Davidsbund, a strange company of supporters recruited in Schumann's mind, to battle the enemies of artistic integrity. If Schumann's compelling life journey – destination lunatic asylum – sounds a bit intense, fear not, Alston is adamant that the piece is 'probably one of the most romantic I've ever created. The music just sweeps you along and the costumes have a hint of 1960s Biba to them – purple and silver, with velvet and long lace dresses.'

Alston follows this strong narrative work with Red Run, which is shorter and episodic, and has the dancers switching pace in a perfect tension between order and chaos. 'It's about a group of people making their way through a hot, dry desert,' explains Alston. 'The dancers perform in a burning golden light to Heiner Goebbels' edgy, jazzy score.'

Water Music is the evening's glorious finale. Fast-moving and intricate, the piece pulses with energy as the dancers literally fly through the air to Jordi Savall's vigorous interpretation of Handel's famous D and G suites.

'I've deliberately chosen three pieces that have impact enough to carry on The Lowry's wonderfully large stage,' says Alston. 'I sit out front for the show because you can actually feel whether the audience is being held – that's important. If we don't get the level of response, I'll change things around.' It appears that Alston has arrived at a perfect balance for the company's latest visit – a hugely entertaining programme from a not-so-old master, who could be sitting right next to you on the night. *Maria McC...*

Fri, The Lowry, Pier 8, Salford Quays, 7.30pm, £8 to £16, con... available. Tel: 876 2000

THEATRE REVIEW

Of Mice And Men ★★★★★

John Steinbeck's classic 1937 novel, Of Mice And Men, is set in the Depression-ravaged Californian agricultural belt. More than just dramatic fiction, it is a profound chronicle, like many of the Nobel Prize-winning author's books, recording the desperate struggles of America's rural labourers. Mark Babych's new production of the author's own stage adaptation is comfortably the best thing the Octagon has done for some time. A wonderfully acted piece of work, it tells the moving story of two itinerant farm workers, George

(Michael Glenn Murphy) and the huge but childlike Lennie (Joe Montana, above left). Running away from the consequences of one of Lennie's innocent indiscretions, the pair arrive at the Tyler Ranch, where they join the hard working, bunkhouse life of other poor dirt farmers. They dream of one day owning a smallholding, a doomed ambition which is violently destroyed. Babych perfectly captures the savage beauty of Steinbeck's work, drawing out its undercurrents of racial prejudice, sexual jealousy and human brutality, but never losing sight of its ultimate belief in the triumph of the human spirit. Montana and Murphy both give beautifully understated performances in this truly magnificent piece of regional theatre. *Brian Wilson*

Until Feb 23, Bolton Octagon, Howell Croft South, Bolton, 7.30pm, mats Feb 6, 7, 13, 20 and 21 1.30pm, Feb 16 2pm, £7.75 to £14.50. Tel: 01204 520661

Macca pupils come together

Criterion

Liverpool Institute for Performing Arts

Is it really three years since Sir Paul McCartney launched his 'Fame' school in Liverpool? Living proof came with this resourceful group of theatre and dance graduates, giving a West End preview of their two student showcases. And in the foyer between the shows their skilful networking over a glass of wine was almost as impressive as the on-stage performance, a credit to head teacher Donna Soto-Morettini, who proudly calls them her "thinking practitioners".

Theatre

This took two forms. **Iain Ormsby-Knox** staged five extended extracts from contemporary musical theatre, interwoven with a drama exercise he called 'three characters in two minutes'. This unwelcome innovation rewards slickness and versatility in the use of accents, but robs us of the chance to assess the student's potential to develop and sustain a role.

But for several students these dramatic vignettes were their chief moment of glory. Auburn-haired **Lisa Ray Arthur** conjured up a Bette Midler character as well as a passionate Shakespeare heroine. Elegant **Anna Dallas** was both an American divorcee and a Sheridan heroine. I noted **Richard Boschetto** both for his Dromio and a Cockney lad. Glaswegian **Iain Davie** was also a convincing LA character from Hurlyburly. Actor, writer and singer **Stephen Griffiths** must hate being described as a McCartney look-alike, but his set included a delightful Liverpudlian moment; as did **Sarah Langton's**, a sunny Cilla in an intimate piece of comedy. Versatile blonde **Sarah Driver** was both a bold, up-front Helena and an upper-class lady in the style of Felicity Kendall, while **Louise Geraldine Fry** offered American and West Country dialects, plus an excellent Shakespearean fragment.

Irish dazzler **Clare Wreath** told a neat tale in her native accent, but was just as effective as an embarrassed gal from the Deep South. **Andrea Marcus** gave us a cynical Beatrice and two north of England characters, while **James Hughes** ranged from Cockney caricature to Neil Simon New Yorker. And all these performers also gave attractive choral support in the musical interludes.

David Tench was too busy supporting the company at the piano to get a crack at this two-minute trial. But I ringed his name for a resonantly tuneful Agony, a superb duet with American actor **Connor Ratliff**, with whom he also shared musical and directing honours for the extracts from Sondheim's Into the Woods.

Among this first LIPA crop was a strong contingent of Scandinavians, including **Elsa Maria Aanensen**, whose green eyes flashed darkly in a brief but thrilling moment from Miss Julie. Blonde beauty **Anna-Karin Larsen**, in black fishnets, looked ready for the West End in a Chicago number. And as one of the afternoon's constant delights, slender Norwegian/American **Lisa McEntire Stokke** had the sweetest, purest top notes in her Godspell solo, was a convincing Englishwoman among her dramatic fragments and shone generously in choral support.

Tall guys **Mark Robbins, Lee Jamieson Cymbal, Paul Cavanagh** and **Gary Charles** also gave effective company support but scored strongly with diverse accents in their three brief dramatic cameos. As did **Jason Nicholls** with a touch of Southern Irish, plus good presentation and an appealing voice for his Godspell solo, while two Welshmen, **Melcal Henson**, equally at home as a Mississippi character, and **Dylan Roberts** as a Cockney soldier, showed a facility for acquiring other useful accents – the latter also featuring musically in Sondheim's Into the Woods.

The Godspell extract featured bold young singer **Emma Bispham** in fine rockin' voice and the big-framed **Kevin Curtin** with a strong rock tenor vocal, who both shone in their dramatic moments.

Stand-out musical item for the girls was Cell Block Tango from Chicago, with diverse but brilliantly characterised performances from **Erica Deakin**, drolly hinting at Madonna, **Helen Barrett** as a witty Chicago babe, and a deliciously sweet **Katy Reeves**, while British actress **Rachel Leskovac** was the most convincingly American in this fine line-up. Another Brit also making a strong claim for American musical roles was **Kate Pinell**, opening the showcase with a disciplined Sunday in the Park number, and closing with comic aplomb and an impressive alto-mezzo solo from Into the Woods.

Most welcome musical spot was a revival of David Shire and Richard Maltby's revue songs for Closer Than Ever, featuring five splendid performers who also registered their talents in the dramatic moments.

Showstopping character singer – Louise McCabe

Louise McCabe literally stopped the show with her brilliant character singing as Miss Byrd in post-coital bliss, a number which won an individual hand at both of the afternoon's performances – this lady will surely go far. Actor and comic **David Stothard**, young and bubbly **Gail Mackinnon** and graceful **Tracy Spencer**, with an impressive CV of professional work, also featured strongly in this set.

And I was especially impressed by **Andrew Langtree**, springy and muscular with a light tuneful tenor, who also held the stage with a Richard II speech. I would couple his name with those picked out by Julia Collier as her expert choice.

A light, tuneful tenor – Andrew Langtree

Dance

Most of the acting company returned to the stage for the dance showcase to reprise their musical episodes as a setting for the contemporary dance troupe, but also to share the exhilaration of a funky ball choreographed by Annette Vetterli.

Barefoot and in brown, green and gold costumes, individual dancers were more difficult to identify by name as they wove patterns of vibrant physicality across the small Criterion stage. But **Mark Franks**, tall for a dancer, stood out not only as a solo male but also for his seemingly effortless ability to become airborne. And one soon identified **Katrina Brackenbury** and **Anna Hudd** as his gifted partners in a trio of shared choreographic talents.

Gifted – Katrina Brackenbur

There was also much to admire in the work of long-haired **Kayte Pitchford**, the eye-catching **Sophie Paratte**, limber **Emma Reid**, Danish gymnast and dancer **Rikke Hojbusk**, **Eve King** with professional show and ballet experience to her credit, and **Tamsin Randall**, who strongly led both jazz and funk numbers.

■ *Because there were no dance producers, critics or agents in attendance, there is no Expert Choice for the dance showcase.*

John Thaxter

Effortless – Mark Franks

Dancer's dream date in Vegas

DANCER Emma Annetts is heading to Las Vegas for a dream engagement alongside international singing star Celine Dion.

Miss Annetts will take to the stage at the Las Vegas Colisseum in March.

The Colisseum seats 4,000 people and is regarded as one of the top venues in the world.

Miss Annetts (23) daughter of Mr and Mrs Les Annetts of Newstead Avenue, Radcliffe, will be part of a 70-strong cast of dancers, musicians and artists who will appear alongside the Canadian superstar.

Bursting

Following auditions in London she was awarded a two-year contract — her first as a professional.

Miss Annetts is one of only three British dancers chosen for the show.

She is rehearsing in Belgium until November in preparation for the show and will then fly out to Las Vegas.

Her mother, Mrs Sylvia Annetts, said: "We are bursting with pride.

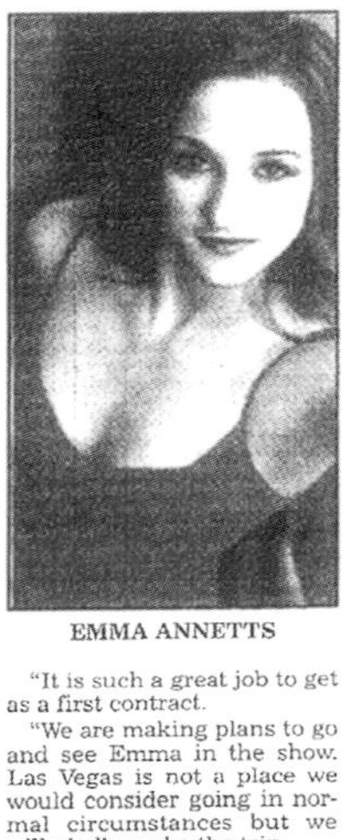

EMMA ANNETTS

"It is such a great job to get as a first contract.

"We are making plans to go and see Emma in the show. Las Vegas is not a place we would consider going in normal circumstances but we will gladly make the trip.

"It's a once in a lifetime opportunity and something we don't want to miss."

Emma, who has been dancing since she was three, did her GCSEs at Radcliffe's Dayncourt School and gained a first class BA honours degree at the Liverpool Institute of Performing Arts which was founded by Sir Paul McCartney.

Gymnastics

Mrs Annetts describes her daughter as very talented, determined and disciplined, a result she says of an early commitment to gymnastics.

From the age of six to 17 Miss Annetts was winning gymnastic medals and trophies as a member of the national development squad and took part in international events in countries including America and Russia.

"But her first love has always been dancing," said Mrs Annetts.

"Her dream is to star in the West End.

"When she got this contract she said she could not believe someone was willing to pay her for something she would do for nothing."

LYNSEY McCAFFREY

My TV Favourites

Lynsey McCaffrey was given her first TV break on Brookside (C4) playing single mum Ruth Smith. After graduating from the Liverpool Institute of Performing Arts, Lynsey moved to London, but has now returned to Liverpool where she lives alone.

What is your current TV favourite?
Sex And The City was my bible in London. It's a great programme.

What do you set your video for?
What, you can set these things?!

Favourite TV show as a child?
Blossom and The Wonder Years. Apparently, as a very young child I loved Basil Brush and Ken Dodd. It went downhill from there!

What is your favourite TV classic?
Surprise Surprise with Cilla Black. I think it was more memorable than favourite – I'd cry through all of it.

Who do you most admire on TV?
Julie Walters for her ability to turn her hand to all mediums and genres and to amaze me in whatever she does.

Your first TV appearance?
At secondary school our choir sang for a series called Voices Raised. I sang a solo and read a poem while sporting an embarrassing fringe that started at the back of my head.

What was your most embarrassing TV moment?
My first interview on T4, which was live. I was sat in a rather "manly" position, forgetting there was a camera on the floor directly in front of me!

What is your idea of TV heaven?
Brass Eye is comic genius. I have a dry sense of humour and watch this show in amazement. I know not to take it seriously but you have to wonder!

Brookside celebrates its 20th anniversary on C4 in November

They love her ja, ja, ja

BEDFORD girl Jemma Endersby is making a bid for pop stardom in Germany.

Jemma was once a member of Bedford Youth Theatre before being picked to attend the prestigious Liverpool Institute For Performing Arts (LIPA) which was founded by Sir Paul McCartney.

She is currently touring and her new album Afterglow, which was released in October last year is tipped for huge success.

Jemma said: "I've been living in Germany since 1999 but come back to Bedford at least twice a year to visit family and friends. I certainly miss the people and the familiarity of the place.

"I used to play in Bedford in a band called The Collective and have many fond memories of gigs there.

Network

"My partner Benny has set up a recording studio in Cologne, which is twinned with Liverpool.

"If there's one thing LIPA taught me, it's how important it is to network in the music industry. I never thought I'd admit it but there is a lot of truth in it.

"One of my most special moments was when Paul McCartney handed me my graduation pin – my legs turned to jelly.

"After giving birth to my son, Finn, in May last year I started touring again.

"I've played Berlin, Rostock, Weisbaden and I also have future performances lined up in Maastricht, Stuttgart and Dresden.

"Apart from performing my own material I have just been accepted as the new soprano in Germany's all-lady Jazz pop group 'Voices Divine'.

"I always thought German wasn't a very nice language but after two years of struggling through the grammar, small talk and the sense of humour, yes they do have one, I've changed my mind."

You can follow Jemma's career by logging onto www.endersby.net

---

Drama student wins West End place – at her first attempt

Fair start to acting career

By Josephine Murray

VICKY ALHADEFF

A DRAMA student from Edgware, who has never appeared on stage before, has landed a part in the hit West End musical My Fair Lady.

Caroline Cohen, who lives in Brockley Avenue, was in her final year at LIPA, Paul McCartney's drama school in Liverpool, when she was offered the role of chorus girl and understudy for the lead role of Eliza Doolittle.

She passed an audition and is now appearing in the musical at the Theatre Royal Drury Lane alongside Dennis Waterman as her father, Alfred P Doolittle.

As well as appearing in the chorus, Caroline is preparing to step in if the actresses playing Eliza Doolittle – Joanna Riding and Katie Knight Adams – are ill.

Caroline, who is 22 years old, said: "The musical is really exciting, brilliant fun. The cast is just lovely. It's such a great show, I couldn't have asked for a better first job. It's always been a dream of mine to be on the West End and it's my favourite show."

She said: "I wasn't ever sure I'd make it, but it was always a dream."

Caroline studied French and Spanish at Birmingham University for a year before going to LIPA. She plans to complete her course and will use My Fair Lady as her performance module.

Her understudy role as Eliza involves speaking with both an upper-class and cockney accent.

Caroline said: "I've lived in London all my life, so it's easy for me."

As part of the chorus, Caroline's roles include a pub customer in A Little Bit of Luck, a prostitute in Get Me to the Church on Time and a race-goer wearing a huge hat at Ascot.

Despite her tremendous enjoyment at appearing in My Fair Lady, fame has not affected Caroline's down-to-earth approach. She said: "It's a job at the end of the day that I go to and then I come home."

Overjoyed: Caroline Cohen's first job in the theatre will be on the West End stage

---

GRADUATES GO ON TO A WIDE VARIETY OF CAREERS

PEUGEOT SONG AD TO BE A SMASH HIT

Lipa course helps rapper's re-mix race up the charts

By CLAIRE STOKER

A TOXTETH rapper is continuing Liverpool's proud tradition of chart success with a top ten single.

Fitzy Fyne, 27, was an unemployed musician when he spotted an ECHO story about New Deal courses at the Liverpool Institute of Performing Arts.

Now his single, Husan, is number seven in the charts.

It first featured in a Peugeot car advert where a young Indian youth reshapes his car by getting an elephant to sit on it – the music has now been remixed with new lyrics by Fitzy as part of Bhangra Nights vs Hasan.

He said: "It was our first project and to have such a huge success so quickly is amazing.

"I appeared live on Top of the Pops with Bhangra Knights and we were flown to Delhi to shoot a video – it was brilliant."

The success of the single led Peugeot to re-release the advert and it has now been voted the best-ever TV commercial by Radio Four listeners.

Fitzy had worked on a few house music tracks before he did the three month Learning Occupational Training course at Lipa.

"Lipa was brilliant – it really gave me an insight into the music industry," said Fitzy.

After the course, he was contacted by a producer in London, Jules Spinner, to help remix the track with Hasan, the Dutch duo who wrote the original song.

Fitzy said: "I added my own verses and vocals, which we sent to Hasan and they loved our version."

The track is set to have a worldwide release and Fitzy is already working on a follow-up single, Punjabi Dayz.

Mat Flynn, head of Fitzy's course, said: "To see a former student appearing on Top of the Pops is tremendous."

LIAM LYNCH
Renaissance man? Whatever

Liam Lynch: socks machine

Pop is littered with those considered renaissance men. Liam Lynch, however, may force some urgent redefinition of the term.

LA-based Lynch, 31, is multi-talented. He writes dialogue and scores music for television and movies. He directs videos, has written songs for the likes of Sum 41 and is working on a feature film with his best friend, the actor and Tenacious D singer Jack Black. But this isn't even what Lynch is most renowned for. That's putting his hand in a sock.

"I made some short video pieces in my flat with two sock puppets and that became The Sifl & Olly Show, which ran on MTV Europe for about two years," he explains. "They would pop up throughout the day. This led to my getting a daily, half-hour show on MTV USA. I did the seasons of Sifl & Olly with my friends like that. It was like a sock puppet version of Reeves & Mortimer."

The Anglocentric reference is no surprise. Lynch conceived Sifl & Olly while studying at the Institute For Performing Arts in Liverpool. He was one of five students hand-picked by Paul McCartney to study with the ex-Beatle on a one-to-one basis. "It changed my life," Lynch says, unsurprisingly.

Now Lynch is ready to put what Macca taught him to practical use. He's released a single called 'United States Of Whatever', a punkabilly blast that manages to condense and send up American youth culture in under three minutes. It is cool.

"This country is so young and cocky," says Liam, explaining the song's inspiration. "Like a 14-year-old with a machine gun – which is probably why our 14-year-olds have machine guns. All I knew was that I was going to say, 'My United States of whatever'... The rest was just made up as I played it. I got lucky and caught some funny moments."

Liam has no plans to play gigs or become a full-time musician, however. The guy is too busy to take any one thing too seriously. Besides, he suspects serious might be boring.

"My bottom line," he considers carefully, "is that Tom Baker was the best Doctor Who."

Er, whatever.

Ted Kessler

'United States Of Whatever' is released on November 18 through Global Warming Records

---

Alexandra Russell is going to Australia to teach young offenders about the arts to help rehabilitate them

PICTURE STEVE REID [042419-73]

Governor tells of benefits of work

ALEXANDRA Russell uses various strands of the arts in her workshops, including video, music, dance, play-writing, live linked performances, and visual arts such as mask-making.

She aims to take the inmates through a verse of Shakespeare and they will analyse it.

She might also take them through a tragedy such as Macbeth or a comedy such as The Taming of the Shrew.

Pauline Johnson, a governor at HMP Liverpool, welcomed drama in prisons.

"It is very positive. Drama in prisons could become part and parcel of rehabilitation," she said.

WESTSIDE FREETIME

Meet the sister act of Les Miserables

LES MISERABLES
The Palace Theatre

WORKING with siblings can be a stressful, but for the Seale sisters, who have just won places in the cast of *Les Miserables*, it's a pleasure.

It's the first time that the cast of *Les Miserables* at the West End Palace Theatre has had sisters in the cast, but the Seales have seen their stage careers follow one another again and again.

Northfields-based Natasha, 27, said: "Our acting careers seem to have worked in tandem. We studied at the same school, both graduated from Liverpool Institute of Performing Arts (LIPA) and we're now appearing in the same West End show."

The duo made their first appearance together at the Palace on Monday night, and although the sisters are close, the experience was, as Natasha put it, a little freaky.

"There are times when we follow each other with solo lines, and our voices do have similar characteristics, so it's a bit freaky."

But according to Natasha the benefits greatly outweigh any downsides.

"There's no competition between us because we've always been really supportive of each other.

"We were obviously both nervous on

STAR TURNS: Rebecca and Natasha Seale tre

MUSICAL

Monday night, but our dressing rooms are next to each other so we can always pop in for a chat if nerves do strike."

But is there any chance that their sisterhood could be damaged by working so closely together? Natasha says not.

"It might too much for both of us if we were actually sharing a dressing room night after night, but we've stud

ied toget
were a ye
other beir

Both sis
parts, Nat
for Eponi
Natash
uating in
to the dai

"I love
relax," Na

"It's go
coffee sh
have the t
anywhere

McCartney school girl graduates to West End

By Ed Harris

SHE ONLY graduated from drama school a few months ago — but already Katie Foster-Barnes has landed herself a plum role in the West End.

She left the Liverpool Institute of Performing Arts, otherwise known as Paul McCartney's Fame school, in July. But on Wednesday she will take to the stage in a new production of a JB Priestley play, Dangerous

Corner, at the Garrick Theatre.

The 21-year-old is just one of several graduates of the institute who have found themselves on the West End stage — rather than starving, in the traditional manner, in a damp garret. Others have landed leading roles in musicals including Spend, Spend, Spend! and Mamma Mia!

But no one is more surprised than Foster-Barnes herself. "I was jumping around and

everything when I heard," she said. "It is my first job."

Director Laurie Sansom had worked with her in Liverpool and remembered her when it was time to cast the role of Betty Whitehouse, a feisty young woman, in Priestley's drama of suspense, murder and passion.

In the production, which is transferring from the West Yorkshire Playhouse, Foster-Barnes will be playing alongside Dervla Kirwan, from

Ballykissangel and Hearts and Bones, and Rupert Penry-Jones, who won an award for Don Carlos with the RSC.

For Foster-Barnes, the next five months are taken care of. After that, who knows? "I have no idea what I will do when it is over," she said. "I would like to try everything."

Whitehouse experience: Katie Foster-Barnes will play the feisty Betty Whitehouse in JB Priestley's Dangerous Corner

---

[D]ANGO WALKER
[Dow]n The Road

[...] The Road / Texas Blacktop
[...]way / The Road You Choose
[...]her Day / All The Miles /
[...]e Life / Modern Day
[...]les / Wild Cowboys / Love
[...]azy Thing / Jose & Jack /
[...]ngwriter / Texas On My

[...]: Lloyd Maines
[...] Music LKU 3756

[...]e Road seems an [...]title for this debut [...] Django Walker as [...]e songs are either [...]it, or have some [...], travelling and [...] gives a semblance [...]ut gives a feeling [...] and a lack of

[...] Choose, All The [...] Songwriter are [...]rd person and [...]rables on the [...]and fame that [...]nity that this [...] for [...]astute [...]ard person in *Modern Day Bojangles* (co-written by Walker and Pat Green) is more subtle and perceptive but only partially successful.

Some of the songs, such as *All The Miles* and *Love Is A Crazy Thing*, are about the weariness,

disillusionment and loneliness of a performer on the road. Coming from someone in his early twenties who is just starting out on his career, one wonders if he is cut out to be a musician. *Down The Road*, with its solid, Steve Earle feel and well constructed lyrics also documents life on the road but far more successfully and from a more positive outlook.

Many of Walker's songs have the feel of a young man trying to imagine situations of which he has little experience. The most successful are the ones that use some autobiographical material such as *College Life* and *Texas On My Mind*, both of which seem to stem from Walker's experiences during his attendance at Paul McCartney's Liverpool Institute of Performing Arts. Pat Green has covered the latter and, according to Rob Patterson's column in CMP, *Texas On My Mind* "has already become something of an anthem with the young crowd."

Walker has a great voice and has put together an excellent band but many of his songs lack a cutting edge and fail to engage on an emotional level. Drummer Noah Watson contributes the folky *Another Day* which has a structure and harmonic subtlety that outshines some of Walker's own compositions.

Walker is the son of Jerry Jeff Walker and it must be a challenge to follow in such a well-known father's footsteps although it must also help with launching the younger Walker's career. A competent debut with much promise but Django Walker needs to cast his songwriting net far wider than his tour bus and hotel room. (No label contact listed.)

Michael Hingston

PERFORMERS HAVE TO
GET PUBLICITY FOR
THEMSELVES – A
TAUGHT SKILL

DAILY STAR, Friday, March 17, 2000 **27**

YOUR BIG HEN'S GONE

by MATT JOHN

BIRDBRAIN student Bernhard Niechotz rules the roost in his motor . . . after covering it in chicken feathers.

Bernhard reckons his Fiat Strada sounds like a big hen's gone every time he lets in the clutch.

He decided a fluffy Fiat was eggs-actly what he needed for a show at the Liverpool Institute of Performing Arts.

He covered his car in a latex film before sticking on the feathers from a chicken factory.

Performance design student Bernhard, 24, from Stuttgart, Germany, explained: "It's weird having people stare at you but it's nice to make people happy."

His next car will probably be a Hen-ry Ford or Hen-sen Interceptor.

Gianni Abruzzese

Readerzone

Oli Bell

What have you got at the end of your garden? If it's anything like mine it'll be a mound of paving slabs waiting to be turned into a patio, but Gianni Abruzzese has something much better. Nestling at the end of his parents' impressive garden, in a small village just outside Bedford, sits the Voodoo Cab, a green Portakabin housing Gianni's project studio. Separated into two areas (a live room complete with drum kit, and a small control room where we did the interview), the Cab is

hired out by Gianni to bands wanting to record tracks or demos — when he's not working as the recording engineer at a Milton Keynes studio, that is.

Musical Beginnings

Gianni's musical roots are familiar enough: he started out on keyboards, before moving onto guitar and bass at school, but never felt completely satisfied with his playing.

"I wanted to be a musician, like most sound engineers, but discovered I wasn't really good enough. So I decided being behind the desk, instead of in front of it, would be the next best thing." Interested in gaining some

hands-on training, he tried to arrange some work experience at local studios, with little success. "I couldn't get any work experience, so I thought I'd teach myself." Armed with a Behringer mixer, an ADAT, and a pair of headphones, Gianni began to learn the basics from his bedroom. "I started doing demos for bands at school, but my parents were beginning to get annoyed with drums banging away in the house, and things like that."

So a run-down Portakabin appeared at the end of the garden and the Voodoo Cab was born. But that was just the beginning of the hard work, as Gianni explains: "First we had to get the building right — it was old and smashed up when it first arrived, and the control room was actually the toilet. We panelled it out, did all the wiring and put the control room window in." Did he have any major problems during the refit? "Leads were the main problem. Because I didn't really understand the difference between balanced and unbalanced back then, I was getting lots of noise and hiss and thought 'Jesus, this is really bad quality, what's going on?' I hadn't done any courses at that stage and was learning as I went along, which I think is invaluable. No-one can sit you in a classroom and teach you everything; some problems you have to sort out for yourself."

Having his own setup soon began to pay off. "Because I was able to find my way around a desk, I managed to get some work experience at a couple of studios, even though I wasn't allowed near the mixer, which was frustrating." As frustrating as it was, Gianni knew he'd found his calling. "Basically, I found I liked engineering better than playing, and wondered how I could get into the industry." After deciding to try for a three-year course in music production and engineering, Gianni set his sights on the Paul McCartney-backed Liverpool Institute for Performing Arts (LIPA).

It was during his time at LIPA that the Voodoo Cab really came into its own. "Every holiday I was back here recording demos for bands, to make the money for the following year's course. It was my holiday job." As well as bringing in some cash, the Cab also gave

infocus

DONNA Steele was only 11 years old when she first stepped into the limelight playing the lead in Annie. More than 15 years later she is preparing as Amanda Holden's understudy in the West End musical Thoroughly Modern Millie. Today, Features Editor **RACHAEL GORDON** spoke to the former King's School girl about her rise to fame.

Everything is going thoroughly well for stage star Donna

IMAGINE putting on a show with some of the world's most well-known faces in the audience.

Imagine former Boomtown Rat Bob Geldof and actor Stephen Fry clapping when you had finished your performance.

And wouldn't it be amazing if Hollywood actor Robert De Niro came up to you afterwards, shook your hand and said: "You were outstanding. I couldn't take my eyes off you."

Well, 26-year-old Donna Steele doesn't have to imagine these things, because they have already happened to her when she took part in the We Will Rock You workshop in front of a host of celebrities, singing some of Queen's best-known hits.

And even now, the former King's School head girl remains modest about her talents and says a lot of it was down to "being at the right place at the right time".

But whether it's luck, or sheer hardwork and talent, Donna Steele is already making her mark in theatreland.

She has already appeared in Peggy Sue Got Married at the Shaftesbury Theatre and The Full Monty at the Prince of Wales Theatre — both in London's West End.

But she feels her latest break – as Amanda Holden's understudy in the Oscar-winning Broadway musical Thoroughly Modern Millie, which opens at the Shaftesbury Theatre in London later this month – is her biggest yet.

Donna said: "I still can't really believe it is happening to me. Every day I'm working with Maureen Lipman and Sheila Ferguson and Amanda Holden. And they are all such talented people. The other day we were rehearsing and I found out Kevin Spacey was rehearsing his new film upstairs.

"One minute I was chatting to Maureen Lipman and the next she was introducing me to Kevin Spacey. I nearly fell over. It just didn't feel real.

"And it's really weird going to the newsagents and buying a newspaper and seeing Amanda in it and then seeing her at work later that day.

"She is a really lovely person, and I just hope when I get to play Millie I do her as much justice as she does."

Donna will make her stage debut as Millie on November 24, when Amanda Holden and Maureen Lipman are taking part in the Royal Variety Performance.

She said: "I can't wa[...]

tremendous opportunity."

But Donna insists she isn't starstruck, and her training a[t] Key Theatre in Peterborough then later at the Liverpool In[stitute] for the Performing Arts fam[ous] school (LIPA) has stood her [...] stead.

She said: "I got to go on a[s] lead quite a few times in Th[e Full] Monty, and to be honest wh[en you] are in the spotlight you ca[n't see] who is in the audience.

"It's no different to bei[ng at the] Key. And when I was at LI[PA they] taught you how to behav[e not] to be starstruck, so it is [no] other people make a bi[g deal of] what you are doing tha[t really] hits home."

Donna grew up in P[eterborough] and lived with her par[ents in] Queen's Drive West.

She made her stag[e at the] age of 11 after auditi[oning for a] part in The Key The[atre's] Annie.

She said: "I hadn'[t done any] productions before, an[d I could]n't believe it when I auditioned an[d] got the lead part. I'd never attempted singing before and it was only when I tried then that my parents realised I had a special talent.

"No one else in my family had ever done any theatre work before."

After Annie, Donna joined the Key Kids, which is now the Key Youth Theatre, and appeared in lots of shows including Oklahoma, Guys and Dolls, Twelfth Night Fever, Much Ado Ron Ron, and Dream Nights.

She also returned recently to play Aladdin and Snow White in two of The Key's pantomimes.

Donna said: "I love coming back to The Key. I had such good times there and made so many friends. It

was there I was taught all the skills I needed from what upstage and downstage meant to basic dance moves. It really is a wonderful place and I have a lot to thank Derek Killeen and Michael Cross for.

"And of course I am extremely grateful to my parents because they have been so supportive.

"Although when I am working, I always try to save, because you never know when you will be out of work. My parents have always backed me 100 per cent. And you need that in this business."

rachael.gordon@peterboroughnow.co.uk

UP AND UP: Donna Steele began her career at The Key Theatre when she was 11, and is now understudy for the lead part in Thoroughly Modern Millie.

AWARD FOR COMEDIENNE

Stephanie's recipe for comic stardom

COMEDIENNE Stephanie Davies is looking forward to performing in front of a wider audience after winning the *Liverpool Daily Post and Echo* award for Best New Talent in Comedy.

Stephanie, who went to Queen Elizabeth II High School and now lives in Liverpool, was surprised at winning the award just 18 months after launching her stand-up career.

She said: 'It's brilliant recognition for me. It shows that people are starting to recognise who I am.'

As part of her prize she won a

bursary of £1,000 which she'll use to help build her profile and put towards travel expenses.

'I don't think it will make a huge difference but it helps me realise that people recognise me and I can ride the wave of publicity.'

The 34-year-old, whose brother Ben presents a show on Manx Radio, has been commissioned to write a radio script for the BBC, something she's looking forward to doing more of in the future.

'People are beginning to take me [ser]ious[...] I'm working

award.

A graduate of the Liverpool Institute of Performing Arts, Stephanie got into comedy while learning about variety at university.

Passing on some words of wisdom to budding comedians she said: 'Observe everything around you, people-watch and put in a twist and a slant.

'Tap into what people think so you have got a mutual understanding. If they can't relate to it, it's not funny.'

Stephanie, a former member of [...] once appeared

alongside Sir Norman Wisdom in an anti-bullying video.

Since graduating she has worked as project co-ordinator of a campaign to encourage people to use stand-up as a tool to promote self confidence.

This is something she knows all about using her energy and personality during her routine, which she describes as observational with a lot of situation comedy.

She said: 'There are a lot of women on the circuit now, they're more willing to try it. A lot more are doing more alternative comedy rather than men-bashing.'

HOW TERRY NETTED EVA, 25, FOR HIS SPECIAL PROJECT

SINGER-songwriter Eva Katzler discovered the power of the internet when former Specials frontman Terry Hall fell in love with her voice.

Eva, a graduate of Paul McCartney's Liverpool Institute for Performing Arts (LIPA), put links to her own site on as many websites as possible.

"Terry was surfing the web and found my stuff," Eva of Pinner, North London, said. "His manager contacted me about performing on Terry's latest project, *The Hour of Two Lights*."

The album, to be released next month, is a collaboration with Asian music pioneer Mushtaq and features Jewish and Islamic musicians.

Eva performs with Hall on the track, *A Gathering Storm*. She was given the lyrics to the song and asked to translate them into Hebrew.

"My father, Ron, was born in Nairobi but lived in Israel until he was 18, so he speaks Hebrew. I got him to translate the song so I could sing it in Hebrew.

"Terry was very normal. Fortunately, I met many great people at LIPA, so we learnt not to get star-struck. Terry taught me a lot about the music business."

The 25-year-old gained a place at LIPA after attending Amersham College where she did theatre studies.

"LIPA was a lot of work – not difficult, but they worked you hard. I met my producer there, he was on a production course."

Eva wanted to be a psychologist but once she got to university, she set her heart on a career in music. Attending LIPA has helped develop her songwriting skills.

Original

"Each student had an eclectic music col[lec]tion," he said. "I listened to some bizarre [music] and learnt many different styles.

Once she graduated, instead of rushing head-long into the music business, Eva heade[d for] Barcelona where she finished her teaching [quali]fication.

"I got my head together in Barcelona," [she] revealed. "I made sure it was what I really [want]ed to do."

She then flew to Munich in April 2001 [to work] on her debut album.

"We finished the album in January," she said. "I signed a production deal with my producer and now just need to licence it to a label.

"I'm so proud of it. If it flops, I don't mind. It's turned out how I wanted it."

The album will all be original material – although Eva is unsure whether to include her cover of *Bridge Over Troubled Water* as it has been recorded recently by Hear'say and Charlotte Church.

Last June, Eva found out what it is like to have a number one when her song *Star*, from her debut EP *Poem* reached the top in the MP3.com charts – deposing multi-Grammy winner Norah Jones. Eva's website — www.evakatzler.com — also gets hundreds of hits a day.

"There is a massive community of people who download random pieces of music – and many of them have downloaded my tracks. Each [day I get] e-mails from all over the world thanking [me for do]ing what I'm doing."

[...] [sh]owing a creative [...] member of

Blonde, Bright and Beautiful

Paul Wilkes releases his first EP this summer after winning critical acclaim for his debut work. Paul took part in the New Deal for Musi... during 2003 at LIP... CAMEO apprentic...

Clubbers website, G... Paul as a genuine ta...

But the 20 year old ... singer/songwriter ea... from Keith Mullin, hi... best known as a me... band, The Farm, sa... work with such a gr...

Paul's first EP, *Blond...* is to be released by ... this summer, follow... autumn.

Since bursting onto ... Paul has played ove... North West and has a tour starting in the summer, taking in performances in England and Ireland.

Photographer: Dave Eva...

ISHMAEL'S NEW CAREER

Ishmael Majid has turned his love of performing arts into a career as a rap artist and dancer.

He was singing in the street with a friend when a passer by complemented him on his singing ability and suggested he should get his voice professionally trained.

Positive Impact were working in partnership with LIPA on the CAMEO project and he joined them as an entrepreneurial apprentice through the project.

One of the highlights of Ishmael's training programme was appearing as one of the Temptations in a musical, *Strictly Motown.* This was produced by Positive Impact and played to a full house at the Liverpool Playhouse.

He did so well during his CAMEO apprenticeship that he is now working with Positive Impact as a mentor and classroom assistant in dance classes and has also launched himself as a freelance tutor, working with a number of organisations. In this work he draws on his own experience to ease teenagers from inner-city communities into the world of song and dance.

He said: "The guy who said I ha... a good voice turned out to be a music producer. I took his advic... and went to Positive Impact and here I am working as a mentor, helping and encouraging people who were learning to be singers and rappers."

Ishmael is also part of a rap clik called Danger Force. His stage name is Statik and the other member of the duo is called Crisis.

Fitzy's top 10 hit

Fitzy Fyne has appeared on Top of the Pops and jetted off to Delhi to record a video, just weeks after completing a FLES Longer Occupational Training course here.

Fitzy's chart triumph, with the hit Husan by Bhangra Knights-versus-Husan, owes its success to an old car and an elephant!

He worked on a remix of music originally written as a backdrop for a Peugeot car advert, in which a young Indian guy re-shapes his car by crashing it into a wall and getting an elephant to sit on the bonnet.

Fitzy, or Raul as he is known in the music world, was enlisted by co-producer Jules Spinner of UK-based Lowered Recordings, to add verses to an instrumental remix by Jules of the original.

The remix went straight into the top 10 and reached number 7, and is now destined for world-wide release. The accompanying video, shot over four days in Delhi, features Fitzy singing and rapping and has been shown repeatedly on MTV.

The hit was such a success that Peugeot decided to re-run its popular advert - already voted the best ever TV commercial by Radio 4 listeners.

Fitzy explained how the hit record was born: "The original was done by two Dutch guys called Husan with the voice of an Indian singer called Raja Mustaq. Jules did a remix and sent me the samples and asked me to work on them. I added my own verses and vocals, which we sent to Husan and they loved our version. We got together to do the single and decided to call it Bhangra Knights-versus-Husan. It was our first project and to have such a huge success so quickly is amazing."

Fitzy is working on two follow up singles with Bhangra Knights, both with an Indian theme and he has other music work in the pipeline.

He said: "LIPA was a brilliant place for me. It really gave me an insight into the music industry and how it works. The learning resources and facilities were just great. It was also terrific to be helped by people who are in bands."

LIPA's Mat Flynn said: Everyone here is delighted with Fitzy's success and to see a former student appearing on Top of the Pops is great. We are sure his success in the music industry will continue."

Photo courtesy of the Liverpool Daily Post and Echo

Bec Phillips calls herself

Queen of Blaggers

Ian Reynolds tried to get a word in

ALL she sent was a head-shot. A girl: flame red hair obscuring one eye, red velvet lips curled in 'in your face' defiance. On the phone she asked: 'how will I know you?' I told her 'don't worry, I'll find you.' So it's a good job that the Fab Bar on Portland Street wasn't crammed to capacity or I'd never have heard the barman say 'Hi Bec' as she walked in. Who says the camera never lies?

'I'm like a chameleon', said the tall brunette, happily.

No kidding.

Bec Peters, 25 (though you'd never guess), is a singer, a model; co-owner of a record label, a band manager; a student at Lippa (The Paul McCartney School of Performing Arts) a script writer, a dancer, a DJ, a... You get the picture? She knows what she wants out of life and she pursues her dreams with the dogged determination of an SAS colonel planning a deadly mission. She's not messing about. Bec wants to be famous - and rich, naturally.

Showbiz mum and dad pulling the strings? 'I always knew what I wanted to do but I was no child prodigy. Mum, (Joan), was the first woman to qualify as a football referee, and dad, (Ronnie), was a professional footballer with Burnley'. Of all the kids who dream of playing football, how many make it? And what kind of woman could break down the walls of a male bastion like football? Chez Phillips, there was no such word as 'impossible'.

THE NON-DEGREE
PROGRAMMES
DESIGNED TO ASSIST
WIDER LIVERPOOL
ALSO ACHIEVE
COVERAGE

POP GETS SERIOUS

Showcase puts local bands in spotlight

TALENT-spotters are set to flock to a series of live gigs by more than 100 Mersey musicians.

Record company scouts from all over the country are expected to descend on Liverpool during the last week of January – to hear 26 local bands.

There will also be the chance to take home a free CD – handed out at the door – featuring groups such as Scooby.

Bonanza

The four-day music bonanza, at The Picket on Hardman Street, marks the end of the "Get Serious" evening course run for local b... by the Liverpo... Perform...

● Finishing touches . . . members of the band Scooby mix a track for the free compilation CD, that will be handed out at the "Get Serious" gigs this month

Art attack

● High hopes . . . (from left) High Five, Ooberman and Jubjub

City's new pop heroes line up for an ECHO night to r...

...ITH all the glitter of the Oscars, the *ECHO* Arts Awards are finally announced this ...nd.

...ll be rolling out the red carpet ...George's Hall to some of Liver...finest musicians.

...d they will be feeling distinctly ...omfortable in their dinner jack...and black ties ... if they bother ...aring them that is.

This year the Best Newcomer cate...ry has been brimming with fresh ...alent.

From the hip-hop of AM to the ...classic pop guitars of Blueseed, right ...through to the party atmosphere of ...Zeb.

Talents

Other bands to be considered were Scooby, Kassius, Nuyen, Hotel, Aquaspacer and Speed.

After much heartache, the short list was trimmed to just three bands — Jubjub, Ooberman and the Hi... Five.

All three are great talents in th... own right and have been causin... real buzz over the last 12 months.

Jubjub seem to have been every... where. They've played almost every... venue in Liverpool as well as Wem... bley Arena.

They played there after making it to the final of a national Battle of

Kirk's date with Atomic Kitten

Kirk Ward has found himself playing as a sessions guitarist for Atomic Kitten following his training under NDfM at LIPA. The 25 year old from Liverpool not only learned the skills of managing a career in music, but found loads of good contacts through LIPA, including one that paved the way for that Kittens work. Kirk has also appeared on radio and is writing a book *How to play the Guitar.* Kirk said: "I was told at LIPA that talent is the minimum requirement in the music business."

Friday Live

EXCLUSIVE

'If I'm going to be a saint, I want to be alive to enjoy it'

ALEXEI SAYLE — PAGE 33

UP AND RUNNING!

...HEIR career is taking off ...— just as their name implies.

Now the ECHO award-winning ...and Up And Running have just ...ecured themselves a place in ...erpool's musical history.

The hard-working lads, who ...his week played their usual ...xhausting schedule of gigs are ...he first band to record an ...bum at LIPA – the recently ...pened Liverpool Institute for ...erforming Arts.

Original Up And Running duo ...'bil Jones and Alex McKenzie ...ave been working on the album ...ith their on-stage band.

Now they tell FRIDAY LIVE ...hat they are proud of this fab ...

Says bass player and vocalist ...lex: "I remember reading about ...he LIPA project in the ECHO ...nd wondering how the whole ...oncept would turn out. But ...eing in there and seeing the ...acilities was eye-opening.

"It's a brilliant complex. The ...students will certainly benefit ...rom it all."

During the recording, the band ...umbled into one superstar — ...inger Jose Feliciano.

Local band notches up a musical 'first' at LIPA

● Studio sound: Up And Running (main picture), producer Will Schilling (above) and Jose Feliciano and Joan Armatrading (inset).

EXCLUSIVE report by PETER GRANT

Says Alex: "Jose was at LIPA to lecture and perform. He came in to tell us how he started writing and spent time with us. He came into our session and listened to a few songs, too.

"He picked out one called *The River* and was really impressed ...

...with Phil's song-writing. And he asked for our card!"

The band completed the recording of their album in nine days — now they are mixing it and it should be in the shops in October.

Says Alex: "Being in the studio was great for us. I kept thinking about who might be using it in the future."

Next week, Joan Armatrading is doing a masterclass and big names such as Phil Collins and hopefully even Paul McCartney himself will visit.

Phil Jones, guitarist, flute and sax-player with the band, adds: "I am very proud that Up And Running are the first artists to make an album at LIPA.

"The facilities there are unbelievable, but perhaps the most impressive thing about the place is the students. There's a real buzz about the place."

American producer Will Schilling, who has worked with the million-selling band Cheap Trick and the legendary Bo Diddely, is confident of the band's growing appeal.

Will, who owns his own studio in Manhattan, saw Up And Running during some gigs in New York and was "knocked out" by their promise and potential.

So President Records flew Will over to Liverpool — and the result is an album the lads and their many fans know them.

...mid...

The His... who came to Live... of it's music scene. No... determined to stay even after ... graduate this summer.

Although they haven't been ...

Liverpool's music scene really has been re-born

At ... has been st... especially to the La... tival. This year it was sho... Guinness and attracted the attentio... of the important music executives in London.

Good luck to everyone who is nom... inated, the results will be announced in Monday's ECHO.

WHO KILLED...... THE ZUTONS

NIKKI DISCOVERS GOLD, PLATINUM AND LIPA

Singer Nikki Belle was just 18 when a song she recorded with a new group Mousse T vs Hot and Juicy climbed to number one in the UK Charts. *Horny,* **led to them appearing on** *Top of the Pops,* **travelling the world doing gigs and earning a gold disc in South Africa and platinum in Australia.**

While she was with Hot & Juicy, they recorded more songs but none of them were released after the smash-hit debut. Six years later Nikki is making a comeback with help from LIPA. She signed up for a New Deal for Musicians course and became an entrepreneurial apprentice with Honey Records through LIPA's CAMEO Project.

Soon after arriving at LIPA, Nikki had stars in her eyes again when she was picked in the backing group for the Eurovision Song Contest. Liverpool duo Jemini became famous as the contestants scoring 'nul points'. But Nikki says the experience was fantastic. She has also backed Atomic Kitten and as a member of Hot and Juicy, played before 80,000 people at the Stade De France in Paris.

Recently two compilations, *Floor Fillers* and *Clubland Exchange,* have been issued featuring Nikki's Scouse House single *Music is my Life.* She is hoping to head for performances in Ibiza during the summer.

Nikki looks back at her incredible experiences and says: "If I had known then what I have learned at LIPA things would have turned out so much differently. Thanks to New Deal and CAMEO I know a lot about contracts, and management and I have been given the chance to network and meet some really helpful and knowledgeable people."

THE SOUND OF MUSIC FOR "VON TRAPP" SISTERS

Beverley

Barbara

Sisters Beverley Ann and Barbara Keenan have had a busy year, playing leading roles in LIPA musical *Life Changes* **and providing backing singing at major gigs in the UK.**

Said Beverley: "We come from a family who love singing. We are a bit like the Von Trapps from the *Sound of Music.* Even my grandmother who is in her 70s loves to sing. Our time at LIPA has taught us so much about the music industry and has paved the way to lots of fantastic practical work experience."

Beverley and Barbara are members of the singing trio Elite, both arrived at LIPA through the New Deal for Musicians programme, and through connections made here they have gone on to work with China Crisis and The Farm. They worked as backing singers with The Farm at two sell out gigs to the 5,000 capacity Brixton Academy in London at the Happy Mondays Reunion show.

Barbara said: "It was the most amazing experience of our lives, to go on stage and see thousands of people. It was a tremendous feeling."

Beverley and Barbara were also delighted to get involved in LIPA's musical *Life Changes.*

As part of the dissemination stage of the CAMEO project, which was part-funded by Equal's European Social Fund, Ged McKenna, Director of Flexible Learning, hit on the idea of using a musical he had been working on with Eddie Lundon, lead singer with China Crisis. The result was *Life Changes*: music and entertainment with an educational message, available in a range of models to suit organisation's requirements, be it education, entertainment or both. The musical focuses on personal development, using coaching and mentoring in a case study format, following the journey of two people from a low point in their lives. The characters realize their aspirations, with a little help from their coaches and mentors – and though song and dialogue their stories unfold.

In addition to using Barbara and Beverley as performers, Chris Phillips, another former New Deal for Musicians student played drums, alongside Andy Stephenson (Performing Arts - Music 2004) on keyboards. Five students who attend LIPA 4:19, LIPA's part-time performing arts academy, took part as singers and Kate McKenna, also of LIPA 4:19 played the role of Passion. The musical was premièred in Liverpool and is set to be performed in London, Birmingham and Manchester.

GRADUATE NEWSLETTER FOUR • SUMMER 2004

See me now

THE LIVERPOOL INSTITUTE FOR PERFORMING ARTS

Taryn on the SONY SIDE OF THE STREET

Taryn Israelsohn imagined a life in theatre films when she graduated (Management 1999). Instead she is rubbing shoulders with some of the hottest names in the music industry, such as Lemar and Charlotte Church.

Taryn is the Personal Assistant to the Vice President of Sony UK and also works for the Director of Sony's A&R Division.

It is a task that makes 27 year old Taryn a Jill of all trades in the music industry and a key member of the Sony team.

Taryn credited LIPA with opening the door of opportunity for her in to big time music management".

continued on page 4.

Jesse reaches for the stars IN CALIFORNIA

California based LIPA graduate Jesse Harlin is working with the stars... *Star Wars* that is.

He is a composer with LucasArts, the company headed by famous director and movie-maker George Lucas.

Jesse, an American, who graduated in Music in 1999, said: "Mostly, I write for videogames. Currently, I'm composing a largely original soundtrack for *Star Wars: Republic Commando*, our new first person shooter."

He is also editing music, including the original John Williams' *Star Wars* scores, for use in new games at LucasArts.

Said Jesse of his time at LIPA: "It was fantastic. LIPA was everything I had been looking for in a college." Later adding: "It was the attention to the business of being a professional musician that made LIPA really special."

● See page 14 for the Big Q&A interview with Jesse.

Sarah's second series with CBBC's Byker Grove

Sarah Lawton had barely finished her degree before making her TV debut playing youth leader Chrissie Harrison in CBBC's popular youth drama *Byker Grove.*

Sarah (Acting 2003) explains: "I auditioned for the part in *Byker Grove* a week before the LIPA Acting Showcase last year and started filming just after the Showcase at the end of June."

Sarah has been signed up for a second series, which is currently in production. *Byker Grove* will be back on our screens in early September.

Sarah says: "It's a fantastic experience for me, I'm improving my camera technique and working with a new director every five weeks which is great for making contacts!"

"I've been involved in a few other projects since I left: a couple of small TV roles, a play and also a short film called *I Am Dead* which won the Northern Film and Media Award and is currently being shown at several film festivals."

DOUBLE ACT

Getting gunged on live TV goes with the territory for Jessica and Laura Thompson (Dance 2000 – professional surname Tilli). This is because the identical twins help to present the Saturday morning popular children's TV programme – CITV's Ministry of Mayhem.

The twins' links have to be delivered in complete unison. Their appearances in the show also involve high energy and bags of enthusiasm. They might not have been quite so enthusiastic about their recent challenge. Both had to endure the gunge tank – at least this was another task they could do in unison!

Snapshots
2001 Graduates

Welcome to the fourth edition of Snapshots, a series of alumni newsletter supplements providing mini work profiles of graduates from LIPA's Higher Education programmes, three years after they graduated.

The 2002 graduate supplement will be issued with the sixth edition of LIPA's alumni newsletter. Graduates will be contacted in spring 2006, however, you can update your profile at any time by contacting Jenny Parkins in alumni relations on +44 (0)151 330 3143, e-mail alumni@lipa.ac.uk, visit the alumni website at www.lipa.ac.uk/alumni or in writing to The Liverpool Institute for Performing Arts, Mount Street, Liverpool L1 9HF, UK.

LIPA
THE LIVERPOOL INSTITUTE FOR PERFORMING ARTS

Nikolai Thøgset, due to start as a technician at a new Community...
after sound, lighting and stage management. Has just returned from Tanzania where he was working as a sound engineer and sound technology teacher ● Jan Holberg (previously Jan Olsen), session bassist in Norway and Head... at Hemne Community Music School. Is writing his... music and performs in a... three LIPA graduates ● Meike Holzmann, pe...
harp... ...ording... ...Wunderbar. Currently promotin...
of Pa... ...com... ...ordinato...
for F... ...ity...
Swiss... ...audio
workst... ...Bellis
in ITV1... had a
season... ...righton
Beach... Radio
● Anna... ...er label
golightly... ...y of events from TV
programm... ...studi...
● Simon Johns, playing M...
to tour Monaco and Lille. Wa...
The G...
the Ba...
for lo...
Publis... ...ces special events, motion grap... scripts and TV productions.
and h...
recen... ...ne, Sh... ...● Lindy LaFontaine, currently
Tech... ...ornia
sang... ...nd. C...
Film...
● Ste... ...r, Founder and E...
(www... ...ces
Devel...
tourin...
album...
key... ...W...
Pro...
withi...
Story...
for...
● Eliz... ...dancer with production company Ope...
Recently performed with Dance In-Tension at the 2005 LEAP dance festival ● Lynsey McCaffrey,

Baby Ingrid

Plus Special Guest, Rachel Taylo...

Neptune Theatre
Monday 15th November, Doors 7pm - 7.30pm Start.

50 - £5 Consession / Student
...kets available from Neptune Theatre Box Office
...over Street, Liverpool
...7097844
...icketmaster.co.uk

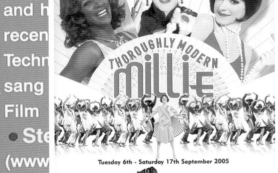

THOROUGHLY MODERN millie

Tuesday 6th - Saturday 17th September 2005

LIVERPOOL EMPIRE THEATRE
A ClearChannel Entertainment Venue

POPCORN
BY BEN ELTON

Liverpool Playhouse

Lucy has been singing the blues

From the blues to Old Blue Eyes, Lucy Davies has been singing and dancing her way round the country in two different styles of UK touring shows, in her first year out of LIPA.

Lucy – stage name Lucy Dean – moved to London after completing her Performing Arts (Dance) degree in 2004 and won a part in the touring version of the *Blues Brothers Party*. She played solo singer-dancer Sister Sugar in the hit stage musical based on the cult *Blues Brothers* film. Altogether, she took part in 40 performances touring with the production across the UK.

In a complete change of music and tempo, Lucy then landed a part in the UK tour of *The Rat Pack*, again appearing as a singer-dancer. This musical celebrates the songs of crooners Dean Martin, Sammy Davis Jr, and Old Blue Eyes himself Frank Sinatra.

Lucy is signed to Vicious Management and has a number of auditions lined up.

Lucy says of her time at LIPA: "You don't realize how amazing it is to be in such a creative environment until it's gone, so soak it up! LIPA was an amazing, unforgettable experience for me."

liverpool playhouse
WILLY RUSSELL'S
BREEZEBLOCK PARK

A NEW MUSICAL BASED ON THE SONGS OF ABBA®

MAMMA MIA!

PRINCE EDWARD THEATRE

fashion show in February 2006 ● Gareth Delve, Systems Analyst for management and IT consultants Accenture, and freelance web designer ● Vicki Dempsey, backing vocalist for Santa Carla, currently on tour promoting their EP Earworms (www.santacarla... ...ding her debut album due out in 2006 on the Digital Wings label ...

music gossip with the pepsi chart

After last week's power cut at the Pepsi Chart which saw everyone sitting in the darkness, the production team behind the show were extremely thankful that everything went without a hitch. I was glad too, because instead of straining my eyesight in the dark, it meant I could properly see the four guys who make up the band, a1, in all their cute glory! Here to perform of their new single, Like A Rose, the band buzzed about backstage in their usual hyperactive manner, mixing with everyone from the crew to singer Gabrielle. Being a fan of the boys' last three hits, I found out a bit about the much-anticipated new track and how the group came to be.

"Like A Rose is a slushy ballad which will appeal to all the romantics out there. It hits the shops on February 21st and if it does as well as our other songs have, we'll be very happy indeed," said Paul.

The oldest member of the group at 25 (and the one I fancy most!), dark-haired Paul loves performing and is thrilled with the success a1 have had so far. "Before I joined the band, I had loads of different jobs, I modelled for Christian Dior for the Spanish equivalent of the Clothes Show, worked in a burger bar and also as a dancer in a nightclub. But being in a1 is the best job I've ever had. I get to dance, which I really enjoy, I get to sing and meet lots of great people, too. I've always loved music but didn't start singing properly until two years ago when a record producer discovered me in my dad's karaoke bar. He liked my voice, so I did some demo tapes for him, but then I read about an audition for a1 and went for it instead, thinking it would be good experience. Even though my voice isn't trained, I was lucky enough to be chosen and here I am today. My dad's very proud of me, because not only am I living out my dream, but his too! He used to be in a band called the In-Betweens, and he's really helped me appreciate so many different kinds of music."

christian's a1 dream

Although a1 have only been around for just over a year, Christian, the blond, has grown up with music and knows all about the ins and outs of the business. Christian said, "Music has always been a part of my life; my dad used to be a famous pop star in Norway and my grandfather was a violin player in the Chicago Symphony Orchestra. I remember going on tour with my dad when I was three. I'd look out from the curtains and wish it were I singing on stage instead!

"When I was a kid, I used to sit at the piano and bang the keys trying to make nice sounds. When I was ten I began having lessons and eventually started making up my own tunes. But my family never pushed me into music; it was something I wanted to do myself. Then, when I went on an exchange trip to America, I started singing, I was even awarded the highest honour by the state of Kentucky for my achievements in performing arts. Then, after secondary school, I came to England to study at Paul McCartney's 'Fame' school in Liverpool, which was a1's manager (Tim Byrne, the man behind Steps) called and asked if they knew anybody who'd be suitable for the group – and they chose me! I love being in the band and want to work hard to make a1 the best we can be!"

by CHRISTINE DAVIES

You can watch The Pepsi Chart on Channel 5 every Thursday at 7pm and Saturday at 11am, and listen to it live on commercial radio every Sunday between 4 - 7pm. If you would like free tickets for The Pepsi Chart filmed at London's Sound Republic in Leicester Square, please call Powerhouse: 0171 287 0045.
You must be over 18 years old.
Next week: I mingle with 'N Sync, Aqua and Simply Red.

NOMADIC KASPAR SETS HIS ROOTS IN AN ALLOTMENT

The world, as the saying goes, may be a stage, but for Kaspar Wimberley, the stage is a local allotment. Kaspar is Artistic Director with the newly formed Treacle Theatre Company, who are planning a performance next year in a Bristol allotment.

If that sounds unusual, Kaspar's first shot at 'unusual' locations was the Williamson Tunnels beneath Liverpool's Edge Hill area, less than a mile from LIPA.

Kaspar studied Theatre and Performance Design at LIPA, graduating in 2003 and for his final year project he worked with fellow final year design student Susanne Kudielka on *Deeptuned*. This was a classical concert that took place in the labyrinth of tunnels created by the so-called Mole of Edge Hill.

Kaspar explained: "Susanne wanted to do a classical concert and I really wanted to do something outside a theatre that would be exciting and I found this leaflet about the tunnels."

"That project helped me realise what I wanted to do – working in site specific theatre and working with writers on devised performances."

That ambition has now led to the curtain raiser among the cabbage patches and strawberry beds in Bristol.

Kaspar is also working on a puppetry show to accompany an upcoming tour by emerging folk musician Owen Thomas. In August he will be directing the Jersey Arts Centre Summer School and this autumn he will be tutoring a Scenography module at The University of Wales, Aberystwyth.

Kaspar says: "My first year after graduating from LIPA proved an exciting, challenging, unexpected time for me. I have become a nomadic performance artist who seems to be forever packing his bags to collect places, people and ideas that are slowly growing into exciting possibilities for the future."

"My first stop was in Wales where I acted as the Lighting Design Tutor for the University of Wales, Aberystwyth, after which I directed and designed the musical event *Fairplay* in Jersey with Susanne Kudielka as part of National Fairtrade Fortnight. I then went on to design *Lovefuries*, a new touring production by Lurking Truth Theatre Company."

Last year was also marked out for him by winning the top prize in the Jersey Telecom Student Arts competition. His entry consisted of a selection of model boxes for theatre sets, including one for the set of *Sweeney Todd*.

www.treacletheatre.co.uk

LA woman

Lynette Howell (2000 Management graduate) is soaking up the sunshine and enjoying the Hollywood scene in an LA based-dream job in theatre producing.

For her final year LIPA placement Lynette worked for one of the top musical theatre casting directors in London and as a result of that, started working as Production Co-ordinator on a new musical called *Napolean* directly after graduating. The producers - a company called East of Doheny - offered her a job in the States as Head of Theatre and Office Manager. She is now responsible for developing new projects, optioning properties, attaching writers, directors, workshopping and overseeing all aspects leading up to production. She also seeks out investing and producing opportunities in New York and London. Recent shows include *The Full Monty* in the UK and *Flower Drum Song* on Broadway.

She says: "I always loved the arts, primarily theatre, I was in Youth Theatre since I was 13 but after applying to LIPA (originally for acting) and being told that my application was much more suited to the management degree, I decided to interview for management instead. It was the best decision I ever made, I love working with people, I am very organised, and love to organise others. LIPA gave me the chance to try my hand at many different aspects of management – from casting to agenting - both as part of the course and through independent student work. All of that helped me to recognise that I felt the most reward from producing. Bringing all the elements together, and being responsible for helping others work towards a common goal is what drives me. My ultimate goal is to be a film and theatre producer. As my company also produces film, it allows me to continue to learn whilst doing my own job."

NIALL COSTIGAN
Bill

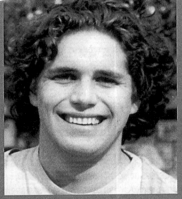

Niall spent most of his early years backstage at either the Everyman or the Playhouse whilst his parents performed at both theatres. He recently graduated from Liverpool Institute of Performing Arts. While training, his theatre credits include Rodney in Seven Stories, Brutus in Julius Caesar, Scaley and Walter Bray in Nicholas Nickleby, The Prince in The Dispute and Mr Rice in Molly Sweeney. He also directed a production of Macbeth at LIPA. This is his professional stage debut.

CATCHING UP WITH ...Connor Ratliff
(1998 Acting)

Connor Ratliff (left) in a scene from Living In Missouri.

"I've ended up as a writer, actor and producer of a feature film called *Living In Missouri*.

I started writing this script during my final year at LIPA. I put it on hold after graduation because there was so much happening. I was doing a play at the Royal Court and when it was nearing the end of its short run, I figured it would be a good time to return to the project.

Working with an American director friend of mine, we put together some money and produced the film on a shoestring budget in late 1999.

Shooting took about 20 days but it took about a year to edit because we had no money and the director and editor were working on borrowed time.

Our rough cut was rejected by Sundance, and then it was rejected by everyone else we showed it to for almost a year. We were about to give up, when all at once we were accepted by three festivals at once.

The movie has now played in Austin, Seattle (where it won Best Picture), Oregon (where we won Best Acting Ensemble), and most recently, San Francisco. We went from being completely unwanted to getting 4-star reviews in major publications."

For more information about the film, please visit www.livinginmissouri.com

No.1 HIT-WRITER

Writer and producer Jos Jorgensen (2001 Sound Technology) has three number one albums under his belt. His songs have been recorded by platinum selling artists in the UK, Europe and in Southeast Asia.

Jos has hit on a winning songwriting formula with long term writing partner Andy Love (Reverb Music). Their credits include *No Pressure* for Lemar, *Baby It's The Weekend* for Blazin' Squad and *Another Bad Goodbye* sung by ex-LIPA student Raghav, a number one in India. Recently, he worked on *This Is My Time*: MOBO nominated R&B singer Terri Walker's latest single and is collaborating with Simon Webbe (Blue) on his first solo album. He has just finished writing and producing Simon's second solo single. Denmark-born Jos says: "I spent a lot of my time at LIPA making contacts with artists and building up a portfolio of songs, then completed a MBA at the University of Liverpool, before securing a publishing deal with Global Talent Publishing." Jos now splits his time between his studio in Brighton/London, an entertainment management agency in China, plus another venture using 3G mobile technology.

Jos also has a connection with ITV1's *X Factor* show. He and Andy wrote and produced *The X Factor's* theme music.

NewWorldMusicGroup, London •Daniel Gifford, freelance Video and Sound Editor. Currently works for VSO where ... is training people overseas in video and sound editing •Nora Gombos ... ospital •Martin Gordon, Web Designer for Ministry of Sou... ...ener, undertaking a PhD ... Metropolitan Univ... ...esigners communicate th... ...endent radio station in Sy... worki... ...ogramme Robinson, a No... Previ... ...r/ producer for a reco... produc... ...documentaries and ... and re... ...Hadfield, Actor, ...ter, Perform... ...organisation. Has also tou... ...currently leading writing workshops •Nichol... ...nager. Currently the Tour Manager ... ...ol City Council. Previous work inclu... ...Eddie Izzard tour •Jesse Harlin... ...ner of Emo Riot Productions, a fi... ...rris, Label Co-ordinator with Li... ...ancer and ... ...Boom Op... ...tbeat, The... ...nician for ... ...Metal •G... ...ool in Shr... ...t MD on ... ...ghton •N... ...wang, Sta... ...nt of Son... ...Krug, wo... ...n New York. He... ...fea... w York Times website •Oliver Latka, Bass Player, Arranger and Copyist. Tou... ...th the production Summer Holiday after a season of Rent at the Prince of W... ...ondon •Michele Lau, teaching abroad and travelling •Samantha Lawson... ...ment Officer, Gillingham... ...Lawson, working with local MC's on various ... ...uding ...ol Student Union Hip Hop night •Geoff Lea, Drum Tutor at Pro ... ...Sound Recordist, ...don ...music ...val ...as, ...eld, ...ople ...rtin ...Has ...at the ...dying ...e Fear Academy... ...ompany •J... ...erience •Ja... ...Strange Real... ...ions in East Yorkshire, offering locat... ...hire for music and theatre, technical support for events and Arts in Education workshop... ...itchell, freelance Stage Manager •Timothy Moss, writing and performing with his band Pulse •Wyn Moss, appeared in the West End production of Mamma Mia! at the Prince Edward

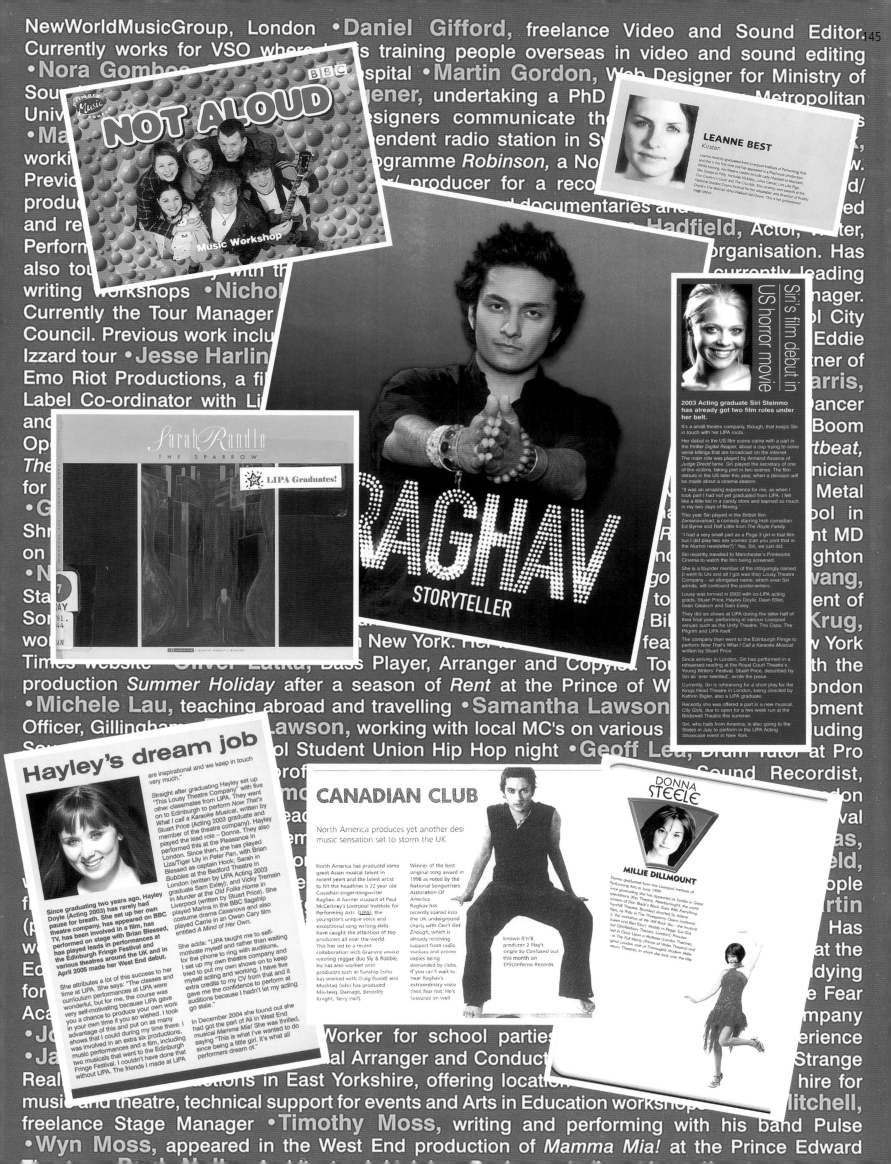

NOT ALOUD

Music Workshop

LEANNE BEST
Kirsten

Leanne recently graduated from Liverpool Institute of Performing Arts and this is her first time she has appeared in a PlayHouse production. While training, her theatre credits include Sally Bowles in Cabaret, Polly in Our Country's Good, Nicholas Nickleby, Julia Carson, Live Like Pigs, The Crucible. She recently won awards at the National Student Drama Festival for her adaptation and direction of Roddy Doyle's The Woman Who Walked into Doors. This is her professional stage debut.

RAGHAV STORYTELLER

SarahRandle
THE SPARROW

⭐ LIPA Graduates!

Siri's film debut in US horror movie

2003 Acting graduate Siri Steinmo has already got two film roles under her belt.

It's a small theatre company, though, that keeps Siri in touch with her LIPA roots.

Her debut in the US film scene came with a part in the thriller *Digital Reaper*, about a cop trying to solve serial killings that are broadcast on the internet. The main role was played by Armand Assante of *Judge Dredd* fame. Siri played the secretary of one of the victims, taking part in two scenes. The film debuts in the US later this year, when a decision will be made about a cinema season.

"It was an amazing experience for me, as when I took part I had not yet graduated from LIPA. I felt like a little kid in a candy store and learned so much in my two days of filming."

This year Siri played in the British film *Zemanovaload*, a comedy starring Irish comedian Ed Byrne and Ralf Little from *The Royle Family*.

"I had a very small part as a Page 3 girl in that film but I did play two sex scenes (can you print that in the Alumni newsletter?)" Yes, Siri, we just did.

Siri recently travelled to Manchester's Printworks Cinema to watch the film being screened.

She is a founder member of the intriguingly named (I went to Uni and all I got was this) Lousy Theatre Company - an elongated name, which even Siri admits, will confound the poster-writers.

Lousy was formed in 2003 with co-LIPA acting grads, Stuart Price, Hayley Doyle, Dean Elliot, Sean Gleason and Sam Exley.

They did six shows at LIPA during the latter half of their final year, performing in various Liverpool venues such as the Unity Theatre, The Casa, The Pilgrim and LIPA itself.

The company then went to the Edinburgh Fringe to perform *Now That's What I Call a Karaoke Musical* written by Stuart Price.

Since arriving in London, Siri has performed in a rehearsed reading at the Royal Court Theatre's Young Writers' Festival. Stuart Price, described by Siri as 'ever talented', wrote the piece.

Currently, Siri is rehearsing for a short play for the Kings Head Theatre in London, being directed by Kathrin Bigler, also a LIPA graduate.

Recently she was offered a part in a new musical, *City Girls*, due to open for a two week run at the Bridewell Theatre this summer.

Siri, who hails from America, is also going to the States in July to perform in the LIPA Acting Showcase event in New York.

Hayley's dream job

...are inspirational and we keep in touch very much."

Straight after graduating Hayley set up "This Lousy Theatre Company" with five other classmates from LIPA. They went on to Edinburgh to perform *Now That's What I call a Karaoke Musical*, written by Stuart Price (Acting 2003 graduate and member of the theatre company). Hayley played the lead role – Donna. They also performed this at the Pleasance in London. Since then, she has played Liza/Tiger Lily in *Peter Pan*, with Brian Blessed as captain Hook; Sarah in *Bubbles* at the Bedford Theatre in London (written by LIPA Acting 2003 graduate Sam Exley); and Vicky Tremain in *Murder at the Old Folks Home* in Liverpool (written by Stuart Price). She played Marina in the BBC flagship costume drama *Casanova* and also played Carrie in an Owen Cary film entitled *A Mind of Her Own*.

She adds: "LIPA taught me to self-motivate myself and rather than waiting for the phone to ring with auditions, I set up my own theatre company and tried to put my own shows on to keep myself acting and working. I have five extra credits to my CV from that and it gave me the confidence to perform at auditions because I hadn't let my acting go stale."

In December 2004 she found out she had got the part of Ali in West End musical *Mamma Mia!* She was thrilled, saying "This is what I've wanted to do since being a little girl. It's what all performers dream of."

Since graduating two years ago, Hayley Doyle (Acting 2003) has rarely had a pause for breath. She set up her own theatre company, has appeared on BBC TV, has been involved in a film, has performed on stage with Brian Blessed, has played leads in performances at the Edinburgh Fringe Festival and various theatres around the UK and in April 2005 made her West End debut.

...she attributes a lot of this success to her time at LIPA. She says: "The classes and curriculum performances at LIPA were wonderful, but for me, the course was very self-motivating because LIPA gave you a chance to produce your own work in your own time if you so wished. I took advantage of this and put on as many shows that I could during my time there. I was involved in an extra six productions, two musicals that went to the Edinburgh Fringe Festival. I couldn't have done that without LIPA. The friends I made at LIPA are inspirational and we keep in touch very much."

CANADIAN CLUB

North America produces yet another desi music sensation set to storm the UK

North America has produced some great Asian musical talent in recent years and the latest artist to hit the headlines is 22 year old Canadian singer-songwriter Raghav. A former student at Paul McCartney's Liverpool Institute for Performing Arts (LIPA), the youngster's unique voice and exceptional song writing skills have caught the attention of top producers all over the world. This has led to a recent collaboration with Grammy award winning reggae duo Sly & Robbie. He has also worked with producers such as Sunship (who has worked with Craig David) and Mushtaq (who has produced Mis-teeq, Damage, Beverley Knight, Terry Hall).

Winner of the best original song award in 1998 as voted by the National Songwriters Association Of America, Raghav has recently soared into the UK underground charts with *Can't Get Enough*, which is already receiving support from radio stations and promo copies being demanded by clubs. If you can't wait to hear Raghav's extraordinary voice then fear not. He's featured on well known R'n'B producer 2 Play's single *So Confused* out this month on TPSL/Inferno Records.

DONNA STEELE

MILLIE DILLMOUNT

Donna graduated from the Liverpool Institute of Performing Arts in June 1999 since graduating she has appeared as Estella in *Great Expectations* (Key Theatre, Peterborough); the world premiere of *Don Black's Black Goes With Everything* (Churchill Theatre, Bromley) directed by Arlene Rips; as Polly in *The Threepenny Opera* (national); the workshop of the *Will Rock You - the musical* (Queen and Ben Elton); Maddy in *Peggy Sue Got Married* (Shaftesbury Theatre, London); Princess in *Once Upon a Mattress* (Landor Theatre); in *The Full Monty* (Prince of Wales Theatre) and original London cast of *Thoroughly Modern Millie* (Shaftesbury Theatre), in which she took over the title role.

Chucho Merchan • Ed Millett, Head of Music Research for Recall, placing music on adverts. Co-founded artist management company Lunch with fellow graduate Alex (professional name Andrea Harvey), Pastoral Support Worker with prim... ...refu... Fring... Teat... ...working as an actor for the ...y for the last year and a h... a le... Assi... spec... for ... • Ja... proj... Fest... and ... • A... office and operations in India • A... • Lynden O'Neill, performing w... production of Miss Saigon • Rebe... design and production of sets an... educational projects. Most recently ... Cunard's QE2 and QM2 ocean line... (www.esk... the Young... internet d... filming fo... Man), ho... after sch... Liverpool... • Samu... directed t... for Die B... Cliff Brad... February)... theatre fe... Institute (... • Vanes... advertisin... across the... freelance arts worker. Runs p... visual arts and community ... production of the Queen and ... for Adlib Audio • Mark Ro... University College Chester. Pe... • Tim Rowland, establish... comedy. He writes, dire... at the Burgess Hill Theatre.

Trollspeilet • Helen M... ...ence her PGCE in S... • Rosie Morris, worked ...ust setting up a session ...udio • Dirk Neuhof, free... ...ng, Technical... Re... ech... ...ppa... al (S... ...in G... ...w No...

RICHARD'S JOB HAS THE X FACTOR

Working alongside the man known as 'TV's Mr Nasty' has been a fascinating introduction to the music industry for LIPA Management graduate Richard Jones.

In his final year, Richard was offered a work placement by Tim Byrne, founder of London-based TForce Management. It is the company that handles the performers that Simon Cowell mentors on the hit television show The X Factor. The placement has led to a full-time job for Richard, who soon starts working on the next series of the show. This year Richard had the job of accompanying the winner of the first series, Steve Brookstein, on a three-week promotional tour. He also tour-managed the X Factor Live Arena tour in February.

● So what does Richard really think of Mr Nasty? Turn to page 3 to find out.

LIPA PLACEMENT LED TO X FACTOR JOB FOR RICHARD

continued from front cover

Working life for Richard Jones involves being collected in a chauffeur driven car at Heathrow Airport and whisked away for meetings with celebrities such as Simon Cowell.

He has already started making arrangements for a tour next year for acts that will battle it out in the forthcoming series of The X Factor.

In his final year at LIPA Richard did a work placement with TForce, based in Shepherds Bush for his Arts Manager module. It saw him working with Simon Cowell on the first series of The X Factor.

TForce founder Tim Byrne was so impressed with Richard he offered him a full-time job once he graduated.

The work experience and the job he was given meant Richard was gaining first hand experience working with some of the biggest organisations in music.

...e tasks handed to Richard ...company the winner of The ...Steve Brookstein, on his three-...otional tour. Richard had to ...adio and television stations, ...V's This Morning, MTV and ...elp arrange personal ...by the man who won ...tes in a nail-biting finale.

...of starting his full-time ...as tour-managing The ...rena tour, featuring acts ...It meant working on ...d nightly audiences of

...working with Ben ...o material and he has ...on an extensive UK ...September he will ...second series of The ...longside Simon ...ists. He will then

tour manage the Live Arena Tour in the winter of 2006, once the series has ended, with its usual thrilling finale.

It has been a fascinating year for Richard. "Everything is so professional. The contestants chosen to be mentored for the new series were all taken to Simon's house in Spain for intensive training. I was with them and it was like a boot camp – a lot of hard work, preparing for the new series, but it was a great experience."

"Simon Cowell is really good to work with, and is very friendly and professional. I am so fortunate to have been given a work placement from my time at LIPA," added Richard.

Working with the singers means Richard also gets to go to a procession of celebrity parties, attended by showbiz journalists and performers from the television and film industry. Richard's aim is to ensure TForce's artists get good exposure on the celebrity pages.

Of his time at LIPA, Richard says: "I really enjoyed my time there. The contacts and experience I gained at LIPA definitely helped me to get my foot in the door. Since leaving LIPA I have been extremely lucky, but feel that is down to having my degree and being given the confidence to try and make it in the tough entertainment business by lecturers and fellow students."

Amy's career shunts along the fast-track

Tropicana

Just one year after graduating, Amy Griffin (Theatre and Performance Technology 2004) is delighted to be working as a Production Manager for Shunt Theatre Company. She says: "I never expected to be in this role just a year on from graduating, by now I would have imagined that I would be working in more of an assistant capacity."

Shunt Theatre Company was formed in 1997 and works largely site specifically incorporating theatre, dance, visual art, sound, video and circus. A year ago they moved to the Shunt Vaults at London Bridge - a 70,000 square foot labyrinth of archways that had been a bonded wine vault for the last 100 years. In September they began performing Tropicana, a collaboration with the National Theatre.

Amy discovered a preference for working on site specific productions, rather than on productions based in traditional theatre spaces, whilst still at LIPA. Thanks to a contact of one of her LIPA tutors, she managed to get work experience with the RSC during her summer holidays, working on a production in a disused warehouse in London.

She says: "I enjoy site specific work because it throws up more challenges and really keeps you on your toes."

After graduating, she moved back home to London and volunteered to work as part of the stage management team on Tropicana, attracted to the challenges of Shunt's unusual venue. After six weeks she was employed full-time as their Stage Manager.

After a few months with Shunt Theatre Company she was recommended to work on Urban Expansion Theatre Company's UK tour of Once Upon A Time In Wigan, as their Company Stage Manager. Amy seized the opportunity and worked on this production from February to June, then was invited back to work at Shunt Theatre Company again but this time as their Production Manager, running the performances of Tropicana five nights a week.

The two productions have taught her very different sets of skills. She says: "The tour really helped me develop my people skills. It was a demanding tour. I was acting as the central contact between all the venues and the company."

CROSSROADS present... what If...? a piece for one actor-dancer performed by Simone L. Hueber

...ncertain h... ...sdom, daftness and self defeat ...Integrat... ...y and rowing visual environment. ...and text explode in a cloud of unknowing. The first integrated solo production by Crossroads.

Performer/ Choreographer: Simone Leona Hueber
Text/Co-Direction: Richard Willacy Scenography: Jobst Moritz Pankok & guests

17 January 2001 8pm The Bloomsbury Theatre
15 Gordon Street, London WC 1
BOX OFFICE 020 738822 Tickets £ 10 (£8 concs.)

with best regards, Simone xxx

the place

Bloomsbury Theatre

resolution!

Printed by JUST POSTCARDS 020-8533 4000

NewWorldMusicGroup, London •Daniel Gifford, freelance Video and Sound Editor. Currently works for VS... where he is training people overseas in video and sound editing •Nora Gombos, Se... •Martin Gordon, Web Designer for Ministry of Sound Digital •Alke... a PhD at Manchester Metropolitan University, researchin... ideas to non-designers •Mario Guala, wor... ...Haavik, working in location s... ...val show. Previous work includ... on sound/ production for NRK w... composed and recorded music... ...tor, Writer, Performer and Dire... ...sation. Has also toured nationa... ...ntly leading writing workshops... ...on Manager. Currently the Tour... ...iverpool City Council. Previous... ...and the Eddie Izzard tour •Jess... ...ing partner of Emo Riot Produ... ...cola Harris, Label Co-ordinat... ...wood, Dancer and Swimmer fo... ...Heyes, Boom Operator in the... ...dale, Heartbeat, The Royal, Whe... ...Drum Technician for the Foo Fig... ...and Chevy Metal •Gareth Ho... ...elford School in Shropshire. W... ...and Assistant MD on Blood Brot... ...tor, Brighton •Nicola Hu... ...in Hwang, Stage Manag... ...President of Sony Music... ...ora Krug, working in i... ...e New York Times web... ...K with the production... ...e, London •Michele... ...elopment Officer, Gi... including Soundbo... ...r at Pro Perc •P... ...cordist, Hammerhead... ...London •Camilla Lø... ...festival •Samantha... ...ucas, Sound Engine... ...sfield, working for Ev... ...eople from socially... ...artin (professional... Has worked with M... ...t the Edinburgh Fes... ...studying for a PGCE to... ...Residence at Cape Fear Academy, No... a Christian Theatre Company •Jocelyn M... ...at the Deva Roman Experience •James McW... •Chris Miley, running Strange Reality Music... ...recording, PA/ engineer hire for music and thea... ...tion workshops •Lisa Mitchell, freelance Stag... ...erforming with his band Pulse •Wyn Moss... ...mma Mia! at the Prince Edward Theatre •Paul Nulty, Architectural Lighting Designer, Indigo Light Planning, London

Meet the Management graduate...
ON TOP OF THE POPS

Jan Burton (Enterprise Management) graduated in 1999 expecting to work for a major record company or in radio. Instead he ended up signing a five-album deal and appearing on Top of the Pops.

The singer-songwriter's fortunes took a dramatic turn when he teamed up with Mike Tournier, one time member of the group Fluke. Their two man group, Syntax, recorded a debut single *Pray,* which won massive praise from some of the country's top DJs including Pete Tong, Digweed, Sasha and Oakenfold.

● Full story continues on page 4.

•Peter Abraham, Hire Manager for Adlite Productions •Kavisha Adapen, Box Office and Duty Manager at the Orange Tree Theatre •Florian Ahrens, freelance Live Sound Engineer and Production/ Tour Manager for bands including Status Quo, Lila Downs and John Mayall •Ingo Aicher, established Ground Zero Studios in Liverpool, manages the band Vinyl •Ashl... ...loo/ Kaa in *Jungle Book* at the Bull Theatre... ...n and Orion in *Stardus...* ...re Technician •Marti... ...ardill, Online Commu... ...online team •Lena... ...ng in Norway, made h... ...ary *Fish out of Wate...* ...fronting the Boston... ...rk also runs the reco... ...duo Alpine Those... ...eaching at an Adu... ...film work in Nor... ...graduate •Matti... ...Continuity for Me... ...with FX Rentals... ...Brown, Technic... ...dying a postgra... ...nal tour of *Bloo...* ...as lead singer... ...Project Manage... ...olds •Cha... ...work include... ...affairs •Ben... ...aboo •Robe... ...stant Engineer at Strongroom, London. Has worked with Radiohead, Na... ...hop Boys •Mich... ...don •Nicholas C... ...mpton, recently played... ...Saddlers Wells •Joann... ...pool with a local theatre... ...cting and performing in a... ...fessional name Big), So... ...isor with Berkertex/ Littl... ...show on Manx Radio. H... ...Modo and the Blue Bar... ...Singer/ Songwriter sig... ...r second album Afterglo... ...rking on *Treflan,* a perio... ...won five welsh BAFTA... ...*ma Mia!* •Lynsey Eva... ...Technical Director with a... ...Internet Developer in J... ...asis with a local pro stu... ...ltimedia development... ...internet development o... ...ffectively. Recently com... ...Publisher Relations Rep... ...oth soul/ contemporary... ...resenter with the Norw... ...lance TV Art Director, productions include the film *The 51st State* and BBC dramas *Murphy's Law*

Birth of a **great career** for **Katie**

Katie Foster-Barnes has just given birth…. in the television drama *Doctors*. She had already experienced life in the world of hospitals with a part in BBC TV's *Casualty*, her first television role.

This summer a short film in which she took part for Channel 4 will be shown at the Cannes Film Festival.

It's been two hectic years since leaving LIPA for the 2001 Acting graduate. Just months after graduating she was in rep at the West Yorkshire Playhouse and at the Garrick in the West End playing the part of young wife Betty Whitehouse in J B Priestley's *Dangerous Corner*. Katie played alongside Dervla Kirwan *(Ballykissangel and Hearts and Bones)*, Patrick Robinson and Rupert Perry Jones. The play's director was Laurie Sansom, a regular visitor here, who Katie had already worked with when he directed with LIPA students in Liverpool.

Katie also starred in the play *Undercurrents* performed at the King's Head Theatre in London's Islington. It was written by Adam Penford (2001 Acting). Also in the play was Jamie Lloyd (2002 Acting) and Katie's boyfriend Andrew Langtree (1998 Acting).

Banging the drum FOR WOMEN

In the male dominated industry of music technology, Heidi Manning is an excellent role model.

Heidi achieved a first class honours degree in Community Arts in 2000 and describes herself as a community musician "specialising in computer music, music technology, soundscapes, sound sculptures, junk music and experimental music."

She works full-time at MANCAT (Manchester College of Art and Technology) where she delivers a range of training courses for 16 to 19 year olds centring on music technology. One of these is aimed at youngsters who have dropped out of mainstream education. She says, "I find it really rewarding to work with young people who have lost their interest in education and to get them more positive about it."

At weekends and during holidays she continues to work on community music projects. She has worked with all women groups, youth groups, people with disabilities, and also with African Townships. Her projects have included:

- Running audio training courses for women in the West Midlands with Sound It Out
- A number of educational projects with the Hallé Orchestra in Manchester, working with youth groups
- Various projects for 'National Foundation of Youth Music'

She is passionate about women in music and technology and has led and taken part in conferences, research and spoken at events in London, Birmingham, Manchester, Liverpool and Scotland to encourage women into the audio/music technology industry. She has had articles published in community music publications and has also provided music technology training to school teachers, as this has become part of the national curriculum.

She has also developed an award winning interactive CD-rom ...d in schools in Tameside containing the Keystage 3 ...ts the play as a crime investigation, ...sound effects all

Your sounds

Not only is Shih Chin Hang LIPA's first Taiwanese student but as the guitarist for Mayday, a band that has recorded three albums with total sales reaching over 900,000, he is no stranger to the music industry. Stone, as he is more commonly known, graduates from the Diploma in Popular Music and Sound Technology this summer and you can hear tracks from Mayday's latest album by visiting www.mayday-5.com.

To feature your work in Your sounds e-mail alumni@lipa.ac.uk with details of your role, the style of music and how your work can be accessed.

fashion show in February 2006 ● Gareth Delve, Systems Analyst for management and IT consultants Accenture, and freelance web designer ● Vicki Dempsey, backing vocalist for Santa Carla, currently on tour promoting their EP Earworms (www.santacarla.co.uk). Also recording her solo album due out in 2006 on the Digital Wings label (www.bhigi.com) ● Luke Duncan, Manage... ...state Agents 'Your Move Oliver Scarlett' ● Clare-Louise Edwards, established A... ...arts organis... ...unning wo... ...cross North W... ...e Front, a p... ...Theatr Cymru'... ...eted filmin... ...ission, where... ...ays a solo... ...Pop the Panda... ...2 in July... ...e Grown Hollyw... ...Operator... ...agement

● Nick... ...Eiko... ...s a small project... ...mposing... ...n Levi Fri, Urban S... ...eacher... ...continuing to perfo... ...nd vid... ...roduction, provide... ...conf... ...veloping a docume... ...6 m... ...a lead role in Drac... ...in B... ...mned in the West E... ...he Y... ...of Peter Pan with Bu... ...sc... ...n Film Festival this yea... ...BO... ...Sue Johnston and Tim... ...gies (www.m... ...en in new musical Stenhoggeren in Nor... ...aying Simon Withead ● Matthew G... ...radio stations, promotes regular band n... ...t and songwriter for fu... ...an... ...most recent... ...s was followi... ...ence member... ...gigs regularly... ...van, performi... ...ssion

● Paolo... ...reign films into... ...es for Dublin-bas... ...ming projects inc... ...Jason... ...r and performed a... ...ative rock and po... ...pool EP due out... ...ke in ● Lewis Har... ...Music Nottingham an... ...Poor Technology deg... ...at LIPA this September.

Virus alert

Frode Oygard (Sound Technology, due to graduate this July) met an old childhood friend, Fredrik Martol (Sound Technology, who graduated in 2002) while studying at the Institute. Together and with other sound technologists (Tim Way and Tord Nikolaisen - graduated 2002; Sturle Strauss Lisaeth due to graduate this July), the group decided to start their own music production company so that they'd have a job to go to when they left the Institute. Five people would mean five times more work and five different music backgrounds and tastes, so more to offer potential clients.

They took Virus Music to MIDEM in January 2003 under the wing of The Association of Independent Music (AIM). Their hundred show reels were snapped up. Eleven clients are already on their recent list; negotiations are underway with nine new clients for writing jingles, supplying new music, remixing and production facilities. Recently, Virus Music remixed using e-mail as the transporter.

Liverpool City Council, MSIF, Prince's Trust, Musicbias and HSBC have allocated financial support.

Check out: www.virusaudio.com o...

Charlotte joins Transitions Dance Company

Every year London-based Transitions Dance Company receives over 200 applications from recently qualified dance graduates competing for just nine places in the company. Charlotte Habib, who graduated from BA (Hons) Performing Arts Dance in June 2003, became the first LIPA graduate to gain a place with this prestigious company starting with them in September 2003.

The company is currently on a six month tour, taking five dance pieces to venues in the UK and overseas. The company has worked with five choreographers including Rafael Bonachela, who choreographed all of Kylie Minogue's dances for her 2002 Fever world tour.

Former company members have established themselves at the forefront of dance practice as dancers and choreographers with companies such as Adventures in Motion Pictures, Alias Compagnie, Siobhan Davies Dance Company, DV8, Rambert Dance Company, the Cholmondeleys and the Featherstonehaughs.

Charlotte says: "I'm so excited about the tour, especially our dates in Asia and Italy. Having the chance to travel to new places whilst performing is fantastic."

And as for Charlotte's next step - since working with the choreographers Charlotte has been offered a contract in Portugal with Miguel Peirera due to start in July 2005.

FULL HOUSES THANKS TO ADAM

Proving that LIPA's management students are ready and able to take on responsible roles in the industry immediately, Adam Burgan bagged a Marketing Officer post at Shrewsbury's main theatre venue, as his first graduate job. He started on Monday 16th June 2003, having attended his last lecture on Friday 13th June. This is the type of role that most graduates would aspire to after they had already been in work for two to five years.

Shrewsbury Music Hall is Shropshire's most popula... entertainment venue. It houses a 384 seated auditorium (550 standing) and is a receiving theat... with a varied programme of dance, drama, come... live music, family shows etc. Examples of recent... include Bob Geldof, The Vagina Monologues, Jeremy Hardy and Jasmin Vadimon Dance Com...

Many light entertainment acts consistently sell... and so he is always excited when the smaller... do well. Adam comments: "I've been working on promoting dance and drama and it's great that the audiences for these types of events a... developing and growing larger. Also I've take... the drama and dance programming from the... Manager (Lezley Picton), which I really enjo...

He adds: "I've been most proud of our pan... though. With 97.2% capacity over 56 perfo... this puts our pantomime as one of the mo... successful in the country and that's some... delighted to be part of."

Our FINNISH first

We recruit students from all over the world and have over 30 countries represented amongst our student body.

Recently, with help from Sennheiser, we conducted a publicity event in Helsinki in Finland, where we caught up with our first Finnish graduate.

Elina Hanhivaara, studied Performance Design at LIPA and graduated in 1998. She has returned to Finland and is working for the Rovaniemi Theater as a stage and costume designer.

Her first production opened on 22nd February 2003. Elina was responsible for designing the costumes for a cast of 13 people, plus the band and choir, along with the set. The piece was premiered in the sixties and is famous for evoking a shift towards the left-wing movement at that time.

The production that Elina worked on modernised the play, setting it in the present day. She says: "I am espec... author and composer, who are both... liked our production very much."

When Elina attended our student re... Finland, she was interviewed by the... ahlfs primetime broadcast on Finnish TV...

She says: "Meeting up with people... nostalgic. Even though LI... time, to me, the spirit and...

Plans for the future – the r... debut looking forward to summe... practice her saxophone. S...pool of trying to find a gallery to... legendary scenic designe... ke in

Since Elina joined us we h... Finnish students studying... Davidow will be our eighth... visit Alisha has accepted a... Poor at LIPA this September.

Players Theatre Company and is a theatre director, freelance workshop leader and an acting tutor for LIPA 4:19 ● Mark Heller, LA-based writer and director. Currently in pre-production for Normal Life which goes into production in the new year. The film is being produced by Silverwood films run by 2000 Enterprise Management graduate Lynette Howell ● Chad Higgins, Head of UK Events for Gyro

Last year co-wrote B-side for Jennifer Ellison's debut single. Recently teamed up with LIPA 98 graduate Chris Anderson and founded the band 'chris and thomas' (www.chrisandthomas.com)

Rachel hits the jackpot

Actress scoops plum West End musical role

BIG CHANCE: *Rachel Leskovac, left, will star as the young Viv Nicholson in Spend Spend Spend alongside Barbara Dickson, above. The real Viv, below, hit the headlines when she scooped a fortune on the pools in the Sixties*

Rachel Leskovac's dad was beside himself when his daughter got her first professional role.

"He kept telling his mates, 'Our Rachel's on TV'," she says. "He was so proud.

"But he started mumbling when they asked him what I was playing. It was a prostitute."

From that inauspicious beginning, on a Crimewatch reconstruction last year, Rachel's career has blossomed beyond

THEATRE with DAVID BEHRENS

her wildest dreams. This week, barely able to conceal her excitement and nerves, the 23-year-old actress and singer set off from Bradford to London to begin rehearsals for a starring role in a new West End musical. She was, as they say in showbusiness, going out there a chorus girl but coming back a star.

Against phenomenal competition, she has been cast as the young Vivian Nicholson in the musical, Spend Spend Spend.

The life story of the celebrated Castleford pools winner who frittered away a fortune in the 1960s, was a smash when the West Yorkshire Playhouse premiered it last year, and its transfer to London has been hugely anticipated.

"I'm in a bit of a daze at the moment,"

admits Rachel. It's barely a year since she graduated from LIPA, the Paul McCartney school of performing arts in Liverpool. When the call from London came, she was with her mum and dad, Peter and Jean Clayton Heights.

"I remember saying to the auditions, 'I don't think I would be too much pressure to be able to handle it'.

Bugsy Malone. But she was not, she says, wholly committed to a career in the theatre.

"When I was 16 I wanted to do a BTEC in performing arts, but I got swayed into doing one in Business and Finance instead. Everyone said it would open doors for me and make me secure financially. At that age you don't really know what you're doing.

"It shocks me now when I hear young girls say they want to be stars. They should be out climbing trees and making dens at their age."

Rachel soon tired of studying business. "It was really boring. I got a job as an office junior with a firm of solicitors in Bradford and another job up at the university. Then I bumped into an old friend who told me she'd auditioned for LIPA, and I asked her for the number.

"It was wonderful, a wonderful experience. They have really good teachers and I met the best of friends. I'd recommend it to anyone."

Among her new friends was the man who would become her boyfriend, David Tench, a pianist and aspiring music director.

"I couldn't have got the part in Spend Spend without David," says as they sent me reaching me.

going

MORE WINNERS

Again current students have been doing us proud in national music competitions.

Lady, Stand Up

Lady, Stand Up is the song that clinched an award for songwriting duo Hilde Wahl (Music student) and Sebastian Von Bischopink (Sound Technology student). They scooped first prize in the R&B / Hip Hop Category of the 2002 UK Songwriting Contest. Hilde says: "We were delighted to have achieved the award particularly plea on th...

Mark eyes his first big signing

Mark Gale (Management 2003) decided to do some unpaid work experience after graduating from LIPA and it paved the way for a full-time dream job in the music industry.

He is with BMG Music Publishing – or Bertlesman as some call it – one of the world's biggest record and music groups. Mark works in the A & R department at its London office.

Said Mark: "I'm working with a roster of about 20 artists and writers, some fairly established and some new acts. I'm also involved in pitching songs for other acts and setting up co-writing sessions. Prospects are looking okay and I aim to sign my first act this year and hopefully have some success, particularly with some of the new acts I'm working on."

Mark tells us he is still in contact with a number of other ex-LIPA students who are doing well in the music business. "Off the management course Julia Jeory is doing really well managing a girl band, Liam Keightley is doing some management and promoting some gig nights and off the Sound Technology course, Joe Hirst has been producing some really good bands."

Mark is pictured bottom right along with members of the band Keane, their manager and the A&R team.

Singing for her supper

Keeping a straight face is one of the trickiest parts of the job for 1998 Acting graduate Gail Mackinnon in her latest role. Gail is supporting Julian Clary as his singer on his national tour entitled *Natural Born Mincer*. Forty-eight dates are booked across the UK, culminating in a performance at the Theatre Royal, Drury Lane in London in June.

This follows hot on the heels of spending a year performing in Boy George's hit musical *Taboo* in the West End. Gail played the role of Big Sue. She remembers it fondly: "It was a great part. I was playing opposite the role of Leigh Bowery, the performing artist. She is based on the real 'Big Sue' who was Leigh's best friend it was very interesting playing a non-fictional character."

Prior to that Gail played the role of Lisa

Ruth's KEY ROLE in NW film industry

Ruth Nicoll has been working in Events and Marketing for BAFTA North since graduating from the Management degree in July 2002.

Much of her time is taken up organising exclusive preview screenings and co-ordinating industry related events; currently the launch of the third series of locally filmed *The Forsyte Saga*.

Recently Ruth represented BAFTA North at the British Academy Television Awards, sponsored by Radio Times, at the London Palladium.

However, it is not all awards and celebrity, Ruth stresses. BAFTA

is a registered charity and relies on outside funding to realise its mission: to promote excellence in the moving image.

Ruth has successfully developed and presented several funding applications on behalf of BAFTA North to North West Vision, the Film Council's regional arm. This funding supports BAFTA North's educational projects such as:
• 'Behind the Scenes': a collaboration with regional production companies such as Mersey TV and Red Productions in encouraging young people to consider a career in the moving image industries
• 'Script to Screen': workshops for local writers developing their craft

• 'In Conversation with...': a series of in depth interviews with industry figureheads such as director of *Trainspotting* and *28 Days Later*, Danny Boyle as well as the controversial award winning director of *The Magdalene Sisters* Peter Mullan.

"All the skills learned at LIPA have been utilised in this job. In April I had to interview the actor Dougray Scott, director Mike Barker and composer Richard Mitchell in front of a BAFTA audience about the feature film *To Kill a King*. If it hadn't been for the presentations I had to make at LIPA I would have wished the ground to swallow me up, as it was, I really quite enjoyed it."

To find out more about BAFTA North's student package or for graduates wishing to join as a full member, please contact Ruth Nicoll at membership, baftanorth@virgin.net or phone on 0151 283 3726.

Jamie goes West - to the West End that is

Jamie Lloyd, who graduated from LIPA in 2002 with an acting degree, has become the youngest ever resident director on a major West End production.

Currently, Jamie is Associate Director with the hit show *Guys and Dolls*, which stars Ewan McGregor and Jane Krakowski from *Ally McBeal* and *Alfie*.

In just its second week at the Piccadilly Theatre the musical had amazing reviews and was a sell-out with queues stretching around the block.

Jamie has also been Resident Director at the Theatre Royal, Drury Lane, where *Anything Goes*, directed by Trevor Nunn, was being performed.

In between Jamie directed in his own right, a chamber musical called *Elegies*, a song cycle that starred John Barrowman from *Anything Goes*, who more recently was a small-screen success in BBC's *Dr Who*.

Said Jamie: "I have had a lot of luck, but you have got to know what to do; you can't mess it up. You have to do a great job."

Jamie was also an associate director on another West End production, *The Solid Gold Cadillac*, starring Patricia Routledge - known to millions for her part in *Keeping Up Appearances*. She has asked Jamie to direct her in a production next year.

WAKING UP TO David Tench

If you're up early enough on a Saturday morning you may have noticed a familiar face on television.

1998 Music graduate David Tench is the keyboard player with Stamford Amp, the five piece house band on BBC1's flagship Saturday morning show: *The Saturday Show*.

David went along to the audition af... friend reco... that he shou... for it. He late... out he was o...

twenty thousand applicants. The audition process lasted a weekend and in addition to the musical auditions, included interviews and group dynamic work.

Before joining Stamford Amp, David had been working solidly in the performing arts industry, in a variety of roles ranging from performing in small jazz gigs to working as Musical Director on West E... shows ...

Larger Than Life

A glittering array of West End, Broadway and film work already populates Morgan Large's CV.

In the two years since graduating with a first class honours degree in Theatre and Performance Design, Morgan, has been working non-stop as a Production Designer or as Assistant Designer.

Morgan has just finished working as Design Assistant to Christopher Oram on *Guys and Dolls*, playing at the Piccadilly Theatre, which stars Ewan McGregor. Fellow LIPA graduate Jamie Lloyd also worked on this production (see article opposite). Previously, Morgan worked with Christopher Oram on *Don Carlos* at the Gielgud Theatre and has now become employed as Christopher's full-time associate. He is currently working on Verdi's *Falstaff* for the Swedish National Opera in November.

One of his first theatre jobs was with Mark Thompson assisting on *Bombay Dreams*. This was a visually spectacular musical, much praised for its lavish sets and costumes, which played in London and at the Broadway Theatre in New York, giving Morgan his first taste of Broadway work. Last year, Morgan also got the chance to work with Tony award-winning designer

Lez Brotherston on *Brighton Rock* at the Almeida Theatre, directed by Richard Attenborough. He has also gained experience of designing for touring productions. These include *Grease* and *Beauty And The Beast*.

As well as working with some of the hottest names in theatre design, Morgan has also been pursuing his own production work. Whilst studying at LIPA, Morgan laid the foundations to set up his own production company, Larger Than Life Productions with fellow LIPA acting student Kate Golledge, who graduated with a first class honours degree in 2002. They have both enjoyed success with the company, which is comprised of two sides: events organisation and theatrical production. Their highlight to date is the showcase of their production of *Six Women With Brain Death* at London's Soho Theatre in January. Having previously produced this for the 2002 Edinburgh Fringe Festival, whilst still at LIPA, where it received five star reviews and was chosen in The Scotsman as their "Best of the Fest" musical, both found it highly rewarding to see it realized in London. Other projects in the pipeline include a performance summer school this summer. They are also currently producing *Ready Steady...Sing!* - a musical by request where audience members decide the destiny of what happens on stage, alongside numerous events.

Somewhere in the middle of all this, Morgan also managed to fit in some film work. He was Art Director on ITV's *Mixers* and *Ninety Second Minute*, which were both shown at the 2004 Cannes Film Festival.

Enjoying her Creature Comforts

Making miniature jogging suits for a herd of wildebeest is a typical task for Laura Savage.

For the last six months Laura (Theatre and Performance Design 2003) has been working in the sets department for Creature Comforts at Aardman Animation - the oscar winning 'stop motion' animation studio based in Bristol, that also created *Wallace and Gromit* and *Chicken Run*.

Laura works in a team of six, painstakingly creating the handmade intricate sets, props and costumes for each of the plasticine creatures, featured in the ITV1 series. Having worked on the Christmas special she was faced with the challenge of dressing the Arab stallion character as a reindeer and also creating the Christmas decorations to adorn the set for Buckingham palace, for a piece about corgis. She says: "I've really enjoyed the work at Aardman Animation – it's a lovely crew to work with. It is high intensity work but it's really satisfying as the end results look really nice."

Since leaving LIPA, Laura has notched up a wide variety of work experience. She recalls: "My first job was in TV, where I had three weeks' paid work experience with designer Alec Walk on a Channel 4 documentary called *Invasion* about the Second World War. I was involved in organising props, doing some prop making and assisting with setting up on location."

She worked with Alec again on *The Bachelor* for BBC3 and has since been employed as Assistant Art Director on two TV programmes, including the ITV1 children's series *The Fugitive*, starring Maureen Lipman. Laura is pictured above in the well set for this programme.

Laura has also been engaged in a variety of theatre work from props making for Bristol Old Vic's *Cinderella*, to set design for ACTA, Bristol's youth theatre. Out of her theatre work so far she is most proud of her work at The Tobacco Factory in Bristol, which houses touring productions and local groups. She designed the set and costumes for their Christmas production of *The Secret Garden* and says: "It was great to realize my own design, seeing that through from start to finish, across the sets, costumes and so on."

She added: "The design part of the course at LIPA was fantastic. I learnt so much in terms of my practical skills and about what is expected from you as a designer in this industry. It gave me a really good grounding which meant that I had a lot to show when I first went for interviews, much more than people would have expected from someone fresh out of university."

•Nora Gombos, Secretary at a Hospital •Martin Gordon, web Designer for Ministry of Sound Digital •Alke Gröppel-Wegener, undertaking a PhD at Manchester Metropolitan University, researching into how designers communicate their ideas to non-designers •Mario Guele, working for an independent radio station in Switzerland •Petter Haavik, working in ... programme ... ity/ survival show. Previous ... neer/ produc... location sound/ production ... en's TV, dram... has also composed and record... mes and CD... ield, Actor, Writer, Performer... Aftathought... organisation. Has also toure... Ladder The... is currently leading writing wo... ndford, a... roduction Manager. Currently ... band Vega... er for Liverpool City Council. P... uction Ma... Stomp and the Eddie Izzard tou... us... founding partner of Emo Riot ... rc... Label Co-... y A... and Swim... Operator i... The Royal... for the Fo... •Gareth... Shropshir... on Blood... •Nicola... Stage Ma... Sony Mus... working i... Times we... productio... •Michel... Officer, Gi... d travellin... ent Soundbo... working ... ding Perc •Pa... t Union ... Pro Hammerhead Television •Simon Li (profess... nal nam... dist, •Camilla Løkvik, Drama Teacher for colleg... don •Samantha Lowden, self-employed Lightin... stival Sound E... in post production at Listen!, an A... cas, workin... pment Trust on a... eld, from ... Als... ople (profe... rtin work... t the Edinb... ying for a... Fear Aca... pany •Jo... ence •Ja... ange Re... e for mu... ell, freela... se •Wyn Moss, ap... performing with his band Pulse Theatre •Paul Nulty, Arch... Mamma Mia! at the Prince Edward Theatre •Paul Nulty, Arch... Indigo Light Planning, London •Andrew Obaka, toured internationally with ... n and Dancers •Dean Pendleton, Theatre Technician at LIPA •Nathaniel Perkins, Product Manager for Universal Music •Kathryne Peters, working for a Liverpool based film company •Alastair R W Powers, supporting the tutoring of undergraduates in production skills at the University of Derby. Working

SO
this is Hollywood

Sophie Hoyt headed for Hollywood in search of an acting career but ended up in another side of the industry working as a casting director.

The 2000 Acting graduate is currently with the Discovery Channel. She has also worked for 20th Century Fox, CBS, Universal, and MTV.

Said Sophie: "Being on this side of the fence is fascinating, giving me insight into what really goes on behind the scenes when it comes to casting. As an actor, it has taught me a lot about what not to do in auditions."

A fringe benefit has got to be the fact that she's living in a gorgeous apartment, just five minutes walk down Hollywood's famous Sunset Strip.

Of the job, she says: "It's extremely gratifying when

you find somebody who is genuinely lovely and has so much depth and talent. I know first hand how it feels to be rejected or cast in something, so to pass on that wonderful emotion is great. My acting experience has also set me in good stead for understanding peoples' nerves and being able to see through them. It's very rewarding."

"I never forget that I came here in the first place to be an actor, though and I'm realising that to get that job 'knowing' somebody really helps."

She jokes: "So hey, if they don't cast me in an acting role I can cast myself."

TAKING A BITE OF THE BIG APPLE

Nora Krug has certainly made her mark in her chosen profession as a freelance illustrator and animator in New York. Her portfolio contains published work in the New York Times, Polygram Records magazine and on Japanese TV, plus a number of the top specialist art publications in the States. She... up a variety of prest...

A & R Anna works with TOP RECORD STARS

Anna Schulte (Music 1999) has landed a job as an A & R with record company Mute.

The job has brought her into contact with big name groups and performers such as Nick Cave, Depeche Mode, Cabaret Voltaire, Throbbing Gristle, Goldfrap...

Erasure and Flood. Her duties include looking after the archive and all of the mastertapes at Mute, plus the typical A and R co-ordination tasks such as booking studios, hotels and transport for artists.

She says: "It's lots of...

However I still want to work on my own music. I have been, and am involved in several bands, and am currently working towards my own album! When I reflect about LIPA I really had three amazing years there. I loved the course and the people."

Life on both sides of the desk

Nick Pemberton (Sound Technology 2002) was appointed UK Sales Manager for Audient on 1st December ... He started off being responsible ... performance range ... over all ... LA ... arket.

Nick is happy in his new role. He says: "I am selling products that I really believe in at the cutting edge of the technology. Having been at the front end as an engineer, that means that I can relate to the customer from the same side of the desk. I also keep up my freelance work, to keep my toe in the water, which is something that Audient is very supportive of."

In February he returned to LIPA to take part in a friendly showdown between Yamaha and Audient as part of the Sound Technology programme's industry week.

The event was called "The working benefits of analogue versus digital in the live arena", with Nick presenting the case for analogue.

He says: "It was a really positive event with a very fair debate. I was pleased with the fact that a really high proportion of LIPA students came up to me after the event to find out more about our latest Aztec desk."

Recalling his time as a student here, Nick says: "LIPA helped me mature both in my skills as a technician and also as a person...

Sealed with a kiss

Lauren is the latest member to join the cast of S4C's welsh language television drama Amdani, securing the role of Ceri Steffan within weeks of completing her degree.

The drama is set around a female rugby team in the Welsh town of Amdani, Ceri along with her father has moved from Cardiff to start a new life following the death of her mother.

Sharing an intimate kiss with fellow female rugby teammate wasn't how 2002 Acting graduate Lauren Phillips (pictured left) had envisaged her first television appearance.

"After graduation, I joined the cast of the new musical Police Story. Within two weeks of completing the show I'd landed a part in the TV drama. They'd asked me at the audition if I'd mind kissing another women, but it was great to be considered for such a challenging role."

Miss Saigon brings Brew back to his Liverpool roots

Working as a sound technician in the musical *Miss Saigon* gave Brew (James Breward) the chance to return to his LIPA roots in Liverpool.

James (Sound Technology, 2002) started work at Autograph Sound Recording in London after graduating, carrying out maintenance on their Sound Hire Stock.

Within months, though, Brew started work as a theatre technician at the 400-seat New Wolsey Theatre in Ipswich. He was responsible for all the music events and sound designs for most of the theatre's productions. As the Christmas Panto *Aladdin The Wok And Roll Musical* approached the then Senior Technician left, and Brew became the operator for the show's two-month run. He then operated and engineered *Leader Of The Pack*, the Ellie Grenwich Musical, a co-production with Theatre Clwyd in North Wales. When the show moved to North Wales Brew became the Production Sound Engineer.

Brew also worked for other companies on one-off gigs.

In June 2004 he left the New Wolsey to become Number 2 Sound Operator on Cameron Mackintosh's touring production of *Miss Saigon*. He has since toured the country as one of the three sound engineers, working on the musical, including that memorable visit to the Liverpool Empire.

Brew plans to become a freelance sound engineer in the near future, working with Autograph as well as other for *Miss Saigon* theatre tours, and events.

He is also trying to find the time to plan his forthcoming wedding!

"Without LIPA I would not even have the aspirations to be where I am now. I stand behind a Digico D5t, the latest digital mixing desk to reach musical theatre. There's a lot of new technology, which without the grounding I gained at LIPA, I doubt I would understand, or have been offered the position in the first place," he says.

Amy Smith takes on America

Singer songwriter Amy Smith has just returned from her first tour in America, where she received some rave reviews plus BBC Radio 2 airplay. She is currently touring Barfly venues across the UK with her band, which features two LIPA graduates. They are soon to embark on a 12 date support gig for Simply Red at places like the Manchester MEN, Birmingham NEC and the Royal Albert Hall.

Immediately after graduating from LIPA's Performing Arts Music degree in 2003, Amy, whose full name is Amy Newhouse-Smith, got her first gig with the Australian Pink Floyd Show, the world's number one Pink Floyd Tribute Band. She toured with them as a featured Backing Singer around the UK for six months, and performed the female solo on the *Great Gig In The Sky*. Their biggest gig was at the Summer Pops in Liverpool (audience of 5,000). They invited her to go on tour with them in America but at that time she got signed to Universal Music Publishing and decided to make her eponymous band the priority.

She says: "When I started at LIPA I knew I wanted to work in music as a singer but I didn't know what direction to go in. LIPA gave me three years to try different things and work that out. Thanks to the excellent singing teachers I got to know my voice and what I could do with it. Being around other students who are incredibly talented and are really serious about studying music makes all the difference. Experimenting together really helped to influence me and two of my band members are LIPA graduates - Philipp Moll (bass player) and Chris Graham (drummer)."

Amy Smith and her band are with Air Management – the team behind Jamie Cullum's rise to fame and have done support gigs for Jamie, as well as for Tom Baxter and KD Lang.

In March Amy and her band embarked on a tour of America, including performing in New York, LA and at the SXSW Festival (South by Southwest festival in Austin, Texas. This is featured on BBC Radio 2 and is one of the biggest international festivals for unsigned and recently signed acts.

New Frontier Artists Limited is due to release her first EP *The Landing Tapes* shortly. Find out more at: www.amy-smith.com.

RUNNING UP THE CAREER LADDER

An informal chat with a guest lecturer at LIPA put 2001 Performance Design graduate Sion Clarke on the first step of the ladder to a career in des... After four years ...

As Art Director on *Grange Hill* Sion works two months ...

A triumphant return

Photographer: Chris Brown

LIPA's production of Jonathan Harvey's stage play *Beautiful Thing* at the National Student Drama Festival at Scarborough this year scooped three awards.

Julie Kearney (Theatre and Performance Technology graduate from 2003) achieved the Stage Electrics Award for Lighting Design, while final year acting students Kevin Kemp (left) and Paul Stocker (right) achieved the Judges' Award for Acting. The overall production received the Festgoers award for best performance.

The cast who first performed the show in LIPA's 2003 Spring season, included graduating acting students Jane Riley, Sian Polhill-Thomas, Jordan Cluroe, Stuart Reid and Jonathan Phillip-Morgan (Director). Both the cast and the creative team behind the production gained more from the experience than the coveted awards, as Iain Ormsby-Knox, Head of Acting, explains: "Adrian Gee (Assistant Designer) and a first year was offered a placement designing the summer season at the Stephen Joseph Theatre in Scarborough. Jordan Cluroe and Kevin Kemp were invited to take part in the playreading for the International Student playscript competition. All six of the cast were asked by Hampstead Theatre new writing department to take part in staging several mini performances at the end of the festival; Gjermund Andresen (designer) had lengthy discussions with a designer which included possible future ventures and the same can be said of sound designer Neil Haris".

We congratulate them and salute their achievement.

CATCHING UP WITH ...Jobst Moritz Pankok

(2000 Performance Design)

Photographer: Christian Schön

"Over the last two years I've been working freelance as a scenographer for Europe's only professional gypsy theatre company: the European Rom Theatre Pralipe. Our latest production *Sheherezade* was a co-production with Spanish theatre company Teatro del Velador. The performance was based on 1001 Nights and our ensemble was joined by a cast of Spanish actors and dancers. Although the focus of my work has been on scenic design and construction, I am also heavily involved in production management and I've even been lucky enough to perform with the company. As well as bringing the European Rom Theatre on tour in the UK this summer, I am setting up my own production company Circulo Produktion, so I can combine my work as a designer and a production manager."

LIPA IN PICTURES

8 THE PEOPLE

Degree for peers with love from Sir Paul

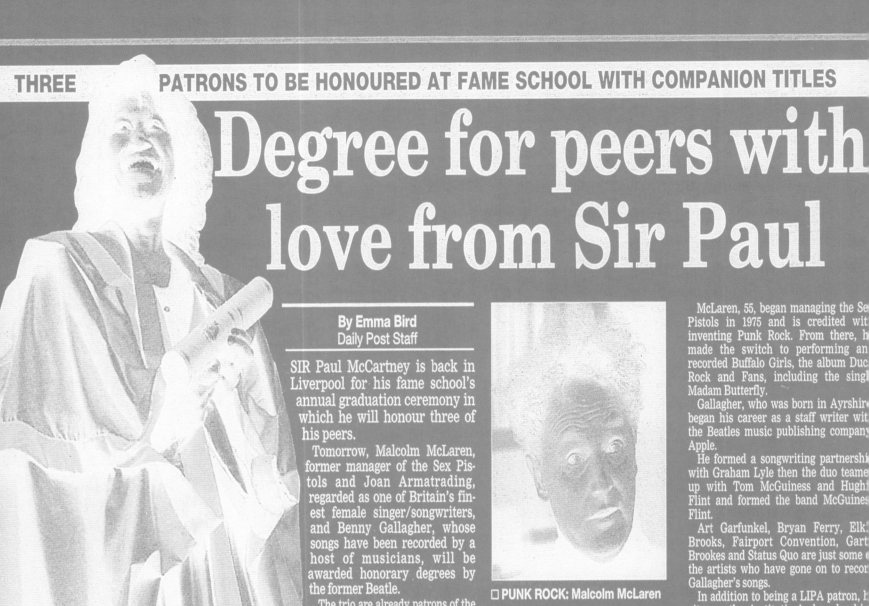

By Emma Bird
Daily Post Staff

SIR Paul McCartney is back in Liverpool for his fame school's annual graduation ceremony in which he will honour three of his peers.

Tomorrow, Malcolm McLaren, former manager of the Sex Pistols and Joan Armatrading, regarded as one of Britain's finest female singer/songwriters, and Benny Gallagher, whose songs have been recorded by a host of musicians, will be awarded honorary degrees by the former Beatle.

The trio are already patrons of the Liverpool Institute of Performing Arts and have long-standing links with college. All three of them regularly make trips to the city to hold masterclasses and deliver lectures.

Now McLaren, Gallagher and Miss Armatrading's commitment will be further recognised when they pick up their Lipa Companion titles. Only one other has been awarded.

For Ms Armatrading the honour comes just one month after being made an MBE. Three years ago, she received an honorary fellowship

☐ **PUNK ROCK: Malcolm McLaren**

from Liverpool John Moores University for her work with young people.

The West Indian-born singer launched her career when she was 14 and her mother bought her an acoustic guitar from a pawn shop.

Since then, she has had a string of now-classic hits, including Whatever's For Us, Love and Affection, Drop the Pilot and Me, Myself, I.

One of the highlights of her career occurred in February 1988 when she performed at Nelson Mandela's 70th birthday tribute concert at Wembley Stadium.

McLaren, 55, began managing the Se Pistols in 1975 and is credited wit inventing Punk Rock. From there, h made the switch to performing an recorded Buffalo Girls, the album Duc Rock and Fans, including the singl Madam Butterfly.

Gallagher, who was born in Ayrshir began his career as a staff writer wit the Beatles music publishing compan Apple.

He formed a songwriting partnershi with Graham Lyle then the duo teame up with Tom McGuiness and Hugh Flint and formed the band McGuines Flint.

Art Garfunkel, Bryan Ferry, Elk Brooks, Fairport Convention, Gart Brookes and Status Quo are just some the artists who have gone on to recor Gallagher's songs.

In addition to being a LIPA patron, h sits on the institution's board whic seeks to elevate the standard of mus and education in the UK and abroad. H is also the founding director and chai man of the Performing Artists Med Rights Association."

Spokesperson Corinne Lewis said th honorary degrees were being awarded recognition of outstanding contributio to the world of arts and entertainmen linked with a contribution to the worl of learning."

emma.bird@liverpool.co

☐ **HONOUR: Joan Amratrading, who received herJMU degree last month, will now receive a Lipa Companion title tomorrow, along with Malcolm McLaren and Benny Gallagher**

8 THE PEOPLE

Building Department

John Coady (Buildings Manager)
John Clensy
William Savage

LIPA Bar

Sophie Swan (Manager)
Simon Williams

Cleaning Staff

Phil Wallace (Supervisor)
Julie Fenlon
Julie King
Paul Lomax
Josephine Marlow
Pauline Mensah
Julie Moon
J. Don Panambo
Eileen Rainford
Pauline Wood

Catering Staff

May Dunbar
Paula Fyne
Julie King
Eileen McAlley

Finance Staff

Katharine Dimmock (Senior Finance Manager)
Glenise Brandreth
Christine Hardy
Not pictured:
Angela MacFarlane

Flexible Learning & Enterprise Staff (FLES)

Jean Barton
Paul Codman
Mat Flynn
Keith Henessy
Eddie Lundon
Keith Mullin
Gary Owen
Kate Wilson
Not pictured:
Peter Hooton

LIPA 4:19

Kerry Watkins (Programme Leader)
Sylvia Boardman
Joanne Cook
Jordan Cluroe
Alison Gorton
Helen Griffiths
Laura Kelly
Jane Lewis
Chloe Oxlade
Hannah Peel
Andrew Stephenson
Alex Vlahou-Tsaousi
Charlotte West

Not pictured:
Simon Caughey
Sam Exley
Cora Gosling
Anne-Marthe Havikbotn

ICT Staff

Ben Faulkner (ICT Systems Officer)
Mark Pritchard
Paul Grimshaw (Web Manager)

Learning Services Staff

Clare Holmes (Learning Services Manager)
Gillian Campbell
Tracey Maher
Akilah Newton
Emma Walsh
Hossnieh Sargazi
Carol Turner
Robert Hughes (Learner Support Manager)
Not pictured:
Faye Cowburn

Security Staff

David Gardner (Security Supervisor)
Tom Freeland
Graeme Lloyd
Alan Mills
George Peters
Robert Freeman
Diana McFarlane

Technical Staff

John Attewell (Lead Technician)
Paul Adams
Aaron Brown
Mark McKenny

Production Staff

Mike Brown (Production Manager)
Toni Bate
Mary Lamb
Stella Okafor
Dean Pendleton
Pete Stormont
Not pictured:
Mark Murphy

Marketing & Student Recruitment Staff

Dawn Bebb
Rachel Bradbury
Laura Campbell
Cath Cullen
Ellie Ellis
Linda Flynn
Richard Gellar
Sarah Goodyear
Julie Martin
Darren Murphy
Jenny Parkins

Sheila Payne (Admin Officer-Academic)
Christine Webster
(PA to the Principal & CEO)
Not pictured:
Karling Chan (HR Officer)

Higher Education - Music

Martin Isherwood (Programme Leader)
Arthur Bernstein
Steve Berry
Clare Canty
Gary Carpenter
Helen Davies
Mat Flynn
Eddie Lundon
Paul Mitchell-Davidson
Mark Pearman
Tim Pike

Not pictured:
Dane Chalfin
Mike Walker
Keith Mullin
Paul Walker
Dan Sanders

Higher Education - Community & Disability Arts

Lee Higgins (Programme Leader)
Mat Smith

Higher Education -
Art & Music Entertainment Management

Phil Saxe (Programme Leader)
Maria Barrett
Jeremy Grice
Dave Pichilingi

Higher Education -
Theatre Performance & Design Technology

Joe Stathers-Tracey (Programme Leader)
Neil Marcus
Kathy Sandys
Ashley Shairp

Higher Education -
Acting

Ian Ormsby-Knox (Programme Leader)
Terry Besson
Steve Buckwald
Gillian Lemon
Nick Phillips
Lise Olson (Programme Leader, Postgraduate Acting)
Not pictured:
Jo Blowers

Higher Education -
Dance

Evelyn Jamieson (Programme Leader)
Jenny Blake
Neil Fisher
Mary Prestidge
Virginia Taylor
Not pictured:
Jacqui Jones

162

Higher Education - Sound Technology

Jon Thornton (Programme Leader)
Mark Atherton
Chris Layton
Peter Philipson
Gordon Ross
Paul Stakounis

LIPA Council

Flo Clucas (Chair of Council)
John Causebrook
Mick Elliott
Tony Field
Viv Gee
Jonathan James-Moore
Ian Jones
Roger Morris
Jean Myers
Steve Rotheram
Humphrey Walwyn
Alison Wild

Not pictured:
Mark Featherstone-Witty
Rupert Grey
David Hughes
Ken Ridings
Sir George Sweeney

LIPA Directorate

Mark Featherstone-Witty - Founding Principal & CEO
Ray Adams - Director of Administration & Personnel
Giles Auckland-Lewis - Director of Higher Education
Jackie Fisher - Director of Finance
Corinne Lewis - Director of Marketing & Student Recruitment
Ged McKenna - Director of Further Learning & Enterprise Support
Ken O'Donoghue - Director of Information Services & Technical Support

2000	2001	2002	2003	2004	2005
Anthony Field	Joan Armatrading	Thelma Holt	Stephen Bayley	The Bangles	Guy Chambers
	Benny Gallagher	Anthony Wilson	Barbara Dickson	Ken Campbell	Robin Gibb
	Malcolm McLaren		Anthony Everitt	Tim Firth	Alec McCowen
			Nickolas Grace	Terry Marshall	Tim Wheeler
			Andy McCluskey	Arlene Phillips	
				Willy Russell	
				Jon Webster	

THREE PATRONS TO BE HONOURED AT FAME SCHOOL WITH COMPANION TITLES

Degree for peers with love from Sir Paul

By Emma Bird
Daily Post Staff

SIR Paul McCartney is back in Liverpool for his fame school's annual graduation ceremony in which he will honour three of his peers.

Tomorrow, Malcolm McLaren, former manager of the Sex Pistols and Joan Armatrading, regarded as one of Britain's finest female singer/songwriters, and Benny Gallagher, whose songs have been recorded by a host of musicians, will be awarded honorary degrees by the former Beatle.

The trio are already patrons of the Liverpool Institute of Performing Arts and have long-standing links with college. All three of them regularly make trips to the city to hold masterclasses and deliver lectures.

Now McLaren, Gallagher and Miss Armatrading's commitment will be further recognised when they pick up their Lipa Companion titles. Only one other has been awarded.

For Ms Armatrading the honour comes just one month after being made an MBE. Three years ago, she received an honorary fellowship from Liverpool John Moores University for her work with young people.

The West Indian-born singer launched her career when she was 14 and her mother bought her an acoustic guitar from a pawn shop.

Since then, she has had a string of now-classic hits, including Whatever's For Us, Love and Affection, Drop the Pilot and Me, Myself, I.

One of the highlights of her career occurred in February 1988 when she performed at Nelson Mandela's 70th birthday tribute concert at Wembley Stadium.

☐ **PUNK ROCK: Malcolm McLaren**

McLaren, 55, began managing the Sex Pistols in 1975 and is credited with inventing Punk Rock. From there, he made the switch to performing and recorded Buffalo Girls, the album Duck Rock and Fans, including the single Madam Butterfly.

Gallagher, who was born in Ayrshire, began his career as a staff writer with the Beatles music publishing company, Apple.

He formed a songwriting partnership with Graham Lyle then the duo teamed up with Tom McGuiness and Hughie Flint and formed the band McGuiness Flint.

Art Garfunkel, Bryan Ferry, Elkie Brooks, Fairport Convention, Garth Brookes and Status Quo are just some of the artists who have gone on to record Gallagher's songs.

In addition to being a LIPA patron, he sits on the institution's board which seeks to elevate the standard of music and education in the UK and abroad. He is also the founding director and chairman of the Performing Artists Media Rights Association."

Spokesperson Corinne Lewis said the honorary degrees were being awarded in recognition of outstanding contributions to the world of arts and entertainment, linked with a contribution to the world of learning."

emma.bird@liverpool.com

☐ **HONOUR: Joan Amratrading, who received her JMU degree last month, will now receive a Lipa Companion title tomorrow, along with Malcolm McLaren and Benny Gallagher**

LIPA offers Companionships to notable arts and entertainment professionals who have participated in the life of the Institute by sharing their skills and knowledge. Right: Joan Armatrading and Malcolm McLaren.

Above: Mark Featherstone-Witty, Jon Webster, Willy Russell, Michael Steele (The Bangles), Sir Paul McCartney, Vicki Peterson (The Bangles), Terry Marshall, Arlene Phillips and Tim Firth.

Left: Tim Wheeler, Sir Paul McCartney, Robin Gibb, Guy Chambers and Mark Featherstone-Witty.

Lea Anderson	Phil Harding	Simone Rebello
Joan Armatrading	John Harper	Corin Redgrave
The Bangles	Kit Holmes	Phil Redmond
James Barton	Thelma Holt	Lou Reed
Jennifer Batten	Hootie and the Blowfish	Peter Reichardt
Paul Bentley	Eleanor Hudson	Seth Riggs & David Stroud
Ed Bicknell	Christian Ingebrigtsen	Eryl Roberts & John Ellis
Lord John Birt	Damian Jackson	Willy Russell
James Burton	Trevor Jackson	Prunella Scales
Ken Campbell	Glyn Johns	Louise Schultz
John Causebrook	Julian Kelly	Prof. Jorg Sennheiser
Guy Chambers	Bill Kerr	Will Shillington
Tracy Chapman	Paul Kilvington	Max Stafford-Clark
China Crisis	David Laudat	David Stark
Thomas Clough	Gerd Leonhard	Alison Stephens
John Dankworth	Martin Lowe	James Taylor
John Dell	Cameron Mackintosh	Dave Tolan
Barbara Dickson	Barry Mason	Cathy Tyson
Zoltan Dikame	David Massingham	Jürgen Wahl
Joe Duddell	Alec McCowen	Rick Wakeman
Sir Ben Elton	Andy McLuskey	Jerry Jeff Walker
Brian Eno	Ian McNabb	Bruce Wall
Jose Feliciano	Mel C	Mark Ward
Tony Field	Ramesh Meyappan	Dionne Warwick
Tim Firth	Bob Mincer	Jon Webster
Dawn French	Gerri Moriarty	Tim Wheeler
Tish Garland	Steve Morse	Richard Wilson
Mel Gaynor	Jim Muirhead	Amy Winehouse
Paul Geary	Beth Nielsen Chapman	Jah Wobble
Robin Gibb	Craig Ogden	John Woodward
Lee Gibson	Alan Parker	Robert Worby
Steve Gilbert	John Patrick	Peter Wylie
Nickolas Grace	John Preston	

Elsa Maria Eike Aanensen	Ashley Alymann	Alexander Arnesen	Richard Badendyck	Martin Barbour
Lena Irene Aarstad	Madeline Amer	Ragnhild Arnestad Monness	Christian Badzura	Richard Barbour
Hans Aaseth	Philippa Amer	Meshaun Arnold	Sunnuva Baek	Emily Barden
Yemi Abisola	Shaunaid Amette	Joanne Ashbridge	Pernille Baggeranas	Rachel Bardill
Jennifer Abraham	Gavin Amor	Marie Ashbridge	Aaron Bailey	David Barker
Nicole Abraham	Hilde Amundsen	Thomas Ashbrook	Donnaleigh Bailey	Katharine Ruth Barker
Gianni Abruzzese	Manos Anastasiou	Gillian Ashcroft	Gary Bailey	Lauren Barker
Andrew Adams	Maria Anastassiou	Philippa Ashley	Vincent Bailey	Paul Barker
Jean Paul Adams	Carl Anderson	Robert Ashley	Gemma Bain	Philippa Barker
Olivia Adams	Christopher Anderson	Katie Ashmore	Matthew Bainbridge	Rupert Barksfield
Holly Adamson	Guro Anderson	Dean Ashworth	Victoria Baines	Emily Barlow
Kavisha Adapen	Natalie Anderson	Megan Ashworth	Rachael Baio	Michelle Barlow
Yannick Aellen	Sarah Anderson	Dorthe Aske	Adam Baker	Simon Barlow
Shalique Ahad	Jayni Anderton	Lauren Askew	Britney Baker	Luc Barnes
Florian Ahrens	Gjermund Andresen	Wasilios Asmanidis	David Baker	Keith Barr
Ingo Aicher	Rebecca Andrews	Marit Aspen	Ewan Baker	Stephanie Barr
Keiko Akamatsu	Gabriel Angeles	Jennifer Aspinall	Jessica Baker	Gregory Barratt
Yoshio Akeboshi	Christopher Angell	Carly Athawes	Laura Baker	Katherine Barret
Maria Akpan	Emma Annetts	Cain Atherton	Phillip Baker	Helen Susanne Barrett
Charles Albin	Jakob Anthoff	Daniel Atkinson	Havard Bakken	Henry Barrett
Haley Alderson	Sofia Antunovic	Joanna Atkinson	Puchi Balanza	Janet Barrett
Ida Alfstad	Mark Apicella	Brita Atlesdotter Hansen	Peter Baldwin	Katherine Barrett
Georgia Ali	Kristina Appel	Tom Aubrey-Fletcher	Rachael Baldwin	Matthew Barrie
Oda Alisøy Søvig	Madeline Appiah	Jostein Austvik	Jamie Ball	Paul Barron
Charlese Allen	Jerry Appleyard	Barry Avison	Stephen Ball	Heidi Barrow
Jonathan Allen	Cristina Aragon Juarez	Zara Awan	Caroline Ballard	James Barrow
Katie Allen	Jacob Archer	Robin Axford	Francesca Bandino	Simone Barry
Kelly Allen	Samantha Arends	Ayca Ayabakan	Richard Banks	Louise Barry-Desmond
Queen Allen	Harry Arkwright	Anna Ayers	Alexander Baranowski	Jake Bartle
Victoria Allen	Paul Armitstead	Richard Babington	Simon Barber	Andrew Bartlett
Adam Alton	April Armstrong-Bascombe	Nina Backman	Jacques Barbot	Joanne Bartlett

LIPA Students continued

Gareth Barton
Chelsea Barton
Anna Barzotti
Nicholas Baskerville
Chloe Bass
Krizia Bassanini
Kellie Bateman
Mercedez Bateman
Joe Bates
Mark Francis Bates
Louise Batey
Jonathan Bath
Olivia Battle-Williams
Lyndsay Baudains
Sarah Bauman
Conor Baxter
Rebecca Baylis
William Baylis
Megan Beadman
Alice Beal
Shane Beales
Megan Beales-Cox
Adam Beaney
Mark Beaney
Elizabeth Beasley
Amanda Beattie
Victoria Beaumont
Jessica Beaumont
Amy Bebbington
Michael Bebbington
David Beck
Jule Beck
Christiane Becker
Christiane Becker
Hayley Beddard
Ghillan Bedford
Christopher Beebee
Christopher Beech
Adrian Beentjes
Nathan Beeston
Kim Begley
Sally-Anne Beighton
Dunstan Belcher
Dale Bell
Nicola Bell
Louise Bellairs
Nicola Belle
Paul Bellman
Stacey Benbow
Thomas Christopher Bendall
Leonie Bennett
Abbie Bennett
Daniel Bennett
Lauren Bennett
Matthew Bennett
Paul Bennett
Phil Bennett
Sandra Bennett
Lea Bensasson

James Bentley
Patricia Beranek
Rune Berg
Stein Berg
Anne Berhus Hansen
Anthony Bermudez
Marco Bernardis
Elizabeth Bernstein
Antony Berryman
Aimee Berwick
India Best
Leanne Best
Natasha Bevans
Nyaradzo Bhebhe
Ruth Bias
David Bibby
Sabine Bickel
Rebekka Biedermann
Aleksandra Bienkowska
Matthew Biggins
Jason Wesley Biggs
Katherine Bigler
Marcus Bilal-Jones
Erlend Bilsbak
Philip Binks
April Bird
John Bird
Julia Bird
John Birss
Joachim Birzele
Elisa Bishop
Emma Bispham
Jan Petter Bjerke
Trym Bjonnes
Torgeir Bjordal
Merete Bjorgvik
Alan Black
Matthew Black
Robin Blake
Adele Bland
Matthew Blank
Millie Blankstone
Gareth Blazey
Abigail Blears
Jamie Bleasdale
Kristian Blindheim
Arild Blomkvist
Gudrún Blöndal
Anthony Blundell
Ian Blundell
Christopher Boardman
Lewis Boardman
Nicole Boardman
Jutta Bobbenkamp
Simon Bobbett
Jessica Bockler
Daniella Bodansky
Joseph Bodansky
Elizabeth Boddy

David Boerke
Nadine Bogan
Christopher Bogg
Nathan Boggon
Gabriel Bogle
Aaron Bogucki
Melissa-Christin Bohlsen
Nicolas Bohnet
Clinton Boland
Hannah Bold
Clare Bolton
Marcus Bonfanti
Luc Bonnet
Philip Booker
Sam Boomer
Elizabeth Boorman
Alison Booth
Lindsey Booth
Marianna Booth
Nicola Booth
Sudhiro Booth
Louise Booty
Clare Borg
Sascha Borg
Solveig Borgen
Nina Borgner
Grethe Børsum
Daphne Bos
Richard Vincent Boschetto
Cara Bostock
Natalie Bosworth
Peggy Botebol
Philip Bottomley
Terence Boughton
Henry Bourne
Amanda Bowen
Lakisha Bowen
Victoria Bowen
Dean Bowers
Andrew Bowes
Jaida Bowles
Gemma Bowman
Jenna Boyce
Stephanie Boyd
Margaret Boyle
Elaine Boyling
Alexander Braathen
Emma Bracey
Katrina Brackenbury
Antonia Bradford
Gary Bradley
Helen Bradley
Michael Bradley
Stephanie Bradley
Jasmin Bradley-Broom
Peter Bragg
Victoria Bragg
Ruth Brameld
Espen Branden

Mia Brandon
Christopher Brannan-Haggas
Jessica Brannan-Jones
Pal Bratelund
Elisabeth Breines Vik
Ina Brekke
Justin Breman
Randall Breneman
Heidi Brennan
Lucy Brennan
Abigail Brett
Amy Brett
Benjamin Breuning
James Breward
Carl Brewer
Colleen Brewer
Nicola Brewster
Rowena Bridge
Philip Bridges
Georgina Bridglal
Caitlin Brie
Cherylanne Brierley
Kathryn Louise Brierley
Silje Brievik
Ali Briggs
Rachel Briggs
Christopher Bright
Grant Brisland
Shaun Briston
Matthew Britnell
Charlie Britton
Elspeth Brodie
Gareth Bromilow
Danielle Brook
Christopher Brookes
Natasha Brookes
Sarah Brooks
Stephen Brooks
William Brooks
Marc Broomby
James Brough
Sarah Brougham
Laura Broughton
Cassandra Brown
Aaron Brown
Adam Brown
Alison Brown
Christopher Brown
Duncan Brown
Jay Brown
Joanne Brown
Marc Brown
Mark Brown
Matilda Brown
Sarah Brown
Scott Brown
Sophie Brown
Stuart Brown
Vicky Brown

Zoe Brown
Emily Brownless
Johannes Broziat
Michael Bruce
James Bruns
Andre Brunvoll
Dominic Bryan
Tristan Bryant
Jake Buchanan
Christopher Buckley
Daire Buckley
Megan Buckley
Wayne Buckley
Thomas Buggins
Stephen Buhagiar
Robert Bull
Sigve Bull
Simon Neil Bulley
Gareth Bullock
Steven Bulmer
Anne Bunckenburg
Claire Bunton
Shade Buraimoh
Caprice Burcher
Adam Burgan
Anthony Burge
Guy Burgess
Ashley Burke
Olivia Burke
Taylor Burke
Frances Burkinshaw
Gail Burland
Ranjit Burman
Christopher Burns
James Burns
Liam Burns
Martin Burns
Raymond Burns
Adam James Burton
Edward Burton
Jan-David Burton
Paul Burton
Lynn Buschhueter
John Busow
David Butcher
Craig Butler
David Butler
Ruth Butler
Sean Butler
Daniel Buttner
Katie-Louise Buxton
Angela Byrne
Penny Byrne
Robert Byrne
Ryan Byron
Joanne Bywater
Christopher Caffrey
Molly Caffrey
Penelope Caffrey

Andrew Cain	Ryan Chappell	Carl Cockram	Selina Corradi	Nancy Cunliffe
Jennifer Cain	Christopher Charalambides	Robert Coe	Laura Corradi	Robert Cunliffe
Rachel Caine	Gareth Charles	Gabrielle Coffey	Camila Cortés	Stevelane Cunnane
Charlotte Caisley	Gary Charles	William Cogger	Macarena Cortés	Anne Cunningham
Paul Callighan	Sarah Charles	Berel-Anne Cohen	Anthony Cosgrove	Sarah Cunningham
Sita Calvert-Ennals	Thomas Malcolm Charnock	Caroline Cohen	Garvan Cosgrove	Daniel Cunningham
James Cameron	Chelsea-Louise Lincoln	Catherine Colbourne	Andria Cossy	Wesley Cunningham
Christopher Campbell	Hsin-Yi Chen	Austin Cole	Niall Costigan	Colin Curbishley
Emma Campbell	Paul Cherry	Andrew Coleman	Christopher Cottam	Lawrence Curran
Harry Campbell	Jack Cheshire	Kate Colledge	Eleanor Cotterell	Fae Currie
Jessica Campbell	Jodi Chhapi	Phil Collier	Stephen Cotton	James Curry
Mark Campbell	Sophie Chin	Michael Collighan	Abby Coulson	Darren Curson
Terence Campbell	Shih Chin-Hang	Benjamin Collins	Mark Cousins	Kevin John Curtin
Gary Canning	Edward Chinn	Denise Collins	Andrew Cowan	Dan Curtis
Isabelle Canning	Matthew Chisholm	Ian Collins	Sarah Cowan	Ella Curtis
Ben Cannings	Hyo Choi	Imogen Collins	Faye Cowburn	Kia Curtis
Joseph Capes	Boyan Chowdhury	Lauren Collins	Jason Cowdell	Richard Curtis
Jon Caplin	Rachel Chowings	Martyn Collins	Damon Cowell	Russell Curtis
Margaret Carlin	Jamie-Leigh Christian	Saffron Collister	Taylor Cowell	Shaun Curtis
James Carnell	Brianna Christianson	David Colohan	Miles Cowie	Michelle Cutler
Helen Carpenter	Artemis Chrysovitsanou	Patrick Colohan	Benjamin Cowper	Jamie Cymbal
Charlotte Carr	Andrew Chu	Naomi Combes	Ellen Cox	Hakan Dadasbilge
Alina Carrasco-Toft	Fu-Ying Chu	Gregory Combs	Peter Coyle	Martin Daester
Ben Carrick	Dominic Chung	Maria Commander	Katie Coyne	Patrick Dahle
Molly Carroll	Margareth Cielicki	Martin Conneely	Gemma Craddock	Petter Dahlgren
Hugh Carruthers	Katherine Clague	Matthew Connelly	Saskia Cradock	Nina Dahlklepsvik
Wayne Carthy	Simon Clancy	Craig Connet	Charlie Cragg	Andrew Daley
Darren Cartwright	Amanda Clark	Lydia Connor	David Craig	Megan Daley
Lisa Carver	Frank Clark	Sheldon Conrich	James Craven-Hodgson	Anna Maria Dallas
Graham Casey	Katherine Clark	Michele Conroy	Charlotte Crawford	Lisa Dalton
Lynsey Cassels	Rhian Clark	Milana Constantinescu	Louise Crawford	Callum Daly
Julian Cassia	Katherine Clarke	Joanne Cook	Colleen Crawley	Caroline Daly
Hannah Cassidy	Alexandra Clarke	Nicholas Cook	John Creggy	Melissa Daly
Lucy Cassidy	Benjamin Clarke	Peter Cook	Catherine Crick	Sally Daly
Millie Cassidy	Emile Clarke	Tanya Frances Cooke	Terry Cripps	James Dangerfield
Mariona Castillo Garcia	Frank Clarke	Daniel Cooklin-Smith	Giuliano Crispini	Steven Daniels
Ben Castle	Hayley Clarke	Kate Cooklin-Smith	Erin Crivelli	Francesca D'Anna
Daniel Castree	Myles Clarke	Lorna Cookson	Nicholas Crofts	Abigail Darby
Camilo Castro Llach	Patrick Clarke	Rachel Cookson	Colin Cromby	Caroline Darby
Jasmine Catherall	Sion Clarke	Felicity Cooper	Paul Andrew Crompton	Sam Darby
Lauren Catherall	Vanessa Clarke	Clare Cooper	Joanne Cronin	Annie May D'Arcy
Thomas Caton	Gary Clarkson	Emily Cooper	Ian Cropper	Jack Darell
Charlotte Catterall	Christina Clayhills-Henderson	Philip Cooper	Gary Cross	Claire Dargavel
David Catterall	Nicola Clayton	Sophie Cooper	Paul Cross	Julia Dark
Vannessa Catterall	Ray Clayton	Stephen Cooper	Cheryl Crossan	Christopher Davey
Isobel Cattrall	Annie May Clearkin	Tom Cooper	Michael Crossey	Alisha Davidow
Simon Caughey	Patrick Clearkin	Alyson Coote	Carly Crowder	Helen Davidson
Peter Robert Caulfield	Martina Clement	Amanda Cope	Claire Crozier	Holly Davidson
Paul Cavanagh	Jazmine Clements	Faye Copeland	Elizabeth Crudginton	Ian Davidson
Robert Cavill	Lisa Clifford	Paula Anne Coppell	Mark Crudginton	Ian James Davidson
Zac Cawdron	Alex Clucas	Scott Corbett	Holly Cullen	Iain Alexander Davie
Aaron Cawley	Jordan Cluroe	Amy Corcoran	Vincent Cullinan	Adam Davies
Stephen Chambers	Sarah Coakley	Lauren Corcoran	Jeff Cullum	Andrew Davies
Heyling Chan	Amy Coats	Liam Corcoran	Richard Cullum	April Davies
Matthew Chandler	Sophie Cobain	Antonia Corish	Simon Cullwick	Carl Davies
Paul Chandler	Louise Cobb	Grace Corish	Paul Cumine	Clio Davies
Matthew Chang	Joseph Cochrane	Josie Cork	Laura Cummings	Emma Davies
Charlotte Chapman	Stephen Cockbain	Hollie Corkhill	Stephen Cummings	Francesca Davies
Zoe Chapman	John Cockerill	Henrietta Corlett	Jennifer Cummins	Gareth Davies

LIPA Students continued

John Davies
Karen Davies
Kirsti Davies
Lisa Davies
Lucy Davies
Mark Davies
Molly Davies
Owain Davies
Rachael Davies
Rebecca Davies
Siân Davies
Stephanie Davies
Stephen Davies
Stuart Davies
Tom Davies
Ben Davila
Camille Davila
Andrew Davis
Carl Davis
Emma Davis
Michael Davis
Paul Davis
Dee Davison
Jonathan Davys
Abigail Dawson
Mahala Dawson
Ashley Day
Iain Day
Joseph Day-Evans
Sarah Daykin
Alicia De Banffy
Dominique De Beaufort
Enrique De Dios
Annette De Goumoens
Mercedes De Graaff
Lee De Pablo
Kerry Deacon
Rachel Deadman
Erica Deakin
Paul Richard Deakin
Jonathan Deamer
Rosie Deane
David Dearden
Christopher Deas
Alexandre Decoupigny
Lauren Deegan
Sandra Dehler
Marcel Delrue
Alex Delve
Gareth Delve
Stavros Demetraki
Abby Dempsey
Catherine Dempsey
Marilyn Dempsey
Vicki Dempsey
Chloe Denis
Zoe Denis
Zetia Dennis
Letitia Denny

Geoffrey Dent
Claire Denton
Simon Denton
Rachel Denyer
Sina Derkum
Charley Desborough
Lars Devik
Drew Devine
Jessica Devine
Keira Devine
Mark Devine
Paul Devine
John Dey
Jaswinda Dhami
Caroline Dhenin
Isobel Diamond
Maeve Diamond
Melanie Dickenson
Gareth Dickie
Sarah Dickson
Morgan Dietkus
Henning Dietz
Barney Dillon
Claire Dillon
Tony Dimeck
John Dineley
Andrew Dixon
Callum Dixon
Marie Dixon
Benjamin Dobie
Charlotte Dobie
Philip Dobie
James Dodd
Christopher Doherty
Jennifer Doherty
Sophie Doherty
Leyton Dohnahue
Daniel Dolan
Simone Dollmann
Emma-Jane Dolphin
Aaron Dolton
Michael Dolton
Nicola Donithorn
Anna Donnelly
Lauren Donnelly
Paul Donnelly
Theresa Donnelly
Hannah Donoghue
Sebastian Donoghue
Isobel Dooley-Kelly
Amber Doran
Gina Dorkins
Adam Dougal
Brendan Douglas
Christopher Douglas
Derek Douglas
Helen Douglas
Peter Douglas
Abbey Dowdeswell

Lauren Dowdeswell
Rebecca Dowey
Ross Dowling
Matthew Downton
Hayley Doyle
Kelly Doyle
Judith Drake
Faye Draper
John Draper
Adam Drennan
Rebecca Driscoll
Sarah Jennie Driver
Stuart Drummond
Jade Drury
Olivia Du Monceau
Rebecca Duckworth
Rachel Duerden
Alan Dufton
Luisa Duggan
Ellis Duke
Nadya Duke
Scott Dulson
Amy Dunbavin-Robertson
Elliot Duncan
James Duncan
Joanne Duncan
Luke James Duncan
Matthew Duncan
Benjamin Dunderdale
Rachel Dunican
Rhian Dunkley
Alastair Dunn
Michael Dunn
Robert Dunn
John Durham
Alexandra Dwyer
Nicholas Dwyer
Marcus Dyer
Rory Dyer
Elizabeth Dykes
Russell Dyson
Jessica Eaden
Isabella Eagle
Niamh Eagle
Julie Eales
Kate Earlam
Lynne Earls
Hannah Eastwood
Lisa Edelman
Gary Edgar
Kim Edgar
Su Edison
Isobel Edmeston
Kelsey Edmonds
John Edon
Sophie Edwards
Clare-Louise Edwards
Helen Edwards
Ian Roy Edwards

John Edwards
Lyndsay Edwards
Richard Edwards
Sarah Edwards
Vicky Edwards
Nina Victoria Eek
Bobbi Effanga
Ashleigh Egan
Niamh Egan
Emma Louise Egerton
Heidi Eggesvik
Frode Eggum Have
Eric Eichenlaub
Johannes Eidelberger
Cristofer Eikenes
Tommi Eisele
Kjersti Ekman
Rebecca Elbs
Jonas Ellenberg
Christina Ellinas
Ian Phillip Ellington
Dean Elliot
Rebecca Elliott
Adam Ellis
Ronald Ellis
William Ellis
Dawn Ellis Hoult
Barry Ellison
Jamie Ellison
Jennifer Ellison
Jessikha Ellison
Nick Ellison
Georgina Elman
Simon Eltringham
Elisabeth Elvsveen
Jemma Endersby
Edvard Eng
Vera Engelhardt
Kristian Engeseth
Tiril Englestad
Elizabeth Ennis
Sirin Enol
Rachel Entwistle
Andrew Entwistle
Hannah Epps
Simon Eraker
Ross Erickson
James Eriksen
Martin Ermen
Nathan Erskine
Luis Escriva De Romani
Mark Espley
Frank Essery
Klara Estberg
Katherine Evans
David Evans
Gareth Bryn Evans
Gemma Evans
Jacob Evans

Jake Evans
Jamie Evans
Lynsey Evans
Miriam Evans
Rebecca Evans
Stuart Christian Evans
Tamsin Evans
Corin Evans-Pritchard
Heather Ewing
Sam Exley
Janet Eyre
Kim Eyres
David Ezra
Johannes Fabry
Emma Fadden
Rebecca Fadden
Anja Fagerli
Joanne Fahy
Ben Fair
Nick Faircloth
Jennifer Fairclough
Beth Fairweather
Eiko Falckenberg
Elizabeth Falconer
Sarah Falconer
Artis Falkner
Samuel Falle
Anne Fallmyr
Sophie Fallon
Martin Family
Georgia Fanning
Imad Farajin
Daniel Farish
Alexandra Farkic
Ben Farmer
Chelsea Farrell
Dibylle Fassler
Benjamin Faulkner
Joe Faulkner
Simone Favell
Giacomo Fazi
Ebony Feare
Peter Fearns
Thomas Featherstone
Simon Fee
Andrew Fegan
Izabella Feld
Peter Fell
Mark Felming
Gary Feltham
Sara Felton
Mark Fenna
Adam Fenton
Michael Fenwick
Karey Ferguson
Rebeca Fernandez Lopez
Paul Ferns
Marta Ferre Guardiola
Lauren Ferrier

Joshua Ferrigan
Ben Fewson
Jake Field
Alexander Fielding
Darnell Fielding
Tempany Fielding
Hannah Fillis
John-Mark Finch
Darren Finn
Oliver Finn
Patrick Finn
Sean Finn
Beth Finnigan
Matthew Fishel
Kirsty Fisher
Thomas Fisher
Helen Fitton
Catherine Fitzgerald
Rowena Fitzgibbon
Edwina Fitzpatrick
Louis Fitzpatrick
Timothy Fitzpatrick
Gia Fitzsimons
Robert Flanagan
Desmond Fleet
Chandra Fleig
Tobias Fleischer
Gerard Fleming
Louise Fletcher
Peter Fletcher
Stephen Fletcher
Sueleen Fletcher
Peter Flynn
Sandra Fogler
Abby Foley
Jacob Foord
Richard Forber
Lucy Ford
Mark Ford
Matthew Forde
Robert Forde
Krystal Ford-Murray
Carl Formby
Ryan Forrest
Catherine Forshaw
Rebecca Forsyth
Charlotte Fortune
Jennifer Foster
Ben Foster
Katharine Foster
Katie Foster
Neil Foster
Shona Foster
Eleanor Foster
Gethin Foulkes
Isabelle Foulkes
Peter Fovargue
Bradley Fowell
Jonathan Fowkes

David Fox
Emma Foxall
Paul Foxcroft
Aja Frais
David Francis
Mark Franks
Stuart Fraser
Melody Frayne
Anna Frazer
Tommy Fredvang
Barry Freeman
Brian Freeman
Janet Freeman
Joanna Lesley Freeman
Andrew French
Claire French
Janet French
Jonathan French
Martin French
Neil French
Richard French
Richard Friemann
Alesha Friend
Joanne Froggatt
Simon Froggatt
Luis Frontana
Benjamin Frost
Sasha Frost
Stina Frosterod
Amy Fry
Darren Fry
Louise Geradline Fry
Sam Fry
Graham Fryer
Joel Frymire
Henning Fuchs
Africa Fuentes Cardial
Andrew Fugle
Lauren Fujii
Simon Fuller
Jørn-Bjørn Fuller-Gee
Wayne Fullwood
Robert Fulop
Peter Fulton
Ruth Fung
Katie Funk
Marianne Furevold
William Furey
Lisa-Ellen Furniss
Angelica Furrer
Jonas Furrer
Martine Furulund
Declan Fyans
Fitzgerald Fyne
Kade Fyne
Miah Fyne
Craig Gaffney
Mark Gale
Diane Gallacher

Natalie Gallacher
Thomas Gallagher
Andrew Gallant
Rhoda Gallardo
Giancarlo Gallo
Michael Gamble
Vishal Gandhi
Kristian Gangflot
Matthew Gant
Natasha Gant
Louise Garcia
Rodrigo Garcia
Trinidad Garcia Espinoza
Shelbie Gardiner
Anthony Gardner
Oliver Gardner
Natalie Garner
Rosy Garner
Samantha Garner
William Garner
Alex Garnett
Amanda Garnett
Matthew Garrett
Lesley Garrigan
Mimoza Gashi
Leanne Gaskill
Jack Gavin
Michael Gay
Adrian Gee
Beatrice Gehrmann
Shie Geller
Tony Georges
Francesca Georgeson
Stephanie Georgeson
Peter Georgiou
Kate Geraghty
Ralf Gerhardt
Tracy Gerlach
Gabriella Gerrard
Emily Gervers
Matthew Gest
John Gibbe
Faye Gibbons
Lydia Gibbons
Seth Gibbs
Simon Gibeau
Charles Gibson
Chris Gibson
Jessica Gibson
Kate Gibson
Katie Gibson
Matthew Gibson
Robert Gibson
Daniel Gifford
Sian Gifford
Julia Gilberton
Laura Gilchrist
David Gilday
Monyca Giles

Julian Gill
Joanna Gillespie
Claudea Gilligan
Gabrielle Gilligan
John Gillon
Megan Gillon
Tony Gilmore
Etienne Girard
Rachael Gladwin
Natalie Gleave
Caroline Gledhill
Chris Gledhill
James Gledhill
Rachael Gledhill
Sean Anthony Gleeson
Jonathan Richard Glew
Amy Glossop
Aimee Glover
Aran Glover
Samuel Goddard
Gemma Godfrey
Julia Goebel
Luke Goetze
Lael Goldberg
Jonathan Goldby
Katie Louise Golledge
Nora Gyulay Gombos
Jefferson Gonzalez
Mark Goodall
Amelia Goodman
James Gordon
Martin Gordon
Michelle Gorrod
David Gorst
Sarah Gorton
Victoria Gotham
Stephen Goudie
Dickon Gough
Jason Gough
Jamee Gould
Thomas Gould
Lucy Goulding
Tommy Govan
Sarah Govier
Andrew Gower
Jorg Gradwohl
Gunnar Graewert
Alexandra Graham
Caroline Graham
Christopher Graham
Ian Graham
Lucy Graham
Michael Graham
Susannah Graham
Paris Graham-Jones
Portia Graham-Jones
Emily Grainger
Christopher Grant
David Grant

Kyle Grant
Thomas Grant
Louise Grantham
Therese Grasdal
Gaute Grav
Anna Gray
Barry Gray
Laura Gray
Priscilla Gray
Paolo Greco
Rebecca Greeb
Jamie Green
Darren Green
Richard Green
Selina Green
Steven Green
Timothy Green
Toby Green
Zoe Green
Jonathan Green
Jolyon Greenaway
Daniel Greenhow
Alex Greenslade
Ian Greenway
Joshua Greenwood
Mark Greenwood
Elizabeth Grefsrud
Ben Gregory
Christine Gregory
Lauren Gregory
Justin Gregson
Martin Greil
Karina Gretere
Andrew Grevey
Tony Grey
Joshua Gribben
Stein Grieg Halvorsen
Amy Griffin
Megan Griffith
Christopher Griffiths
David Robert Griffiths
Elizabeth Griffiths
Garry Griffiths
Helen Griffiths
Lee Griffiths
Leslie Griffiths
Liz Griffiths
Nicola Griffiths
Oliver Griffiths
Rachel Jean Griffiths
Stephen Griffiths
Rebecca Griffiths
Richard Grimley
Rachel Grimshaw
Ruth Grindrod
Jean Grobler
Christine Gronsleth
Alke-Christiane Groppel-
Wegener

LIPA Students continued

Oliver Gross
Simon Gross
Anna Grotelueschen
Lorraine Grout
Rebecca Grove
Ian Grundy
Mathias Grunwaldt
Kathrine Grzeschik
Spencer Guainiere
Mario Guala
Florian Gubisch
Haraldur Gudmundsson
Thomas Guest
Manuel Guix
Ayesha Gumbhir
Alex Gummer
Joerund Gundersen
Tor-Einar Gundersen Rogn
William Gunn
Lucy Gunning
Mirjam Gurtner
Christina Gusthart
Stephen G Williams
Lars Haakonsen
Gerrit Haasler
Stella Haastrop
Petter Haavik
Charlotte Habib
Robert Hack
Andrew Hackett
Leah Hackett
Simon Christopher Hadfield
Stacie Hadgikosti
Marina Hadjilouca
Daniel Hadley
Nadin Hadorn
Sonoko Haga
Christopher Hagan
Emma Hagan
Knut-Oyvind Hagen
Daniel Haggis
Youssef Haghegh
Ewan Hails
Darran Hailwood
David Jason Hain
Kimberley Hale
Helen Hall
Jennifer Hall
Jon Hall
Kjetil Hallre
Michael Halls
Matthew Halsall
Steven Halstead
Christina Halvorsen
Yuka Hamamoto
Shereen Hamdadou
Helen Hamer
Mark Hamilton
Raymond Hamilton

Claire Hammett
Martin Hammil
Josh Hammond
Marine Hamou
Richard Hampson
Robert Hampton
Sang-Yong Han
Chris Hanby
Kenneth Hancock
Martyn Hand
Nicholas Handford
Christopher Handley
Gemma Hands
Katri Elina Hanhivaara
Adam Hanley
Kia Hanley
Stephen Hanley
Katherine Hannible
Havard Hanserud
Nick Hanson
Tay Hanson
Oliver Hardaker
Jens Hardangen
Robert Hardaway
Danny Harding
Kendell Harding
Neil Harding
Dominic Hardy
Esi Hardy
Geraint Hardy
Gayle Hare
Anthony Harley
Jesse Harlin
Ryan Harlin
Jessica Harlock
Carl Harper
Jane Harper
Adelaide Harris
Brett Harris
Jemma Harris
Neil Harris
Rosalind Harrison
David Harrison
Derrick Harrison
Edward Harrison
Hugo Harrison
James Harrison
James Harrison
Laura Harrison
Martin Harrison
Neil Harrison
Nicola Harrison
Owen Harrison
Rosa Harrison
Chelsea Harrison
Jade Harrison
Noel Harron
Grenville Harrop
Joanne Harry

Anthony Hart
Claire Hart
Mark Hartley
Benjamin Harvey
Chris Harvey
David Harvey
James Harvey
Lewis Harvey
Sean Harvey
Octavia Harwood
Russell Haselhurst
Antony Haselton
David Haslam
Gavin Hassan
Liza Hassan
Ingvild Hasund
Alicia Hatton
Mads Hauge
Morten Haugerud
Endre Haukland
Line Haukland
Kjell Haune
Rainer Hausmann
Anne-Marthe Havikbotn
Kate Havneivik
Roland Havranek
Alex Hawkins
Jason Hawkins
Dean Hawksford
Gerard Hawksworth
Rebecca Hawley
Chris Haworth
Carrianne Hayden
Kristy Hayes
Samantha Hayes
Stephen Hayes
Greg Hay-Moulder
Leanne Hayward
Claire Hazelgrave
Helen Hazelgrave
Andrew Heard
David Hearn
John Paul Hearne
Rachel Heath
Bethany Heath
Janine Heath
Rebecca Heath
Ross Heaton
Sarah Hebb
Steven Hedley
Rainer Heesch
Claire Heffernan
Bianca Hehir
Andreas Heidu
Niko Heimolinna
Thomas Heister
Martin-Alejandro Heizmann-Blanco
John Heldt

Nicola Heldt
Mark Richard Heller
Marte Helleseter
Florian Helmbold
Christopher Hemmings
Luke Hemmings
Tale Hendnes
Alicia Henigan
Emma Henigan
David Hennessey
Keith Hennessy
Sophie Hennessy
Tamira Henry
Katherine Ann Henrys
Joanne Henshaw
Meical Alexander Henson
Lauren Herandez
Nicholas Herbert
Colin Heron
Florian Herrmann
Johanna Herron
Kaya Herstad
Stephen Heslin
Julia Hesselberg
Kati Hetmaincyzk
Zoë Hewitson
Elaine Hewitt
Daniel Hewitt-Teale
Naomi Heyes
Nathan Heyes
Robert Heyes
Dwain Heywood
Emma Hickebottom
Liam Hickey
Thomas Hien
Kyle Higginbotham
Emma Higginbottom
Chad Higgins
Nathan Higgins
Daniel Higgott
Conrad Hijazi
Christian Hildebrand
Sara Hildebrand
Andrew Hill
Mark Hill
Paul Hill
Phillip Hill
Lauren Hillary
Joanna Hillier
Stephen Hillman
Stefanie Hilty
Daniel Hinchliffe
Christopher Hine
John Hines
Bonny Hinton Cook
Bethany Hinton-Lever
Sophia Hinton-Lever
Daniel Hipshon
Jun Hiragushi

Sara Hirn
Siobhán Hirrell-Naylor
David Hirst
Joseph Hirst
Christian Hitchen
Kjetil Hjornevik
Elizabeth Hobson
John Hobson
David Hockenhull
Wiley Hodgden
Beth Hodgson
Carl Hodgson
Yngve Hoeyland
Erling Hoff
Denise Hogan
Nikolai Hogset
Bryn Holding
Simon Holgate
Andrew Holland
Grace Holland
Robert Holland
Amy Holland- Rathmill
Damion Holling
Mark Hollingworth
Helen Holmes
John Holmes
Judith Caroline Holmes
Nicholas Holmes
Nicola Holmes
Asbjorn Holmseth
Charlotte Holroyd
Fiona Gaynor Holt
Emma Holwill
Meike Holzmann
Yoko Honda
Daniel Honey
Anthony Hopkins
Daniel Hopkins
Emma Hopkinson
Rebecca Jocelyn Horn
James Hornby
Patrick Hornby
Drew Horner
Rachel Horobin
Adam Horrell
Eirik Horremsbakk
Lewis Horrocks
Sarah Horrocks
Adam Horton
Emma Hothersall
Wibke Hott
Christopher Hough
Nolan Hough
Daniel Houghton
Richard Houghton
Sophie Houghton
Anne-Marie Howard
Caroline Howard
Gareth Howard

Lucy Howard	Suzanne Hyland	Frode Jenssen	Claudia Jones	Richard Kemp
Thomas Howard	Michael Imerson	Hans Jenssen	Kirsten Jorgensen	Michael James Kemsley
Kate Howden	Ingi Ingason	Oyvind Jenssen	Peder Jorgensen	Rolan Kendrick
Peter Howe	Christian Ingebrigtsen	Julia Jeory	Daniel Josman	Erin Kristina Kennedy
Kate Howell	Lindsay Inglesby	Shehnaaz Jinwalla	Trevor Jowett	Olivia Kennedy
Lynette Howell	Sophia Ireland	Michael Joel	Alec Joyce	Steven Kennedy
Jamie Howie	Ben Ireson	Ruby Joelson White	Marec Joyce	Faye Kenny
Rebecca Howley	Nicola Irving	Sadie Joelson White	Luke Juby	Michelle Kenny
Davina Howley	Anna Irwin	Natascha Jogimar	So Jung Kim	Richard Kent
Sophie-Claire Hoyt	Stuart Irwin	Lars Johann	Kevin Jungk	Grace Kenwright
Vadzim Hrom	Hannah Isaacson	Anund Johansen	David Junior	Julia-Ann Kerner
Richard Hrytzak	Shintaro Ishikawa	Ingrid Johns	Jeannette Jurgens	Leigh Kerr
Lisa Jayne Hubbard	Hiroyuki Ishizaka	Arne Johnsen	Lauren Kahn	Siobhan Kerry
Mitchell Hubbard	Katsuki Isomichi	Lydia Johnsen	William Kaibanda Baijukya	John Kershaw
Rebecca Hubbard	Eyal Israel	Alice Johnson	Shimpei Kaiho	Tayfun Kesgin
Tim Hubbard	Taryn Israelsohn	Caitlin Johnson	Sayuri Kaizaki	Joanna Ketley
Alexandra Hudaly	Daniel Istitene	Catherine Johnson	Adama Kamara	Julia Kiepiela
Hannah Hudd	Jin Ito	Gabrielle Johnson	Ragnhild Kambo Grov	Eirik Kiil Saga
Carol Huddleston	Kate Ivory	James Johnson	Sarah Kamender	Colin Neil Kilbride
Martin Hudson	Yuichiro Iwasaki	James Johnson	Sophie Kammann	Harriet Kilburn
Rachel Hudson	Andrew Iwediebo	Jonathan David Johnson	Hadley Kamminga-Peck	Lauren Kilgallon
Simone Hueber	Anthony Jack	Martin Johnson	Rachel Kan	Kory Kilgore
Kaspar Hugentobler	Claire Jackson	Robert Johnson	Chun-Tse Kao	Hyoun Yong Kim
Alexandra Hughes	Damien Jackson	Simon Anthony Johnson	Alex Karatzas	Sam Kim
Ben Hughes	Daniel Jackson	Steven Johnstone	Stefan Kasassoglou	Eve King
Christine Hughes	Emily Jackson	David Jolly	Thomas Kasebacher	Henry King
George Hughes	Emma Jackson	Adam Jones	Christos Katsifas	Paul King
Jade Hughes	Jana Jackson	Alison Jones	Eva Katzler	Scott King
John Hughes	Linus Jackson	Aron Jones	Gavin Kaufman	Timothy King
Katherine Hughes	Nicole Jackson	Bethan Jones	Danielle Kavanagh	Lynne Kingsley
Katie Hughes	Peter Jackson	Bryn Jones	Ellie Kavanagh	Billy Kinnear
Laura Hughes	Rebecca Jackson	Catherine Jones	Laura Kavanagh	Roseanne Kinvig
Matthew Hughes	Samantha Jackson	Catrin Jones	Joseph Kavaney	Ane Kiran
Megan Hughes	Aaron Jacobs	Christopher Jones	Annette Kaviani Nejad	Gareth Kirkham
Neil Hughes	Eden Jacobs	Craig Jones	Lee Kay	Natham Kirkham
Rachael Hughes	Terry Jacobson	David Jones	Megan Kay	Marya Kiselova
Rebecca Hughes	Shazmin Jagot	Elizabeth Jones	Thea Kay	Naoki Kita
James Nicholas Hughes	Florian Jakob	Frederick Jones	Nikki Kaylor	Philippa Kitchen
Nicola Hughes	Nicky James	Gareth Jones	Uzma Kazi	Steven Kitchen
Tracy Anne Hughes	Claire James	Harriet Jones	Christopher Kearney	Donna Kitching
Adrian Hull	Edward James	Jacqueline Jones	Julie Kearney	Shafali Klecka
Ian Humphreys	Juke James	Jon Jones	David Kedward	Stian Kleppa
Mark Humphreys	Nicky James	Katy Jones	Barbara Keenan	Daniel Knapp
Sophia Humphreys	Steven James	Laura Jones	Beverley Keenan	Kayleigh Knight
Ian Hunter	Hailey James-Gannon	Lucy Jones	Judith Kehrle	Kizzy Knight
Joshua Hunter	Melisssa James-Gannon	Mark Jones	Liam Keightley	Tom Knights
Kerry Hunter	Iain Jamieson	Michael Jones	Jonathon Keith	Anthony Knowles
Richard Hunter	Jay Jarvis	Michael Robert Jones	Laura Kellerher-Jefferies	Charlotte Knowles
Allessi - Jade Hunter	Franzeska Jasper	Nicholas Jones	Lucy Kellett	Jason Knowles
Brendan Hurley	Mark Jaynes	Paul Jones	Adam Kelly	Sarah Knowles
Ryan Hustuft	Tracy Anne Jeffery	Paul Jones	Ash Kelly	Tony Knox
Jan Hutchins	Joanna Jeffries	Phillip Jones	Craig Kelly	Lars Wrist Knudsen
Katy Hutchinson	Beat Jegen	Rhianon Jones	Michael Kelly	May-Line Knutsen
Tobias Huthmann	Erlend Jegstad	Richard Jones	Richard Kelly	Michael Koderisch
Lee Hutton	Mark Jenkins	Sam Jones	Sheena Kelly	Saori Koenig
Nina Huxley	Alexander Jennings	Simon Jones	William Kelly	Kathrine Kolgrov
Jeremy Hewell	Luke Jennings	Stephen Jones	Emma Kelsey	Ida Helene Kolsto
Laura Hyde	Henrik Jensen	Tobin Jones	Megan Kelsey	Thomas Kongshavn
Beth Hyland	Rikke Jenson	Zara Jones	Kevin Kemp	Maadhav Kothari

LIPA Students continued

Trusha Kothari
Anthony Kowles
Bojana Kozarevic
Stephen Kreilinger
Virginia Krieg
Laura Krier
Kirsti Kristiansen
Tine Kristiansen
Gunhild Kristoffersen
Sigrid Kristoffersen
Simen Krogstie Lagesen
Susanne Kroll
Ella Kronenburg
Jonas Kroon
Otto Kroymann
Nora Krug
Susanne Kudielka
Nick Kudson-Davies
Stephanie Kuebler
Nadja Kuenstner
Jodie Kumble
Oyvind Kurszus
Sarah Kurth
Taichi Kusaba
Olowaseun Kuti
Kristian Kvael
Benedicte Kvinge
Alexandra Lacey
Anissa Ladjemi
Patrick Ladnier
Stephen Lafferty
Lindy Lafontaine
Christine Lagan
Helen Lainsbury
Neil Lamb
John Lambert
Miriam Lamen
Maria Lancashire
Richard Lancaster
Lo Lance
Ian Lane
Victoria Lane
Holly Langley
Nicholas Langmead
Megan Langton
Sarah Louise Langton
Andrew Lardner-Hickie
Morgan Large
Jedidiah Larkai
Terry Larkey
Anna-Karin Larsen
Kine Larsen
Benjamin Laser
Thomas Latham
Oliver Latka
Michele Lau
Håvard Lauritsen
Peter Lausten
Alex Lavery

Amar Lawal
Samantha Lawler
Zoe Lawler
Amy Lawrence
Clare Lawrence
Gillian Lawrence
Paul Lawrence
Gemma Lawrenson
Anthony Lawson
Dein Lawson
Lee Lawson
Samantha Lawson
Sarah Lawton
Sophia Le Gros
Justin Le Tissier
Geoffrey Lea
India Lea
James Leach
Nicola Lean
Richard Lean
Michael Ledwich
Francesca Lee
Rebecca Lee
Suzanne Lee
Rolf Leer
Mark Leeson
Richard Leeson
Craig Lee-Williams
Olivia Leisk
Philipa Leivesley
Moses Lemngh
Katja Lenihan
Steven Lennon
Michael Lerner
Rachel Leskovac
Jonathan Levi
Hannah Levitt
Colyn Lewin
Daniel Lewin
Chantelle Lewis
David Lewis
David Guy Lewis
Ffion Lewis
Jamie Lewis
Jane Lewis
Jonathan Lewis
Patrick Lewis
Rachel Lewis
Rosalyn Lewis
Tyrone Lewis
Simon Li
Leo Licursi
Cordelia Lieb-Corkish
Christopher Lightfoot
Julia Liles
Leif-Magnus Lilleaas
Delaney Liming
Susan Lincoln
Elizabeth Linden

Paul Lindop
Joanne Lindsay
Kathryn Lindsay
Rachel Lindsay
Jennifer Linley
Benita Lipps
Sturle Lisaeth
Meghan Lisi
Laura Little
Callum Llewllyn
Ann Lloyd
Carrie Lloyd
David Lloyd
James Raymond Lloyd
John Lloyd
Matthew Lloyd
Robin Lloyd
Damien Lloyd-Davies
Fiona Lloyd-Davies
Lance Lo
Selina Lo Neng Fong
Richard Lobb
Alexander Loeseke
Sean Loftus
Heidi Løkken
Camilla Lokvik
Leonida Loli
Julie-Anne Lomas
Elin Lomheim
Emma Longden
Hannah Longman
Thomas Longmate
Gavin Longworth
Richard Loosemore
Lara Lopez Parra
Amy Lord
Matthew Lord
Markku Lorentz
Kate Loughhead
Matthew Loughran
Phillip Loveless
Amy Lovelock
Daniel Lowe
Jonathan Lowe
Rebecca Lowe
Carly Lucas
Oliver Lucas
Annabella Lucy
Christopher Luna
Malcolm Lunan
Aaron Lund
Mikkel Lund
Tine Lund
Lasse Lundberg
Jasmine Lundon
Olivia Lunt
Joanne Lusby
Paddy Luscombe
Holly Anne Lyas

Jon Lyddon
Sigrun Lydsdottir
Paul Lynch
Elizabeth Lynn
Gerald Lynn
Danielle Lyon
Jennifer Lyon
Adam Lyons
Bethany Lythgoe
Cameron Lythgoe
Hayley Lythgoe
Merry Macdonald
Jamie Campbell Macfie
Jade Mackay
Gail Suson Mackinnon
David Mackness
Amy Mackown
Carla Louise Maclean
Ewan Macpherson
Leah Macquarrie
Holly Macrthur
Patricia Madden
Patrick Madden
David Maddock
Matthew Maddock
Emma Madge
Emily Magee
Joseph Magee
Danielle Magowan
Alexander Maguire
Laura Maher
Olivia Maher
Antony Mahoney
Jan Maihorn
Graham Main
Simon Mainwaring
Ishmael Majid
Tim Major
Miho Maki
Qabaniso Malewezi
Ian Mallett
Olivia Mallinson
Faye Malone
Dawn Maloney
Leisa Maloney
Liam Maloney
Line Malvik
Hollie Manchester
Lucy Mangan
Saira Mangat
Nicholas Manley
Suzanne Manley
Stuart Mann
Heidi Manning
Georgia Mansell
Colin Mansfield
Leigh Mansfield
Melissa Maples
Maria Mappouridis

Elizabeth Mapstone
Andrew Laura Marcus
Carlin Margaret
James Margetts
Kate Margretts
James Markey
Leonie Marklew
Kathryn Marley
Michael Marr
Lorna Marsh
Chris Marshall
Jamie Marshall
Scott Marshall
Rebecca Martin
Amanda Martin
Elizabeth Martin
Hannah Martin
Jessica Martin
Nick Martin
Robert Martin
Sarah Ann Martin
Allan Martin
Andrew Martindale
David Martindale
Javier Martinez Maya
Fredrik Martol
Pharis Mashava
Lois Maskall
Joanna Mason
Louisé Mason
Melissa Mason
Talulah Mason
Ian Mason-Jones
Carl Massey
Rosa Masters
Daniel Mather
Raghav Mathurin
Steven Mathurin
Laura-May Mattocks
Julius Mauranen
Samuel Maurice
Neil Mawdsley
Elliot May
Jodie May
Susanne Mayer
Brian Mayfield
Julie Mayor
Nwebo Mba
Tim McAdam
Victoria McAdam
Clare McArdle
Martin McBeath
Samuel McBride
James McBroom
Julie McCabe
Louise Helen McCabe
Lynsey McCaffrey
Laura McCann
Rosanna McCann-Scott

Clare Emmanuel McCardle
Neal McCarthy
Symone McCarthy-Jones
Leanne McCaughey
Katy McClelland
Danielle McCormack
Jayne McCormack
Lyndsey McCormick
Christopher McCourt
Hayley McCowan
Martin McCready
Christopher McCrone
Kevin McCue
Aine McDaid
Kim McDean
Liam McDermott
Paul McDonagh
Alex McDonald
Alison Ruth McDonald
Neil McDonald
Joseph McDonnell
Sam McDonnell
Paul McDonogh
Louise McDonough
Anna-Marie McDougall
Hannah McDowell
Paul McDowell
Lisa McEntire Stokke
Ross McFarlane
Stacy McGahan
John McGee
Anna McGeoch
Heidi McGeough
Sean McGhee
Lee McGinty
Rachael McGivern
Emma McGlacken
Sarah McGrath
Alice McGreevy
Peter McGreevy
Caroline McGuinnes
Eugene McGuinness
Paul McGuinness
Rachael McGuinness
Sabrina McGuinness
Sarah Jayne McGuinness
John McGurgan
Tim McHugh
Jonathan McIldowie
John McIntyre
Kevin McKay
Kevin McKay
Andrew McKenna
Gary McKenna
Kate McKenna
Bradley McKenzie
Brenna McKenzie
Lindsay McKenzie
Clare Patricia McKeon

Charlie McKeown
Laura McKeown
Robyn McKeown
Clare McKinley
Alasdair McKinna
Laura McKinnon-Clark
Jamie McLlachlan
Lucy McLachlan
Laura McLaughlin
Katie McLean
Ryan McLean
Stuart McLean
Dean McLeod
Fiona McLleod
Jennifer McLleod
Michael McLeod
Gail Louise McLlintock
Michael McLoughlin
Michelle McManus
Jocelyn Louise McMillan
Ross McMillan
Keri McNabb
Michael McNamara
Vanessa McNamara
Shona McNeil
Tom McParland
James McWilliam
Adam Meade
Sophie Meadley
Christopher Meara
Chris Meehan
Audun Melbye
Heidi Melgard
Jake Mellor
Neil Mellor
Nicholas Melvin
Grace Menary-Winefield
Franklin Mensah
Jivvel Mensah
Sophie Mercer
Hannah Meredith
Juri Merker
Anthony John Merna
Keith Merner
Ian Merrick
Joanne Merritt
Jordan Metcalf
Andrew Metcalfe
Geoffrey Metcalfe
Jordan Metcalfe
Paul Metcalfe
Ramesh Meyyappan
Christina Michael
Dora Micheals
Patrick Michel
David Mildenberg Posner
David Miles
Hector Miles
Nicola Miles

Christopher Miley
Philip Millburn
Aaron Millen
Adam Miller
Alexander Miller
Georgia Miller
Jasmine Miller
Katie Miller
Edward Millett
Gregg Milligan
Joanne Mills
Deborah Milner
Laura Milns
Ashley Milward
Sang-Yong Min
Erik Minde
Andrea Lesley Minns
Sanaya Minocher-Homji
Emma Minshull
Sergio Minski
Khera Missen
Lee Mitchell
Sarah Mitchell
Scott Mitchell
Russell Mitchison
Philip Mitov
Hakon Moe
Hilde Moe Høiesen
Alan Mogan
Dror Mohar
Sarah Moir
Matthew Moldowan
Philipp Moll
Belinda Mollokwu
Ellie Molloy
Erin Molloy
Grace Molloy
Heidi Molloy
Liam Molloy
Lois Molloy
Paul Molloy
Elizabeth Molloy
Redd Moneypenny-Cole
Scarlette Moneypenny-Cole
Daniel Monk
Darren Monoghan
Luke Montague
Thomas Montgomery
Anna Moody
John Moonan
Alexandra Mooney
Elizabeth Mooney
Linda Mooney
Jason Moor
Paul Moorcroft
Dale Moore
Gary Moore
Kirsty Moore
Ruby Moores

Chloë Moores
Michael Moorhead
Andrew Moorhouse
Helen Moors
Natasha Morais
Sebastian Morawietz
Caleb Morgan
Emma Morgan
James Morgan
Jonathan Morgan
Julie Morgan
Kelly Morgan
Rosemary Morgan
Sophie Morgan
Thomas Morgan
Tracey Morgan
Gabriel Morgan-Munro
Christopher Morland
Rebecca Morrell
Andrew John Morris
Jade Morris
Karla Morris
Rosemary Morris
Sean Morris
Simon Barry Hywell Morris
Suzanne Morris
Andrew Morrisey
Robert Morrison
Richard Michael Morse
Rahel Morten
Espen Mortensen
Russell Morton
Rebecca Moruzzi
Charles Mosesson
Timothy Moss
William Moss
Brogan Moss
Ella Moss
Digby Mothes
Matthew Moxon
Paul Moyes
Natalie Moyse
Adam Muddle
Justin Muir
Clare Mulcahey
Orla Mullan
Russell Mullen
Patrick Muller
Paul Muller
Robert Muller
Christopher Mullin
Lauren Mumby
Brenda Murphy
Christopher Murphy
Eden Murphy
Emily Murphy
Greg Murphy
James Murphy
James Murphy

Jeremiah Murphy
John Murphy
Jon-Paul Murphy
Katie Murphy
Mark Murphy
Matthew Murphy
Richard Murphy
Robert Murphy
Sara Murphy
Sarah Murphy
Christopher Murray
Craig Murray
Lauren Murray
Norman Andrew Murray
Richi Murray
Seán Murray
Jessica Murray
Sophie Muscatelli-Gibson
Adam Muskett
Timothy Mvula
Nicola Naden
Torunn Naevdal
Ayako Nakane
Seiji Nakano
Akiko Nakashima
Andrew Nash
Zoe Naylor
Leagha Naylor
Shaun Naylor
James Neale
Kate Neave
Philip Needle
Scott Negus
Amanda Neild
Rory Nellis
Billy Nelson
Kate Nelson
Mai Nemoto
Birgit Nerheim
Beate Nes
Vegar Nesset
Truls Nesslin
Jon Netton
Dirk Neuhof
Andrew Neve
Gary Nevitt
Amy Newhouse-Smith
Sarah Newman
David Stuart Newman
Jennie Newman
Hannah Newson
Akilah Newton
Amy Newton
Chloe-Rose Newton
Sara Newton
Chloe Nezianya
Eric Ng
Kenneth Nichol
Jason Alan Nicholls

LIPA Students continued

Pip Nicholls
Caroline Joy Nicklin
Ruth Nicoll
Stuart Nicoll
Bernard Niechotz
Liam Niederst
Emilie Niermans
Mio Niikawa
Tord Nikolaisen
Hollie Noades
Valerie Noell
Kieran Noel-Paton
Jurgen Noetzel
Michael Nolan
Michael Noonan
Ellen Noone
Nurhayat Noor Mohamad
Einar Norberg
Alexander Nordgaren
Elisabeth Nordgaren
Ragnhild Nordset
Vidar Norheim
Matthew Ronald Norley
Sara Norlin
Christopher Norman
Michael Norman
Natalie Norman
James Norris
Jonathon Norris
James Norton
Andrew Norwood
Peggy Norwood
Emma Nowell
Helen Nugent
Paul Nulty
Sarah Nunn
Uzo Nwanaga
Laura Nydegger
Linn Nystadnes
Paul O'Para
Rebecca Oakes
Michael Oates
Goran Obad
Andrew Obaka
Dirk Oberlander
Miriam Obrart
Chloë O'Brien
Dashiell O'Brien
Sarah O'Brien
Michelle O' Connell
Catriona O'Connor
Oliver O'Connor
Rachel O'Connor
Thomas O'Connor
Juan Octaviano
Erin O'Dell
Carla O'Donnell
Sandra O'Donovan
Richard O'Dor

Peter Oertl
Michael Ogden
Alan Oglesby
Hannah O'Gorman
John O'Hare
Havard Oieroset
Soile Ojala
Rebecca O'Kane
Erik Okstad
Kelly-Jo O'Leary
Stuart O'Leary
Julian Olivares
Andrew Oliveira
Clare Oliver
David Oliver
Jan Olsen
Bethany Olson
Adeyinka Olushonde
Francesca O'malley
Donna Omar
Paula Omar
Shaun O'Marah
Ryohei Onaga
Mika Onedera
Christopher O'Neil
Erin O'Neill
Claire O'Neill
Lynden Michael O'Neill
Paul Opara
Francesca Ormesher
Hayleigh Ormesher
Michael O'Rourke
Megan Orr
Rachel Orrell
Tim Ortmann
Takashi Osaka
Annie O'Toole
Sean Otty
Terje Overland
Terje Wessel Overland
Tord Overland - Knudsen
Davies Owain
Lucy Owen
Michael Owen
Natalie Owen
Stephen Owen
Timothy Owen
Dafydd Owen-Ellis
Daniel Owens
Olivia Owens
Jeniffer Owens
Patricia Oxley
Andrew Oyeneyin
Frode Oygard
Begum Ozgur
Lynsey Packman
David Pae
Stephanie Paes
Louisa Page

Adam Pain
Alexander Painter
Rebecca Palmer
Jobst Pankok
Kathy Papadopoulos
Sarina Papadopoulos
Sophie Paratte
Scott Pardue
Jennifer Park
Anne-Margaret Parker
James Parker
Jennifer Parker
Louise Parker
Victoria Parker
James Parkes
Jenny Parkinson
Amy Parkinson
Luke Parkinson
Sam Parkinson
Amie Parle
Kate Parle
Leanne Parle
Bhavna Parmar
Chris Parmar
Stephanie Parr
Lee Parry
Richard Parry
Rachael Parry
Rachel Parsons
Sophie Partridge
Dijwar Pasary
Katja Pasquini
Stefan Pasternak
Daniel Pate
Alpnaben Patel
Graham Paterson
Carly Paton
Liam Paton
Andrew Patterson
Steven Patterson
Paige Patterson
Christian Pattinson
Simon Paul
Tiffany Paul
Paula Paulou-Andreaou
Didrik Paulsen
Daniel Pawlowski
Amanda Pearson
Daniel Pearson
Gemma Pearson
Mark Pearson
Steven Pearson
Hannah Peel
Regina Peldszus
Lee Pell
Nicholas Pemberton
Anthony Pendlebury
Adam Christopher Penford
James Pengelly

Karl Penney
James Penter
Faye Penton
Anna Percival
Mark Percy
Heather Perkins
Nathaniel Perkins
Rhea Perkins
Kristina Perner
Nicholas Perry
Mia Perry
Kathryne Anne Peters
Gemma Petrie
Michelle Petrie
Lasse Pettersen
Katrin Pettersson
Joel Phelan
Roy Philips
Tom Philips
Andrew Phillips
Christopher Phillips
Lauren Phillips
Peter Phillips
Rebecca Phillips
Roy Phillips
Sian Phillips
Thomas Phillips
Macimum Pichilingi
David Picken
Simon Pickerill
Adam Pickering
Andrew Pickering
Danica Pickett
David Pickford-Wardle
John Pickup
Alison Pike
Stacey Pike
Adam Pilarski
Charlotte Pimlott
Andrew Pinchin
Tilo Pirnbaum
Daniel Piscina
Kathryn Pitchford
Harriet Pittard
Ulrike Pittroff
Ruth Plater
Jonathan Platt
Andrew Platts
Julia Pledl
Mark Plonsky
Stephanie Pointon
Scott Poley
Sian Lovisa Polhill-Thomas
Daryl Pollard
Alexandra Pomelova
Daniel Pook
Robert Pook
Simon Poole
Tom Poole-Kerr

Richard Popple
Dawn Porter
Jade Porter
Paul Porter
Sebastian Portillo
Thomas Portman
Veronica Posse
Liam Potter
Christa Powell
Emma Powell
Jessica Powell
Tatum Powell
Gary Power
Alastair Powers
Lindsey Powling
Stephanie Powling
Stephen Poynton
Owen Pratt
Clare Prendergast
Gillian Prendergast
Michael Prest
Daniel Price
Natasha Price
Rachel Price
Megan Price
Stuart Price
James Pridgeon
Marianne Prinelle
Noel Prior
Mathew Pritchard
Sean Pritchard
Sally Proctor
Samuel Proctor
Virginia Prout
Clare Prudence
Delroy Prussia
Christopher Pugh
David Pugh
Lydia Pugh
Ray Pulling
Keren Pullinger
Pino Pumilia
Lene Puntervold
David Purcell
Simon Pursehouse
Duncan Purvis
Susan Quick
Amanda Quigley
Ema Quinn
Matthew Quinn
Kelly Quintyne
Jonas Raabe
Wolf Erik Rahlfs
Sazzadur Rahman
Alvaro Ramirez
Paul Ramsden
Tamsin Randall
Michael Randle
Sarah Randle

Lee Range
Daniel Rankin
Samira Rankin
Sally Elizabeth Raper
David Ratchford
Leanne Rathore
Connor William Ratliff
James Rawlinson
Michael Ray
Rachel Raymond
Stephen Rayner
Nicholas Raynor
Richard Reardon
Brime Reatus
Anthony Reber
Peter Reckenfelderbaeumer
Gary Reddock
Leah Reddy
Stephen Redfern
Eleanor Redhead
Laura Redhead
Jayne Reed
Richard Reeday
Matthew Reekie
Thomas Reemer
Katy Anne Reeves
Alex Reid
Andrew Mark Reid
Stuart Reid
Emma Reid
Erik Reiff
Cynthia Remolina Gutierrez
Rebecca Rennison
Annie Reppe
Sophie Reynolds
Carys Reynolds
Edward Reynolds
Emily Reynolds
John Reynolds
Sophie Reynolds
Michael Rhea
Andrew Rhymes
Alexandra Rice
Christopher Rice
Laura Richards
Gavin Richards
Hannah Richards
Kate Richards
Kimberley Richards
Matthew Richards
Carl Richardson
Damon Richardson
Dawn Richardson
Jamie Richardson
Patrick Richardson
Vanessa Richardson
Marlene Richter
Lauren Ricketts
Zoe Riding

Charlotte Rigby
Dean Rigby
Johnathan Rigby
Andrew Rigg
Laura Rikard
Aidan Riley
Alyssa Riley
Andrew Riley
Edward Riley
Jane Riley
Kent Riley
Stephanie Rimmer
Joseph-Jacques Rio
Faye Riozzi
Zoe Riozzi
Isaac Rischer
Mark David Robbins
Beth Roberts
Alice Roberts
Amelia Roberts
Andrew Roberts
Christina Roberts
Daniel Roberts
Dylan Gwilym Roberts
Elizabeth Roberts
Ellie Roberts
Felicity Roberts
George Roberts
Justin Roberts
Philip Roberts
Rebekah-Anne Roberts
Joanne Roberts-Cullinan
Jason Robertshaw
Skye Roberts-Nurse
Lee Robertson
Molly Anne Robertson
Michael Robins
Heidi Robinson
Ben Robinson
Danielle Robinson
Harry Robinson
Irene Robinson
Louise Robinson
Marianne Robinson
Richie Robinson
Justin Roche
Paul Rock
Hannah Rockcliffe
Amanda Rodger
Nadeen Rodgers
Natalie Rodgers
Rocky Rodriguez Jr
Eva Roessler
Autumn Rogers
Christopher Rogers
Hope Rogers
William Rogers
Gwen Rogerson
James Rogerson

Oliver Roll
Rita Rometsch
Philip Ronayne
Maria Maaiyaan Ronen
Paul Rose
Meriel Rosenkranz
John Ross
Abigail Rosser
Christopher Rosser
Chloe Rossiter
Eva Rößler
Christopher Rothwell
Mark Rowan
Hannah Rowbottom
Andrew Rowe
Nicola Rowe
Simon Rowe
Tim Paul Rowland
Mark Rowland
Claire Rowlands
Katrina Rowley
Rachel Rowlinson
Lucy Rowse
Neil Roxburgh
Martin Royle
Ase Røyset
Alistair Ruddick
Leroy Ruglass
Siyao Rui
Jan Rule
Jan Runge
Tina Rupp
Helen Rushforth
Liz Russ
Alexandra Russell
Amy Russell
Nathan Russell
Natalie Russo
Amie Rutherford
Scartlett Rutherford
Chloe Rutter
Andreas Ruuska
Abi'j Ryan
Anthony Ryan
Charlie Ryan
Jacob Ryan
Lucy Ryan
Michael Ryan
Olivia Ryan
William Ryan
Rachel Ryder
Rebecca Ryder
Simon Ryder
Mocci Ryen
Christopher Rygh
Evy-Marie Rygh
Peter Saba
Kyrre Sæther
Christopher Sagar

Harprit Sahota
Julie Salater
Andrew Salida
Zain Salim
Peter Salmang
Tom Salmon
Tony Salter
Hug Salval Torregrossa
Hakeem Samari
Chelsea Sampson
David Edmund Sampson
Emily Sampson
George Sampson
Rosie Sampson
David Samwell
Rachel Sandbach
Jessica Sandbrook
James Sanders
Philip Sanders
Maria Sanderson
Nicky Sanderson
Samantha Sanderson
Wayne Sanderson
Sondre Sandhaug
Jonathon Sands
Jagdev Sanghera
Singh Sanghera
Lily Sanlon
Christopher Sansom
Ben David Sansum
Keshia Santos
Robin Sato
David Sattar
Silke Sauer
David Saunders
Lauren Saunders
Victoria Saunders
Nick Saunderson
Laura Savage
Shaun Savage
Genevieve Say
Laura Sayles
Grace Scanlon
Robert Scanlon
Nicole Scantlebury
Christopher Schaper
Florentine Schara
Samantha Schefele
Bettina Scheibe
Inga Schenck
Dominik Schirmer
Roland Schmidlin
Robin Schmidt
Martin Schmitt
Antonia Schmitz
Matthew Schmolle
Simon Schofield
Thomas Schofield
Daniel Scholes

Ingrid Scholes
Stefanie Schoroeder
Michael Schrant
Holly Schroeder
Xenia Amelie Schuerer
Anna Schulte
Juliane Avelina Schulz-Gibbins
Volker Schuster
Kristoffer Schwarz
Anne Scott
Dean Scott
Nathalie Scott
Pauline Scott
Ross Scott
Johann Scoular
Sophie Scragg
Melanie Seagrave
Natasha Seale
Rebecca Angharad Seale
John Sealey
Sheena Sear
Andrew Searle-Barnes
David Searson
Carl Seary
India Seavor
James Secker
Kevin Seeby
Mia Sefia
Jude Sefton
Mika Seger
Joanne Seggie
Tamasine Seibold
Beatrice Seidt
Daniel Semple
Armin Bodo Sengenberger
Daniel Sepke
Harry Serjeant
Leon Seth
Ben Sewell
Michael Sewell
Matthew Sewell-Rutter
Helen Seymour
Jodie Seymour
Francis Shacklady
Tariq Shah
Daniel Shales
Lisa Shannen
David Shannon
Rori Shapiro
Michael Sharman
Peter Sharman
Kirsten Sharp
Wayne Sharples
Adam Shaw
David Shaw
Jonathan Shaw
Robert Shaw
Lauren Shearing
Rachel Shedwick

LIPA Students continued

Nicholas Sheedy
Carla Sheldon
Catriona Shenton
Denise Shepherd
Christopher Sheppard
Emily Sheridan
Fintan Shevlin
Peter Shewell
Yan Shi
Jaqueline Shiel
Carla Shield
Samantha Shields
Cassidy Shipley
Joseph Shooman
John Shortell
Christopher Shrimpton
Lee Shrimpton
Kieran Shudall
Peter Siawson
Nicky Siebert
Jay Sikora
Ian Sillett
Michael Silverman
Ioannis Simantiris
Brandon Simmons
Marius Simonsen
Emma Simpson
Laura Simpson
Sophie Simpson
Andrea Dawn Sims
Emma Sinclair
Nicola Jane Sinclair
Mick Singh
Hannah Singleton
Stephanie Singleton
Helle Singsaas
Amy Siu
Jodie Siu
Sophie Siu
Martin Sjolie
Brita Skare Malvik
Silje Skaugen Karlsen
Sigrid Skeie Tjensvoll
Karen Skilling
Adam Skinner
Daniel Skinner
Djamila Skoglund-Voss
Sunniva Skorve
Asmund Skuterud
Adele Slachmuylders
Kelly Slack
Edward Slaney
Carol Slattery
Peter Slawson
Olivia Sloyan
Joshua Smales
Michelle Smikle
Adam Smith
Andrew Smith

Andrew Smith
Bradley Smith
Celia Smith
Charlene Smith
Cherie Smith
Christopher Smith
Craig Smith
David Smith
Ellie Smith
Emily Smith
Gemma Smith
Hayley Smith
Helen Smith
Janine Smith
Jay Smith
John Smith
Lauren Smith
Matthew Smith
Michael Smith
Nicola Smith
Rebecca Smith
Richard Smith
Robert Smith
Stephanie Smith
Stevie Smith
Nick Smitton
Franziska Smolarek
Jennifer Snart
Kathryn Sneade
Aaron Snyder
Jennifer Soddy
Audun Søgnen
Robin Sohrabi-Shiraz
Merete Solli
Kerry Solway
Peter Somerville
Alex Song
Michael Soo
Sean Sorby
Maximilian Souchay
Mike South
Michael Peter Southern
Natalie Southern
Lauren Southwick
Jessica Spalis
Jennifer Sparrow
Duncan Speakman
Chris Spear
Marc Specter
Thomas Speight
John Speirs
Alexander Spencer
Gareth Spencer
Sara Spencer
Christopher Spencer-Jones
Jacqueline Spicknell
Timothy Spilman
Georg Spindler
Michael Spink

Gavin Barrie Spokes
Alexander Spreadbury
Daniel Sproston
Karolina Spyrou
Mark Staines
Lindsey Stainthorpe
Jesse Stainton
Neil Stainton
Paul Stakounis
Gemma Stansfield
Andreas Star
Sally Starborg
Andrew Stark
Darryal Stark
Charlotte Stark-Stevens
Benjamin Stead
Mark Stedmond
Rebecca Steel
Donna Lisa Steele
Christopher Stefanciw
Miroslav Stefanovic
Jan Stegemann
Christine Steinmetz
Siri Steinmo
Melanie Stenhouse
Andrew Stephenson
Chiara Stephenson
Ryan John Adam Stephenson
Emma Lucy Stevens
Gayle Stevens
Jack Stevens
Jenna Louise Stevens
Victoria Stevens
Rebecca Stevenson
Ben Stevenson
Robert Stevenson
Charlotte Stewart
Craig Stewart
Harley Stewart
Stephen Stewart
Stuart Stirland
Nicholas Stirling
Chloe Stoakes
Gary Stock
Paul Stocker
Jodie Anne Stockwell
Katy Ellen Stone
Annabel Stoops
Rachel Storey
David Stothard
Kate Stothert
Ben Stott
Charlotte Stott
Rachael Stott
Anna Stranack
Oyvind Strandem
Marianne Stranger
William Stratton
Christian Straukamp

Peter Street
Robert Strefford
Justin Stretch
Vibeke Strom
Vegard Stromsodd
Paul Stroud
Laura Stubbings
Javier Suarez
Darren Suarez
Ashley Suddaby
Ozgur Sulak
Naomi Sumner
Paul Sun
Camilla Sunde
Katie Sunderalingam
Marc Sunderland
Claire Sundin
Bekkie Sunley
Anton Süß
Giles Sutton
Hanna Sutton
Hanna Suzuki
Jodie Svagr
Kristian Sveholm
Shannon Swain
Nicola Swales
Hazel Swann
Paul Swanton
Alyssa Swanzey
Emma Sweeney
Hannah Sweeney
Jason Sweeney
Katie Sweeney
Shakira Sweeney
Dean Swift
Edward Swift
George Sykes
Mark Sykes
Jack Sylvester
Samuel Sylvester
Zachary Sylvester
Zebedee Sylvester
Kim Syvret
Jasmine Ta
Robin Tabari
Lisa Taeter
Ingvild Tafjord
Beccy Taggart
Elizabeth Taker
Gerard-Lee Talbot
Yoshio Tamamura
Matthew Tanner
Stephen Tapscott
Eirin Taraldsvik
Ben Tarbard
Jonathan Tarr
Reuben Tasker
Annette Taubmann
Jennifer Taylor

Adam Taylor
Alice Taylor
Amber Taylor
Barnaby Taylor
Christopher Taylor
David Taylor
Frank Taylor
Leah Taylor
Oliver Taylor
Rachael Taylor
Richard Taylor
Robert Taylor
Tania Taylor
Rachael Taylor
Pascal Tchakouté
Lawrence Telford
Clair Templeton
David Tench
Matthew Tennie
David Terry
Joshua Terry
Cecilie Testman
Mathias Thamhain
Jonas Theis
Alexandria Thom
Chris Thom
James Thomas
Victoria Thomas
Christine Thomas
Craig Thomas
Kyle Thomas
Mark Thomas
Morgan Thomas
Neil Thomas
Owen Thomas
Matthew Thomason
Alex Thompson
Christopher Thompson
David Thompson
Donna Thompson
Gareth Thompson
Jamie Thompson
Jessica Thompson
John Thompson
Jon Thompson
Julie Thompson
Laura Anne Thompson
Mark Thompson
Matthew Anthony Thompson
Peter Thompson
Rachel Thompson
Robert Thompson
Simon Thompson
Sophie Thompson
Stephanie Thompson
Terri Thompson
Theo Thompson
Tia Thompson
Craig Thomson

Roger Thomson
Stephanie Thomson
Elanor Thornhill
Jennifer Thornton
Ellie Thornton
Lindsay Thornton
Chris Thorpe
Joanne Thorpe
Stine Thorsen
Ian Threlfall
Kirsty Tibbetts
Thomas Tichai
Joe Tierney
Stephen Tierney
Joe Tighe
Grant Tilbury
Robert Tilsley
William Tisdale
Rebecca Tjimbawe
Peter Todd
Stuart Todd
Lene Toje
Diane Tomasi
Kyle Tomkins
Ian Tomlinson
Lisa Ann Tomlinson
Paul Tomlinson
Trenton Tomlinson
Paul Tong
Joanna Toop
Jamie Tosh
Roy Tough
Ryan Towers
Ewan Townhead
Annamarie Townsend
Anthony Townsend
Lisa Marie Tremarco
Victoria Tremlin
Matthew Trethawey
Chiara Treves
Emma-Jane Trivett
Paul Tsanos
Takaya Tea Tea Tsukuda
Lucinda Tucker
George Tudor-Williams
Oliver Tuercke
Jessica Tully
Thomas Tunney
Kristin Tunold-Hanssen
Richard Tunstall
Joanna Turbitt
Elizabeth Turley
Scott Turnbull
Anthony Turner
Diane Turner
Luke Turner
Ronald Turner
Richard Turvey
Mari Tvede Lunde

Phil Tweedle
Andrea Tynan
Philip Tyreman
David Tyrrell
Stephanie Tyrrell
Mayuko Uekita
Hajime Ueoka
Hallvard Ugland
Corinne Ullrich
Yoji Umetsu
Samantha Underhill
Ingvild Vaagsether
Bence Vagi
Ben Vale
Maria Valencia
Lena Valla
Rachel Vallance
Ian Van De Waal
Aslak Van Der Lubbe
Elizabeth Van Dooren
Nashwa Van Flute
Peter Van Neste
Rebecca Van Netton
Jens Van Slooten
Karen Louise Vanross
Katharine Varatharajah
Rebecca Varatharajah
Serena Varatharajah
David Vardy
Ruth Varley
John Varney
Arne Vatnoy
Emma Lucy Vaudrey
Ali Vaughan
James Veitch
Nicholas Venceil
Celia Vergara Guerra
Adam Vernon
Jane Veysey
Heather Vickers
Mark Vina
Alexandra Vincent
Robin Vincent
Matthew Vines
Emily Clare Voelker
Fredric Vogel
Kjell Volle Knutsen
Sebastian Von Bischopink
Maya Vovnik
Shai Vure
Johan Wadsten
Signhild Wærsted
Hilde Wahl
Joseph Wainwright
Siri Walberg
Fran Walden-Jones
Alwyn Walker
Andrew David Walker
Django Walker

Isabel Walker
Jayne Walker
Juliette Walker
Lee Walker
Oliver Walker
Paula Walker
Rachel Walker
Valerie Walker
Claire Walls
Matthew Walls
Andrew Walmsley
Barry Walsh
Catherine Walsh
Kathryn Walsh
Laura Walsh
Martin Walsh
Ryan Walsh
Charlotte Walters
Mishell-Ivon Walton
Rachel Walton
Birgitte Wang
Mareike Wang
Christopher Warburton
Helen Ward
Jonathan Ward
Martin Ward
Rachel Ward
Stuart Ward
Nicholas Wardle
Esther Wareham
Paul Wareing
Rachel Wareing
Dawneey Warren
Kerry Warren
Natasha Warren
Dawn Warriner
Mark Warwick
Sean Waters
Angharad Watkeys
Kirsty Watling
Jamie Watson
Peter Watson
Rosalind Watson
Samuel Watson
Simon Watterton
Vanessa Watts
Tim Way
Harriet Webb
Karl Webb
Abbi Webster
Paul Webster
Philip Webster
Rachel Louise Webster
Simon Webster
Teo Wedel
Dyveke Wedel Kuloy
Alison Weedall
Natascha Wegerer
Paul Weichart

Mo Anton Weisskopf
Are Weisten
Chloe Welch
Christopher Welford
Katharine Welland
Robert Wellings
Nicholas Wells
Emma Welsby
Andrew Welsh
Daniel Welsh
Robyn Welsh
Monika Wenke
James Went
Silje Wergeland
Samantha Wesley
Charlotte West
Michael West
Kyle Western
Christopher Weston
Keith Weston
Anthony Wexler
Michael Wharton
Alice Wharton
Laura Wheatley
Clifford Wheeler
Caitlin Whelan
Kathryn Whelan
Christopher Wherely
Sion Whiley
Brennan Whitaker
Simon Whitby
Elizabeth White
Katherine White
Philip White
Stephanie White
Katie Whitehead
Christopher Whitehouse
Robert Whiteley
Tom Whitelock
Kerry Whiteside
Craig Whitfield
Gemma Whitfield
Christian Whitlock
Joseph Whitlow
James Whitmarsh
Craig Whittaker
Dee-Ann Whittle
Mark Whyte
Rebecca Whyte
Scott Wiber
German Wider
Andrew Wierzan
Stephen Wignall
Nicola Wilce
Martin Wilde
Greig Wilding
Helen Wilding
Angelika Wildt
Annette Wilkes

Christopher Wilkes
Paul Wilkes
Alex Wilkinson
Daniel Wilkinson
Phil Wilkinson
Sarah Wilkinson
Christopher Willcock
Rachel Williams
Alex Williams
Alison Williams
Andrew Williams
Angela Williams
Bartholomew Williams
Chloe Williams
Claire Esther Williams
Dale Williams
Daniel Williams
David Williams
Diana Williams
Gareth Williams
George James Williams
Glyn Williams
Jack Williams
James Williams
Jenny Williams
Jorinde Williams
Joshua Williams
Kate Williams
Kelsey Williams
Michael Williams
Tudor Williams
Zachary Williams
Kirk Williamson
Mark Williamson
Emily Williamson
Heláena Williamson
Meg Williamson
Kathryn Willis
Melanie Willis
Gerd Willschutz
Andrew Wilson
Bryan Wilson
Carolyn Wilson
Edward Wilson
Emma Wilson
Helen Wilson
Ian Wilson
James Wilson
Joanne Wilson
John Wilson
John Wilson
Samantha Wilson
Helen Wilson
Kaspar Wimberley
Paul Win
Sonny Winder-Rodgers
Ingrid Windsland
Claire Windsor
Jeremy Wing

LIPA Students continued

Nils Wingerei
Sarah Winkler
Alan Winstanley
Emma Winterbourne
Hayley Winters
Darren Winwood
Ragnhild Wisloff
Simon Withenshaw
Boris Witzenfeld
Phillip Wolfel
Marie-Francoise Wolff
Alexandra Wolkowicz
Lynsey Wollaston
Katherine Wolley
Justin Wong
Rachael Wood

Russell Wood
Craig Woodall
Claire Woodcock
Darren Woodcock
Ariel Woodiwiss
Craig Woodrow
Martin Woods
Daniel Woodward
Jessica Wooley
Ashley Woolfson
William Worgan
Sandy Worm
Andrew Worral
Barry Worrall
Raymond Wortel
Sonya Wratten

Amy Wray
Clare Patricia Wreath
Alex Wright
Andrew Wright
Anthony Wright
Cathy Wright
Christopher Wright
Craig Wright
Marcus Wright
Matthew Wright
Thomas Wright
Wayne Wright
Shan Shan Wu
Kevin Wun
Christopher Wyles
Katie Wymark

Rachel Wynn
Charlotte Wynne
Patrick Wyss
Dai Yajmia
Daisuke Yamashita
Anthony Yassin
Anne Theresa Yates
Iris Yates
Lucy Yates
Paul Yates
Gareth Yearley
Thomas Yeates
Jeff Yellen
Silvana Yemm
Mandy Yeo
Sam York

Greg Young
Thomas Young
Victoria Young
Anette Ystgaard
Sarah Yule
Henning Zacher
Michael Zawadzki
Juan Zelada
Rene Zensen
Marcus Ziegenrucker
Gerd Zinsmeister
Zoe Zinsmeister
Nadia Zuberi
Ariana Zwozdesky

THE PAUL McCARTNEY AUDITORIUM

10cc
Graeme Gouldman
Mark D Ackerma
Paul Adams
Mike & Marsha Adnot
Linda Aiello
Dale Akaki
Daniel Albertson
Edith Anderson
Warren & Jenny Anderson
Gina Ando
Hitomi Ando
Yoshika Andoo
Carol Angell
Brenda & Neil Angwin
Apple Corps
Kazuhiro Arakawa
Dale Araki
Clint Ard
Denise Ard
Hanako Ariyoshi
Hiroshi Ariyoshi
Momoko Ariyoshi
Teruko Ariyoshi
Utako Ariyoshi
Joan Armatrading
Arts Council of Great Britain
Tomoyo Asai
Yukie Asam
ASCAP
Lord Ashdown Charitable Trust
Mark Asperti
Association for Quality &
Participation
K.P. Atherton
Mary Aultice
Naomi Awa
Kazuko Awaji
David Backhouse
Baillie Gifford & Co
Geoff Baker
Janice Baker
Mark Baker
Wayne & Lisa Baker
Ivan Barrow
John Barton
Laurence Bascle
Batesville Veterinary Clinic
BBC Books
BBC Enterprises Corporation
D.Schultz of the
Beatles Club Wuppertal

Maureen Lowry of
Beatles Fans Unite
Betty Lou
& Lauren Beatty
Monica Beck-Simon
Ian Bell
Sharon Bell
Genie Benson
Penny Benz
Ivan Bergamini
Steve Lipman of
Berklee College of Music
Jack Berry
Neil & Michelle Bethrens
Vincent Betremieux
Uta Beuthien
J. P. Bevan
Mark Beyer
Mark Bhaty
Linda Bhaty
Simone Bianch
Biblios Publishers' Distribution
Services Ltd
Vladimiro Bibolotti
A & C Black
Thomas Blewett
Kelvin P Blinston
BMG Music Publishing
BMG Records
Michael Bohn
Gerhard Bohrer
Agnes Bojsza
David Booth
Martin Booth
Ronald Borgon
of Bootleg Beatles
Maurizio dal Borgo
Michael Borries
Sue Boss
Angela & Gloria Bossio
Rachel & John Bowes
Craig Boyer
BPI Ltd
Denise Brailey
Ginger Brannon
Rachel Bremlist
British Gas Plc (North
Western)
British Journal of Aesthetics
Broadcast Music Industries
Julia Brook
Larry Buckla

BUKO
Bart Bullock
Dave & Sheila Bullock
Julie Ann Bullock
Rocco Buonvino
David Burdus
Paul Buswell
Rob & Leonie Butler
Butterworth-Heinemann
Gregg & Dee Byers
Jerrad Lennon Byers
Rita Byrne
Cindy Cabra
Peter Caiaf
Sheila Caldwell
Alan Calleja
Frank Calli
Donna & Terry Campbell
Colin H Reineck
of the Carroll Foundation
Tom Carswell
Hal Carter
Nicholas Carter
Hilary Carter
Hal Carter Organisation
Gregg Casey
Bruno Caspar
Cassell Ltd
Claudio Castagnino
Maria Castro
Tony Catalano
The Cavern
Cavern City Tours
CBS Records Limited
Marcia Cebula
Mary Ann Cedro
Giuseppe Celenza
Centaur Publishing
William Cermak
Rachel Chadwick
Karen Challis
Jayni & Chevy Chase
Jeffrey Chesters
Mary K. Chestnut
Liz Cheyney
Susumu Chiba
Sal Chieto
Jane Chivari
Stuart Christie
Chrysalis Group Plc
Risty Ciarcelli
Stefano Cicchetta

Deborah Kelly of Cigna
Healthplan of NJ.
R. J. Clare
The Clarence Foundation
Brian Clarke
Pat Clingly
CM Artists
Andrew Cobb
Thomas Coen
M. Coffey
Alan Colgan
Claudio Colle
Graham Collier
Andrew Collinge Hair Salons
Jean Collins
Commission for Racial
Equality Publishing
Neil & Dot Conaghty
Condé Nast Publications
Mike Connaris
Paul Conroy
Warren & Jenny Cook
Chery Cooke
Ron, Kyle, Alex
& Jeffrey Cormier
Davis & Diane Cosey
Elvis Costello
Sue Cotton on behalf
of Henry E. Cotton
Courage Ltd
Richard & Jo Court
Alan Cowell
Bea Cox
Tim Cox
Crafts Council
Creative Review
Lisa Hurley of Creative Works
John Crichton
Patricia Crichton
Tony Crisafio
Lolly Cross
Suzie & Gregg Cross
Elisabetta Crovoto
Francesca Crovoto
Ron Cumberland
Fred Curley
Paul Curran
Mark D'Angelis
Robin D'Arcy
Jim D'Asceneo
Robert D'Ella
Anne-Marie DaGraca

Douglas Dale Chartered
Accountants
Brian Daly
Russell & Lori Dameron
Mike & Cindy Daniels
Eveline Danino
Richard Daoud
Astrid Dapra
Ian Darlington
Bill & Mary Dassel
Herschel & Dorothy Dassel
Datateam Publishing Ltd
George Davies
June Davies
N.J. & E.F. Davies
Robert Davies
George Davies Partnership plc
Nelya Davila
Dr. Lawrence Davis
Dr. Randall Davis
Graham & Pauline Day
Russell Daye
John Deacon
Elizabeth Deaton
Ed & Donna DeGrau
Dennis DeHart
Mark Delanoy
Lisa Delfulvio
Debbie Dempsey
Design Council
Valeri Despre
Jenny & Richard Devenish
James Dickson
Marylou Dieringer
Ralph C. DiFronzo
James Dimmock
The Walt Disney Company
Peter Dixon
Tomoe Doi
Carolynne Dougherty
Patrick Dowling
Robert Downs
Jan Doyle
Nicole Drake
Oscar & Roselyn Drescher
Donald Dresser
Volker Drews
Richard Driessen
Cynthia Duff
Joanne Dunn
Richard Dunstrude
Jaqueline Dutton

Donors continued

Robert Dvorak
John Eastman
Eastman & Eastman
Chikara Ebisu
Marion Eckerle
The Economist
Michael Eddins
Ede & Ravenscroft
Leesa Edmonds
Peter Eggerstein
N. Eiko
Lilly Ekberg
Lennart & Ute Eklund
Nigel Elderton
Tracey Ellerton
Tani Ellis
Vivian Ellis
EMAP Metro Publications
Peter Reichardt
EMI Music Publishing
Therese Emken
Melanie Eng
Peggy English
Queenie Epstein
Florence Eskin
Esquire Magazine
Oliver Etzkorn
Evans Brothers
Sumie S. Ezaki
Faber & Faber
John Fairclough
John Falk
Brigitte Unger Soyka –
Ministerium for Famile Frauen,
Weiterbidung und Kunst
Francis Fane
Mick Farley
Roy & Debbie Farr
Evy Featherstone-Witty
Mark Featherstone-Witty
Peter & Jenny Fegredo
Caren Felzer
Rick Fenn
G. P. Fennell
Caroline Ferraro
David Denton Fethers
Laurie Fidler
Scott Fisher
Ariel Figueiras Flavio
Charlie & Debbie Flemming
E. S. Fletcher
F-Multi Media
Jane Fonda
Fonda Films Inc.
A. G. Foote
Noela Foote
Noel Forth
Elizabeth I Foster
Mark Foster

Sir Norman Foster & Partners
Foundation for Sport
& the Arts
Fountain Press
Lowell Fowler
Michael F. Fox
Michael Fox Inc.
Christian Wiedem of
Frankfurter Film Produktion
Don Fraser
Scott Freauf
Free Association Books
Michael Freegard
Samuel French
Herb Siegel of the Friars
Foundation
The Rt. Hon. Lord Jenkin of
Roding For Friends Provident
Christian Frietsch
Teresa Fritsch
Jennifer & Nigel Fry
Hikari Fujii
Setsuko Fujimori
Yuko Fujita
Yukie Fukuoka
George Furrie
Jennie Furrie
Rita Furtner
Michiko Furuta
Keith Leary - Game Audio
Jane & Derek Gascoigne
Christine Gattiker
Kam Gatz
Kelvin Geck
Robin Gehrke
Ron Germeaux
Shelley & Ron Germeaux
Katherine Gethin
Lynda Gilbert
William Giles
Barbara R. Gionfriddo
Roberto Girlanda
Girobank Plc
Sylvia Giustina
John & Edie Glenn
Joan Glover (on behalf of the
family of J. Fethers)
Amy & Paul Goldschmidt
Jose Anibal Gomez
Ilean Gonzalez
Sir Donald Gosling – The
Gosling Foundation
Matt Goss
Erii J. Goto
GQ Magazine
Sylvia Grade
Bonni & Tom Granato
Teresa Grant
Grant Thornton

Graphics World
Mrs. L. A. Gray
Beryl & Victor Greenberg
of Greenberg Glass
Glen Greenway
Martin Greil
P. T Griffin
Russell Griffiths
Ted Griffiths
Connie Grillo
John Groves – Music Makers
Grundig AG
Jurgen Grunk
Guardian Royal Exchange
Charitable Trust
Guinness Publishing
Kazue Gunji
Hans-Peter Gutzeit
Michael & Sonia Guzzardi
Donna & Glen Haar
Rainer Haas
Julie A. Hagan
Sharon C. Hale
Helge Halkjelsvik
Margaret Hall
Mike Hall
Hall & Company
K. Hallberg
Minori Hamada
Sanae Hamada
Tetsuo Hamada
Takashi Hamazaki
Bruce Hamlin
John Hammel
Mariko Hanaoka
Sharon & Mostyn Hancock
Ellanor & Peter Handley
Hard Rock Café
Chris Hargreaves
Harman Pro Group
Harrap
E.C. Harris Project
Management
Olivia & George Harrison
Mr. Hartman
Harvard University Press
Keiko Hasegawa
Grant Hattam
John & Kori Hay
H. Hayasaka
TadaoHayashi
Jane Hayman
Simon & Bronwyn Heath
Scott Heezen
Gary M. Hein
Lieselotte Hein
Heinemann Educational
Mary Lynne Helier
Colin Henry

Delores Hensley
Helene & Steve Herman
Peter Hewett
Chikako Hide
High End Systems Texas Inc.
Kevin Higley
Kan-Ichiro Hikichi
Hillsdown Holdings Plc
Tomiko Hino
Ikumi Joanna Hirano
Jun Hirao
Kiyoko Hirayama
N.Hiromi
Kanji Hiroti
Yoshiaki Hisako
Hobart Manufacturing Co.
David Hockney
Larry Hodgen
Paul & Michael Hodgen
Helmut Hoefle
Mikael Hojris
Roger Appleton & Alison
Holbourn
Bill Hollowell
Hollyoaks Production Co.
Jackie Holmes
Julian Holt Charitable Trust
P Holt Charitable Trust
Debbie & Jim Holtsclaw
Steve Hooper
Joanna Horgan
Kate Horgan
Noriko Horiuchi
Kevin & Denise Houser
Hayes Howsley
Barbara Hoyle
Mark Hudgens
Susan Hudson
Vincent Hugg
Gregg Hurnall
Steve Hutchinson
Nobukazu Igarashi
YukariIgarashi
Hiroyuki Ikeba
David Inman
Hanako Inoue
Kengo Inoue
International Creative
Management
International Music
Publications
The Ireland Fund
of Great Britain
Mitsue Isobe
Genichi Ita
Harumi Ita
Masako Ita
Mitsuo Itoh
Wendi Jankowitz

Jill Jarrett-Waingrow
Leigh Jenssen
Gary Jergler
Billy Joel
Elton John
Penny & Fred Johnson
David Johnston
Barbara Jones
Delyth Jones
Patricia Jones
Jeanette Jones
Waka Joo
Yves Joos
Elaina Joseph
Journal for Quality
& Participation
Ahlmer Juergen
Aoi Kagitani
Kazuyo Kakishita
Yuichi Kakuno
Aki & Rumi Kamebuchi
Yu & Kei Kamebuchi
Kaoru Kamizato
Yukiki Kamoda
Yukiyo Kanayama
Susan & Henry Kane
Kate Feast Management
Mariko Kato
Daisuke Katouno
Tomoko Kawaguchi
Yumiko Kawaguchi
Takeshi Kawamoto
Mieko Kawamura
Mary Keesling
Joerg Keitel
Katie Kelly
Luke Kelly
Andrew Kemble
Sharon Kennedy
Vicki Kennedy
Steve Kernohan
Faye Kershisnik
Hisao Kezuka
Cynthia Kimble
Kenichi Kimura
Shizuko Kimura
Michael King
Emiko Kita
M. Setsuko Kitahara
Kazuhiro Kitoh
Aino Kizu
Edward Klein
Dr. Rene Kleinlutgenbelt
Dorothy Klimasz
Ray Paul Klimek
Guenter Knappe
Renate Knappe
Hiroaki Kobayashi
Vineet Kochhar

Vineet Koga
Isao Koike
Naruni Komatsu
Toshiyuki Kondo
Hirohu Koshinuma
Mitsuko Kotake
Olive Kraft
Olive Kraker
Toni Kraker
John & Rose Kriens
Judy & Mark Krodal
Carroll A Kruger
Alizabeth Krumenacker
Norbert Kryszliewicz
Sachimi Kubota
Tsugum Kudo
Friedhelm Kugele
Mary Kuhtenia
Hiroshi Kusatsu
Chinatsu Kuwana
Young-Ho Kwak
L'Oreal
Catherine La Marca
Marco Landi
John Lanza
Mildred Lanza
Mark & Carol Lapidos
Fred Larke
Larousse Plc
Jochen Laschinsky
Richard Latt
Cecchini Lauretta
Michaell Lavallee
Ron Lavallee Jr
Cindy Lee
James Lee
Karen Lee
Mr. Lehrke
Barbara Leibundguth
Ciancarlo Lena
Peter Leopold
Maureen F. Lerner
Nancy Lester
Gabriella Letterio
Gilles Grosjean of Libra Presse
Lighting and Sound
International
Hans Lingenfelder
LIPA Enterprises
Brenda Little
Liverpool Council of Social
Services (Norwegian Bursary)
Liverpool Document Systems
Liverpool John Moores
University
Liverpool Palatinate
Lloyds TSB
Beth & Jerry Long
Lisa & Joe Long

Stella Longo
J.M. Longworth
Sandy Lopez
Barbara & Jan Lorenc
Ann Lorenzo
Joao Loureiro
John Lucana
Carola Lueth
M. Lumby
Carolyn Lutticken
Maria Luz
Gillian Lynne
Wolf Maahn
Ray & Anne MacGrotty
Dr. Alec G. Mackinnon
Macmillan Publishers
Sharon Madagan
Mariano Ivan Mahia
Mailout
Yasuko Makita
Cheryl & John Maloney
Valencia Maloney
Management Publications
Management Today
Manchester University Press
Gabriele Manenti
Joseph Mannarino
Jerry Marcec
Wendy Marcec
Daman Marsha
Julie Martinez
Akiko Masaakia
Go Masae
Yoshida Masaki
Mason Owen & Partners
Beatrice Mastrorilli
Kotaro Masuda
Kazuko Matsuda
Toyoko Matsudaira
Yoritake Matsudaira
Jun Matsumoto
Hiroko Matsushita
Keiko Matsushita
Deborah-Jane Matthews
Albert Suzanna Maurin
Billy Mawhinney
John & Ana May
Scott & Lauren Maybaum
Nilsen Mayer
Watanabe Mayumi
Mcasso Music Production
John McCabe
Ian McCarthey
Heather McCartney
James McCartney
Kumiko Suwa McCartney
Linda McCartney
Mary McCartney
Michael McCartney

Sir Paul McCartney
Stella McCartney
Sueko McCartney
Keith & Susan McCauley
Camilla McCourt
J. McCullough
Marcia McCurry
Diane & Malcolm McCusker
Ian McDermott
Catherine McDowell
Patrick McGuigan
Christine McGuire
Jaquelynn McIlvaine
Kenneth McKelvie
Ged McKenna
Don McKenzie
Dr. Alec McKinnon
Thomas McLaughlin
John McNally
Andy McNaul
Donna McNaul-Tomlin
Capt'n Meck
& Yellow Submarine
Carol & Steven Mehven
Julie Mellotte
Donna Mellotte
Robert Memery
Fernando Menedez
Uwe Menze
Chris Johnson of
Mercury Press Agency
Guenther Merlin
Merseyside Task Force
Merseyside TEC
Gareth Meyer
Joyce Meyer
John Michaet
Christine Middleton
Manami Mikado
Watanabe Miki
April Miller
Archie Miller
Gary Miller
Kenneth Miller
J. Garnett Miller
Christine Milligan
Aki Minami
Mary & Helen Minor
Megumi Mitake
Mitch Mitchell
Rob & Sara-Jane Mitchell
Susan Mitchell
Masakazu Miyazaki
Hiroshi Mochizuki
Debi Moen - High End
Systems Texas Inc.
Markus Moerl
Pauline Moller
Steve Mollin

Joan Molnar
Moorwood Vulcan
Dan & Eddie Moran
Sarah oran
Thomas Morgan
Y. Mori
Joanna Moriarty
Miyuki Morikawa
Ryoko Morooka
Roger Morris
Donna Mosesian
Angela Mosimann
Dave Moss
Jim Mountzouris
Paige Mozdzen
MPL Communications
Harry Mrocki
Louie Mucci of
Gal. Publishing
Dr. Gerald Mueller
Roberta Mueller
Jennifer Mullin
Multi Media Group
Chris Murphy
Dan & Karen Murphy
Eddie Murphy
Chip Murray
Murray
Music Business
International/Music Week
Music of the World
Music Publishers Association
Music Sales
Music Theatre International
Musicians' Union
Marjorie Myers
Yoke Nakagawa
Patty Nalley
Hiroyuki Naomi
Miyuki Nara
National Arts Collections Fund
The National Magazine Co.
Gloria Navarro
Mark Navarro
NCVO Publications
Eileen Neff
Naomi Negishi
Beth & Mark Nelson
T.W. Nicholls
Liam Niederst
Morten Nielsen
Shigeyuki Nishimura
Masami Nishio
Junko Nishizaki
Meryl & Malcolm Noad
Akiko Nogam
Atsushi Noguchi
Northcote House Publishers
Northern Song Project

Ferninando Novelli
Yoshiko Nozaki
Yoke Nozawa
Gary O'Brien
Herb O'Brien
Stephen O'Donnel
Sammy Oakey
Oberon
Shizue Oe
Hitoshi Ogasawara
T. Ohbayashi
Mamiko Ohsaki
Atsushi Ohtake
Minsin Okamoto
Marcy Old Ham (Lanza)
Joyce Oliveria
The Lady Olivier and
The Olivier Foundation
Patricia Olsen
H. Onagi
Kohtaro Once
Yasuhiro Ono
Emiko Oohata
Paul Oginsky
of the Weston Spirit
Nobuyoshi Oosawa
Orange Amps
Cristiano Orlani
Yukie Osa
Toshio Otake
Rumiko Otani
Andrea Ott
Masahiro Ouchi
Scott Overfelt
Nick Owen
Jim Painton
Marcel Pal
Gudrun Palm
Frank Palmeri
The Rudolph Palumbo
Charitable Foundation
Inuo Panda
Pannell Kerr Forster
Joanne Paragi
Dominique Parent
Christopher Parez
Manuela Parisini
Carmin Pascuzzi
Evelyn Passik
Raj Patel
Gareth Pawlowski
Becky Payne
Paula Payne
Bergen Peck
Gert Pederson
Peer-Southern Music
Sal Pellettiere
Suzie Penley
Pepsi Cola UK

Donors continued

Ronald Perelman
Raul Perez
The Performing Right Society
Harriet Linda Perry
Personnel Publications
T. Peters
Peter Petrel
Jennie B. Petrillo
E. Petzol
Phaidon Press
Steve Phillips
Jorie Gracen – PhotoOne
Jenni Piattelli
Drusila Natalia Piovera
Pitman Publishing
Luke Pittorino
Jens Plachetka
Barry & Karen Plant
PLASA
Ian Plater
Robert V. Plath
Thomas Pochert
Polygram International
Music Publishing
Polygram UK
Tony Pomeroy
John Pope
Kia Portafekas
Terry Porter
The Post Office Group
Kathleen Posthumus
Matthew Powell
Prescot Property Consultants
Frances Preston
John Preston
Princeton University Press
Ann Proctor
Steven Purcell
Q Magazine
Her Majesty the Queen
John Rago
Paul Raider
Ralph Lauren – The Polo Ralph
Lauren Corporation
Rob & Gayle Rappaport
Richard Hobhouse on behalf
of the Trustees, Rathbone
Bros & Co.
Paul Ratterman
Terry Ratterman
Dietmar Ruttger
Jonathan Simon
Margo Langford – Recording
Industry Ass. of America
Mary Ann Redfield
Brian J. Parker
of Reepham High School
Ken Regan
Anja Rehm

G.B.Reid
John Reid Enterprises
Mrs. Wilma Reid
Linda Reig
Jos Remmerswaal
Ann Renshal
RESKA Terrapin Productions
The Revlon Foundation
Enrica Ricciuto
Cheryl Richards
Karen Richie
Jack Richman
Mr. Riethmueller
Michael Riley
Marjorie Ripp
Ritz AV
Maria A Rivera
Rivera Global Record
RKW Ventilation
Linda M. Robbins
Jean Roberts
N.D. Roberts
Jeann M Robertson
Joyce Robertson
Jane & Rob Rogers
Simon & Wendy Rogers
Rolling Stone Magazine
Marye Romme
Rondor Music
Hans Roosenbrand
Robert Rose
Charles F. Rosena
Harry & Rose Rosenay
Rotary Club of St. Albans
Michael Rothaug
Karen Rothman
Karen Roy
Mike Kirkham of the Royal
Bank of Scotland
Royal Bank of Scotland
Molly Rubin
Brenda Ruscco
Robert Rush
Marian Rushby
David Rushworth of
Rushworth Music House
Alice Russos
Bernard Ryan
James & Berlinda Ryle
I. Sachiko
H. Sagawa
Natsue Sagawa
Keiji Saida
Kishor Saint-Jean
Hiroko Saito
Fusako Sakai
Noriko Sakakibara
Shuichi Sakamaki
Kyoko Sakaue

Sonja Sakolowski
Ryuichi Sakurai
Sawako Sakurai
Patti Saldutti
Masahiko Sang
Rolf Sanner
Koji Saotome
Yuki Sarashini
Perino Sartori
Mika Sasaki
Hitoshi Sato
Junko Sato
Kaya Sato
Kohtaroh Satoh
Nigel Satterley
Mikako Sawada
Betsy Scattergood
Gerd Schabdach
Bob Schacherl, President of
High End Systems Texas Inc.
Mr. Schaefer
Mr. Schaek
Burkhard Schaeling
Harald Scheitler
Larry & Connie Schleusner
Juergen Schmeitz
Stefan Schmid
Elena Schmitz
Sara B. Schneider
Joanne & Gren Schoch
Hank & Elaine Schoeffel
Eddy & Sandrine Schoenfeld
H.F. Schroeder
Britta Schulte-Bieting
Evelyn Schwarz
Dagmar & Peter
Schwarzwalder
Tanja Schwerer
Joy & Paul Scofield
Geoff Scott
Sachiko Sekiya
Nadia Semczuk
Hannelore Sevecke
Wolfgang Sevecke
Chris Shanks
Joan Shatter
Scott Shaw
Janice L. Shenko
Clare Sherman
Yoko Shibasak
Takashi Tomoko Shibata
Yoko Shimamura
Chikako Shimizu
Hajime Shimizu
Katsuichiro Shimizu
Ritsuko Shimoda
Nishikawa Shin
Aiko Shioyasu
Hideko Shira

Ikuko Shiraishi
Kaori Shoji
Wil Shore
Paul Simon
Ralf Frier Simon
Christian Simon
Christi Simons
Peter Sissons
Slavik
Joanna Sledzinski
Wayne Sleep
Barry Slocum
Hannah Sluis
Edwina Smith
Jeffrey J. Smith
Susan Smith
Stan Snellemann
Sony Music Enterprises
Sony Music International
Yve Soos
Dottie Spathis
Spendant Works
Spotlight Publications
David & Glenys Spottiswood
Roberta Spreafico
Monika Stache
Michael Stack of ASCAP
The Stage & Television Today
Richard Starkey
Jake Staunton
Stefan Stegmayer
David Stein
Friedlinde Steiner
Monika Steiner
Jerry Stelmach
Heidrun Stengel
Mrs. Barbara Stettler
Garnett Stevens
Jean Stevens
Eric Stewart
Matthias Storb
Edward Storey
Studio Audio & Video
Michael Sudds
Mr. Suessmeier
Lorraine Suppa
Andreas Sutter
Asami Suzuki
Hidek Suzuki
Toshio Suzuki
Greg Swan
Peter Taft
Etsuko Takahashi
Keiko Takahashi
Naomi Takahashi
Taku Takeishi
Yayoi Takeuchi
Daigo Tamada
Kazuko Tamai

Hiromi Taokeda
Roger C. Tavener
Tavener & Son
Harry Tavitian
Masao Tawaraishi
Miwa Tayano
Yasuhide (Paul) Tayano
Iain Taylor
Jo-Beth Taylor
John Taylor
Mark Taylor
Roger Taylor
TDK
George Tebbens
Yuji Tgakegawa
Thames & Hudson
Cindy & Scott Thayer
Gunnar Madsen of ROSA –
The Danish Rock Council
David Thomas
Grace & Sonny Thomas
Margaret Thompson
Cindy Tivador
Yumiko Tomioka
Tsuruse Tomohiro
Total Research
Isao Ohashi Toyama
The Training Agency
Kathy Trosko
Yuko Tsuchiya
Shiomi Tsukizawa
Izumi Tsutsumi
Yoko Tsuzi
Keiichi Uchida
UCL Press
Edwina Upmann
Mayumi Usukura
VAG UK
Tony Valente
Michael Valiante
George & Chris Van der Veken
Don Van Schaick
Ron Vance
Will Vandermark
Eddie & Linda Veltman
Ann Verdi
Andrew Veres
Dorothy GreenlaghVeres
Y.F. Verlander
Roge Verte
Radio Victoria
Virgin Music Group
Virgin Records Limited
Franziska Voellmy-Huwiler
Inge Vogel
VickiVogel
Pirschel Volmar
Rainer Vornholt
Ralph Vuono

David Wailer
Dave & Elaine Wainscoat
Kaori Wakabayashi
Debbie Wakeford
Patricia Wakeman
Yukie Wakikawa
George Walker
Jo-An Walsh
Humphrey Walwyn
Elizabeth Dean Wanderer
War Memorial Fund
Chris Warner
Warner Chappell Music
James Warnock
P.J. Harvey of
Washbourn & Garrett
James A. Wasson
Kazuya Watanabe
Motonobu Watanabe
Nobuyuki Watanabe

Toshiyuki Watanabe
Yuri Watanabe
Jeff Watson
John & Sethina Watson
Mr. & Mrs. K. Watson
Joy M. Waugh-O'Donnell
Mary Wears
Diana Weaver
Michelle Webb
Josiah Wedgwood & Sons
Weidenfield & Nicholson
Claudia Wein
Josef Weinberger
Ina Weinhold
Leonie Welch
W.A. Wellsted
Alexis Weston
Dr. Fernande Weyrich
Dr. Rainer Weyrich
John Whale

John C. Whalley
Beatrice Wiessler
Rainer Wiggenhauser
Nicole Wilde
Toyah Willcox
Kim Willet
Linda Willet Willet
Judy Williams
L.E.D. Williams
Nancy Williams
Roger Williams
Barry & Ivy Wilson
Derek Wilson
Paul B. Winn
Chery Winslow
John Winson
J. Winsor
Elke Wirth
Madlen Wirtz
Deborah Wise

Robert Wise
Randy Witt
Andrea Witthohn
Adam Witts
Lord Andrew Howland for
Woburn Charitable Trust
Rihm Wolfgang
Sir Brian Wolfsen of
Wembley Plc
Mary Wood
Chris Wooden
Mark S. Woodin
Woolwich Building Society
Woolwich Building Society
Bridgid & Ronald Woss
Susan Wright
H. Yaeko
Kieko Yamad
Yamaha Kemble Music UK
Frank & Helen Yamakoshi

Lois Yamakoshi
Kenji Yasuda
Bob Yates
Shannon Yates
Bruce Yelle
Janet Yelle
Beverly Yem
Naomi Yoda
Chiaki Yokoi
Yumi Yokota
Eiko Yoshimoto
Leslie Anne Young
Young Presidents
Tanya Young-Womack
Youth Arts Network
Hiroto Yui
Yuki
Gubbs Zollo
Zomba Music
Julie Zurlino Zongaro